THE
JANEWAY

50 Years of Caring for Children

Dr. Rick Cooper

BOULDER
PUBLICATIONS

Library and Archives Canada Cataloguing in Publication

Cooper, Austin Richard, 1942-, author
    The Janeway : 50 years of caring for children / Richard Cooper.
ISBN 978-1-927099-86-5 (softcover)

    1. Janeway Children's Health and Rehabilitation Centre--History.
2. Children--Hospitals--Newfoundland and Labrador--St. John's--History.
I. Title.

RJ28.S24C66 2017   362.19892009718'1   C2017-901605-9

Design and layout: Todd Manning
Front cover design: John Andrews
Editor: Stephanie Porter
Copy editor: Iona Bulgin

Printed in Canada

We acknowledge the financial support of the Government of Newfoundland and Labrador through the Department of Tourism, Culture and Recreation.   Newfoundland Labrador

We acknowledge the financial support for our publishing program by the Government of Canada and the Department of Canadian Heritage through the Canada Book Fund.

Royalties from the sale of this book will be donated to the Janeway Foundation.

For Dr. Clifton Joy

CONTENTS

Part III: Research at the Janeway

Part IV: Perinatal Program

Part V: Medical Education

Part VI: Janeway Foundation

INTRODUCTION

At 11 a.m. on August 9, 1966, the Dr. Charles A. Janeway Child Health Centre officially opened in a former World War II American military hospital in Pleasantville in the east end of St. John's. The extensively refurbished building was ready to serve children from across the province.

It was a remarkable achievement. At the time, Newfoundland was an impoverished province with fewer than 500,000 residents, many isolated communities, and limited transportation. The creation of "the Janeway," as it became known, had been opposed by the Newfoundland Medical Association (NMA), most St. John's physicians—including several pediatricians—health minister Dr. James McGrath, and the leader of the provincial government opposition, Dr. Noel Murphy. Most local physicians recognized the need for improved pediatric services but felt they would be better located in a wing of the existing General Hospital in the east end of St. John's.

The MacFarlane Commission, which had been appointed by Memorial University of Newfoundland to investigate the feasibility of a medical school, had also recommended against a children's hospital. Little public support was evident. In a broader context, the concept of a free-standing pediatric hospital—one that was geographically, financially, clinically, and administratively independent from other health facilities—was controversial. The accepted wisdom was that such hospitals should be integrated into larger medical centres with more resources and close affiliations with medical schools.

Support for the endeavour, however, came from several crucial quarters, including Premier Joseph Smallwood, five or six local physicians, and several prominent Canadian pediatricians. The "Brain Commission," a Royal Commission on Health led by British neurologist Lord Russell Brain, fully endorsed the establishment of a free-standing provincial children's hospital. Rallying the support for it would never have happened without the dedication, hard work, perseverance, and vision of St. John's pediatrician Clifton Joy.

From the beginning of his pediatric career in 1954, Joy had been convinced that Newfoundland needed a central pediatric hospital where children from around the province could be referred. Joy wanted local pediatric medicine expertise to develop and did not believe that treating children on a wing of the larger General Hospital would provide the best environment for that.

When the American military hospital building beside Quidi Vidi Lake was turned over to the provincial government in 1961, Joy recognized his opportunity. While other medical leaders argued that the Pleasantville hospital should become a rehabilitation and convalescent hospital, Joy and his colleagues believed in its potential as a children's hospital. Smallwood eventually supported Joy's vision, and Joy's dream became a reality.

Opening a children's health centre in the east end of St. John's in the 1960s was a gamble. Not only was refurbishing the building expensive but it would also be isolated from the proposed medical school and health sciences centre farther uptown. But it paid off: from its early days, the Janeway was an efficient, modern, well-staffed, and well-equipped hospital. It earned a national reputation as an excellent academic pediatric health centre and was embraced by Newfoundlanders and Labradorians, fulfilling all of Joy's hopes and expectations.

Questions remain: should the government have put the children's hospital in the Pleasantville site or waited for the construction of a new health centre, where the Janeway would move in 2001? The province's economy improved greatly in the 17 years after confederation in 1949 and, with modern public health initiatives, access to better health care, better nutrition, and a better educated population, was a provincial pediatric hospital justified? Why did so many physicians oppose the proposal? And why wasn't there more public support, considering the high infant mortality and incidence of pediatric diseases? I examine these questions in this book.

The American military hospital in Pleasantville, future site of the Janeway, in 1960.

In 1991, Donald E. Kelland, retired administrator of the Janeway, published *The Dr. Charles A. Janeway Child Health Centre: The First Twenty-Five Years, 1966–1991*. It is an excellent reference book about the Janeway—its history, its staff, and the patients and their families—in which Kelland details how a vacated military hospital became a modern children's hospital. Twenty-five years later, I believe there is more to say.

While I refer to Kelland's book in several places, I wanted to take a different approach to telling the story of the Janeway. I will examine the state of child health in the early part of the 20th century and its influence on the establishment of the Janeway. I will take readers on Joy's incredible journey by investigating the struggle of a small number of pediatricians as they convinced the government of the value of a children's hospital—and all of the controversy, politics, disappointments, and successes that ensued. In 2001, the new Janeway Child and Women's Health Centre was opened adjacent to Memorial University's medical school and the adult Health Sciences Centre; I will investigate the decisions behind the creation of that centre and its continued influence on child health. I often refer to the two locations simply as the "old Janeway" (in Pleasantville) and the "new Janeway" (Health Sciences Centre).

I also wanted to document the changes in child health care that have been implemented by tracing the evolution of each of the Janeway's departments and programs and to acknowledge the excellent care provided by its health

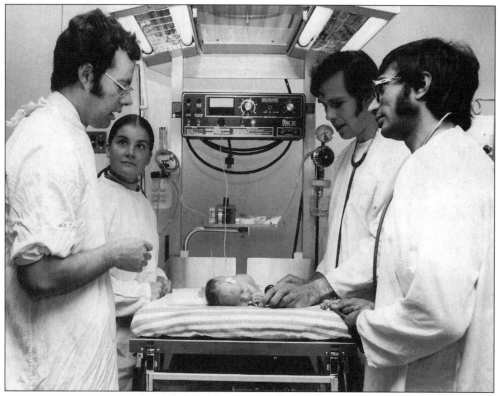

The author (left) teaching in the old Janeway, 1976.

care team. The development of varied programs, with the full support of the provincial government and the regional health care authority, Eastern Health, is a success story.

Part I details the events leading up to the establishment of the Janeway as a stand-alone pediatric hospital and its 2001 move to a newly constructed hospital attached to the Health Sciences Centre. The story was not always easy to unravel and I consulted many primary sources, including newspaper and journal articles, meeting minutes, House of Assembly transcripts, and personal communications. A list of references is found at the back of the book. Parts II and III relied heavily on input, and sometimes written contributions, from health care professionals; unless otherwise noted, the text is written by me.

The Janeway had limited resources when it opened but, through tremendous technological advances, the adoption of an evidence-based approach to pediatric medical care, and the recruitment of skilled physicians, nurses, and health care workers, it has developed into a modern, highly respected tertiary-care centre. Without the vision and perseverance of Clifton Joy and the hard work, dedication, and expertise of the many professionals who walked its hallways, the Janeway would never have evolved into the first-class teaching health care centre that it is in 2017.

PART I

JOURNEY TO THE JANEWAY

THE WAY IT WAS

William Murphy was born a healthy, full-term baby in St. John's on August 11, 1942. He was the third son for his parents. For the first few days of his life, William, who was bottle-fed, thrived. At about one month of age, however, he started vomiting and had frequent, watery stools. Despite the best efforts of the family physician and the parents, William's condition continued to deteriorate. He became listless and pale and started to lose weight. About a week after the onset of the symptoms, he was very weak, ashen, and mottled. He died on September 14, 1942.

I know William's story well; he was my first cousin and we were born in the same year. His parents were devastated. Not a day went by for my aunt and uncle without their grieving for their lost son. William was one of the many thousands of children who died of gastroenteritis in Newfoundland in the 20th century.

The life of most children in Newfoundland and Labrador in the first half of the 20th century was miserable, restrictive, and unhealthy. Many factors contributed: poverty, over-dependence on the fishery, isolation, ignorance, and poor government. Many communities lacked roads, electricity, and indoor plumbing. Farming was limited, and nutritious food, such as fruits and vegetables, was scarce, especially in the winter in the outports. A large part of the province was isolated and people were unable to travel or ship goods easily. Health care facilities were scattered, and most people in rural areas did not have access to a physician or nurse. The average educational level was low; it was not until 1942 that education of all children was legislated. Access to up-to-date literature and modern methods handicapped many health care efforts. The government had incurred extensive debts financing troops for World War I and building a railway and paper mills. The international depression in Canada, the US, and Europe greatly affected the economy, especially in St. John's.

In 1934 the Dominion of Newfoundland was basically bankrupt and the British government introduced commission of government. This form of government brought some improvement in public health, and cottage hospitals were built. Some developments, including more jobs, came with the arrival of the American and Canadian military in 1939 and Newfoundland's confederation with Canada in 1949.

Certain indices attested to the poor economy and the hardships faced by children of the province and indicated that child health care was of a lower standard in Newfoundland than elsewhere in Canada. The infant mortality rate—the death of an infant in his or her first year—is an indicator of child health and prosperity. Newfoundland and Labrador had a high infant mortality rate compared to the rest of Canada until later in the 20th century (see Table 1).

Infectious disease is another marker of child and population health. The worst of these in Newfoundland was tuberculosis; many of those who died of tuberculosis were parents whose children were left in desperate circumstances. Gastroenteritis was common, and even in 1963, 100 Newfoundland and Labrador children died from this disease. Diphtheria was a common cause of death in older children (see Table 2) until a vaccine program was introduced. Initially the vaccine was given to diphtheria contacts, but in the early 1950s a comprehensive provincial immunization program was introduced and the disease was eliminated by the 1970s. Whooping cough (pertussis) was listed as a common cause of death; however, some of these cases may have been pneumonia or tuberculosis.

Malnutrition in Newfoundland and Labrador children is well described in the literature and government papers. Beri-beri, or thiamine deficiency, vitamin B6 deficiency, vitamin C deficiency causing scurvy, vitamin A deficiency causing blindness, and vitamin D deficiency causing rickets were prevalent. The diets of many residents, particularly in rural communities, were poor in

TABLE 1: Infant mortality.
Deaths per 1,000 live births for selected years.

Year	#s per 1,000 NL	#s per 1,000 Canada	#s per 1,000 Other
1901	136		UK 151 St. John's 153
1912	171		UK 95 St. John's 140
1920	136.0		New Brunswick 134.9
1931	132.6	84.7	Saskatchewan 62 Ontario 61
1936	112.7	64	Saskatchewan 55 Ontario 50 St. John's 96.7
1942	97.0	54	St. John's 107
1949	53.3	47	
1956	43.4	32	Quebec 41 Ontario 25 Saskatchewan 28
1965	31.1	20	St. John's 19.4
1975	17.3	13.1	
1987	7.59	7.3	
1995	7.9	6.1	
2006	5.3	5.0	

TABLE 2: Diphtheria-related mortality for selected years.

Year	Deaths
1900	59
1910	41
1920	82
1928	22
1938	5
1948	8

Diphtheria after 1950

9 deaths after 1950
Last death: 1973
88 cases after 1950
Last case: 1976

fresh vegetables and meat. Many children in the first half of the 20th century suffered from malnutrition.

Obstetrics and newborn (or neonatal) care was also deficient; newborn mortality—death in the first 30 days after birth—and stillbirth rates were high.

After confederation with Canada, child health care improved in Newfoundland and Labrador, as it did in other provinces. The overall economy improved and, with better transportation, more foodstuffs were available and parents began receiving a "baby bonus" for every child. Public health was always a priority, but poor economic conditions had prevented the government from providing adequate service. After confederation, public health services greatly improved and better screening for tuberculosis, malnutrition, and dental caries (a marker of poor nutrition) was implemented. A very aggressive immunization program was also started.

Child Health Care in Newfoundland before 1965

In 1898, the first children's ward in Newfoundland was established at the General Hospital; between then and 1966, several unsuccessful attempts to establish a dedicated pediatric hospital were made.

The Women's Patriotic Society, originally formed during World War I to perform voluntary works, responded to the locally high rates of infant mortality and assumed responsibility for child welfare in St. John's in 1919. Society members were prepared to establish and operate a children's hospital in Waterford Hall, a house that they had run as a convalescent hospital during the war. St. John's mayor William Gilbert Gosling had directed considerable financial support to child welfare initiatives but not enough to open Waterford Hall as a children's hospital. Instead, the Society opened a "Little Hospital" for sick babies in a private home at 54 LeMarchant Road with five cots for infants, a day nurse, and three unpaid probationers; it operated from May to October 1920, when it closed at the request of Mrs. Marshall, the homeowner.

The St. John's Clinical Society met in December 1926 and resolved that the City of St. John's needed a children's hospital and that David Baird's private home on Circular Road was suitable, in terms of layout and location. Baird generously offered it for use as a children's hospital; however, it was up to the City to operate and maintain it. The project did not receive approval.

Prior to 1966, sick children were generally treated in wards and beds in public and private religious hospitals. The pediatric ward at the General Hospital, established in 1898, was expanded in 1947 to include a second ward. The wards were in a building block of two floors at the rear of the older part of the hospital. The lower floor (Victoria Ward), which housed children aged two to six, consisted of a main ward and a covered veranda running along part of one side. The upper floor (Alexander Ward), occupied by infants and children up to two years of age, consisted of a main ward and a small nursery.

The Fever Hospital, a 52-bed wooden building on Connor's Field at the southwest corner of the General Hospital grounds, opened in April 1905; it closed with the opening of the Janeway in 1966. The only isolation hospital for infectious diseases in Newfoundland, it admitted a wide variety of cases from all parts of the island, but particularly St. John's. Most of the patients were children with "pediatric" problems such as fever, pneumonia, and gastroenteritis and not major public health concerns like diphtheria, typhoid, or tuberculosis. The orthopedic hospital, a wooden building constructed by the Royal Canadian Navy in World War II as a temporary hospital, was a part of the General Hospital. Its children's ward, in operation until 1966, was partitioned into a section for children less than six years old, and a smaller section for boys from six to 13. Girls older than six were housed in the adult female ward.

The Grace General Hospital, a private general hospital operated by the Salvation Army, with an emphasis on obstetrics, opened in 1926. It had enough beds to care for 150 adults and 46 children and a newborn nursery with 55 bassinettes and incubators. Children's beds there in the 1950s were scattered throughout the building: the wards (two on the fourth floor and one of the

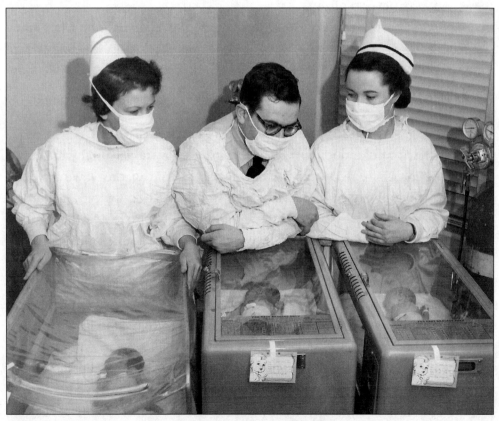

In 1955 triplets were born and cared for at the American military hospital.

first), a collection of rooms on the second floor, and beds in additional wards and rooms. A private general hospital operated by the Roman Catholic Order of the Sisters of Mercy, St. Clare's Mercy Hospital, was built in 1928 and expanded in 1930, 1940, 1962, and 1972. In the 1950s most children were treated in the 28-bed children's ward on the first floor. A newborn nursery contained 40 bassinettes, two isolates, and four incubators. In 1962 a pediatric ward was opened on the seventh floor.

In 1956 the provincial Department of Health submitted a proposal to have 50 additional pediatric beds added to the General Hospital. The proposal, which suggested building a pediatric wing, was enthusiastically supported by many St. John's physicians. However, with plans circulating for a children's hospital, as well as for a new site for the General Hospital and a medical school, these bed were never realized.

In 1957, 183 hospital beds were available for children in St. John's, but many were deemed unsatisfactory—and in some instances unsafe—because of overcrowding and fire hazards associated with the wooden construction of the Fever and orthopedic hospitals.

Plans for a New Child Health Centre

After Newfoundland joined Canada in 1949, its overall economy improved and more health care resources became available. In 1949, the Newfoundland government's total expenditure on health was $5,538,000; by 1965, it had increased five-fold, to $28,580,000. The infant mortality rate fell, fewer children died from tuberculosis, and immunization rates rose. Vaccine-preventable illnesses had virtually disappeared by the 1960s.

Despite this, there was still room for improvement. In 1954, Clifton Joy, a 32-year-old Newfoundland pediatrician, returned to St. John's from Boston, where he had spent the final year of his pediatric training at the Boston Children's Hospital Medical Centre. Joy had been a resident physician in pediatrics at the Montreal Children's Hospital and had spent a year as a fellow in ambulatory pediatrics with prominent American pediatrician Charles A. Janeway in Boston. Janeway, who had previously travelled to Newfoundland on vacation, spoke to Joy about the province's high rate of infant mortality, suggesting that considerable work was needed to improve the situation. Joy, too, was deeply concerned about the lack of hospital facilities for children in his home province; according to his family, Joy's goal had always been to open a provincial child health care centre. The province's pediatric population was significant—in 1955, fully 40 per cent, about 173,000, was under the age of 16.

In 1957, Joy, on behalf of the NMA, chaired an ad hoc committee struck to survey the province's pediatric hospital facilities. The resulting report pinpointed many issues of concern, including ward overcrowding, an inadequate number of beds, a lack of outpatient facilities, a lack of qualified personnel, and increasing numbers of children being admitted to hospital. The report, with its long lists of criticisms and suggestions for improvement, laid the groundwork for a proposal for a child health centre. The report was generally accepted by physicians and government—though no doubt some parties would have taken offence to some of the observations and assessments.

The Children's Health Service

In October 1955, the provincial government introduced a plan to partially cover the cost of child health care in the cottage hospitals, the Grenfell hospitals (in Battle Harbour, St. Anthony, and elsewhere), the general hospital in Twillingate, and some St. John's hospitals. The province inaugurated a Children's Health Service in 1957 which covered the cost of hospitalization, outpatient diagnostic services, and medical care for hospitalized children. This innovative and progressive initiative provided basic hospital coverage for children up to 16 years of age (43.2 per cent of the population in 1964)—according to Smallwood, Newfoundland was the first province in Canada to introduce a free health scheme for children. This improved access to health care was intended to be implemented in five phases: hospitalization, outpatient diagnostic services, hospital medical care, dental and optical care, and office and ambulatory visits. Only the first three were implemented.

Two formal presentations from the NMA addressed the Children's Health Service: a speech to the annual meeting of the NMA by Dr. Harry Roberts, Canadian Medical Association representative (published in the Association's 1960 newsletter); and, a 1965 brief to the Brain Commission from Dr. Norah

Elphinstone Browne, chair of the special study committee of the NMA for the Children's Health Service.

Roberts was critical of the Children's Health Service and was concerned that the plan had been hastily assembled. He noted that in 1935 the commission of government had set up the cottage hospital system, which offered needed services to isolated areas, and the government owned and operated the General Hospital, the Hospital for Mental and Nervous Diseases, and the St. John's Sanatorium (the "San," for tuberculosis patients). Medical professionals thought that this was to be the extent of government involvement in health care and were surprised when the premier announced in a December 1955 telecast that his government would provide a complete health service for all children under 16. Roberts commented, "Perhaps it was just a brainwave—one of the many which have burst in the heavens over Newfoundland in the past 10 years." He quoted from an editorial in the St. John's *Evening Telegram*: "The remarkable aspect of Mr. Smallwood's statement was its emergence from out of the blue. There have been no preliminary statements, no discussion, not even any special demand."

The introduction of the Children's Health Service in 1955 brought a substantial increase in hospitalizations. In 1957 Smallwood announced that the government would supply free medical and surgical services for all hospitalized children. According to Roberts, physicians were concerned, because no plans had been made for expansion. He believed the Children's Health Service would contribute to overcrowding because it was "free," and he had concerns about poor planning, overcrowding, and insufficient pediatric beds.

Elphinstone Browne reviewed the Children's Health Service's history, achievements, deficiencies, and acceptance by (or lack of) physicians in a formal brief. She also made recommendations, noting that too few beds were available (in 1964, 2.16 beds per 1,000 children). The fifth stage of the plan—office and domiciliary visits—should not be implemented, as it would create too much demand for trivial and non-urgent conditions. Providing drugs free or at a fixed fee, however, would encourage more treatment at home and earlier discharge from hospital.

Elphinstone Browne further advocated that the Children's Health Service program be expanded to include the Grenfell hospitals, a communication clinic, expanded in-patient services, better laboratory services, more pediatricians, greater ease of referral to consultants outside the province, and improved outpatient facilities. In 1964, the Children's Health Service covered the cost of hospitalization and outpatient diagnostic services but not dental, optical care, office, or domiciliary visits. Physicians were paid fee for service, which did not include the Fever Hospital, Hospital for Mental and Nervous Diseases, St. John's Sanatorium, or the Grenfell hospitals.

The Children's Health Service improved pediatric patient care in all areas: in-patient, outpatient, and diagnostic services. With improved consulting services, referrals from cottage hospitals were easier. The many deficiencies of the service, however, included a lack of dental and eye care, unnecessary admissions, prolonged length of stay (in 1961, the average hospital stay was 13.7 days; in 2010, 4.2 days), long waiting times for appointments, and delays in obtaining consultations with other doctors (due to a shortage of specialists in certain departments). Some health officials felt that unnecessary admissions and the long length of stay were sometimes caused by physicians or parents abusing the system.

An increasing birthrate, too few pediatric beds, a lack of child health specialists, the geographically scattered resources in St. John's and the province, and the increased demands of the Children's Health Service all contributed to a significant crisis and greatly increased the need for expanded facilities and a provincial child health centre.

A New Site for a Children's Hospital

A lack of pediatric beds was recognized as a problem by the Newfoundland government in the mid-1950s. D.L. Butler, the Department of Health's administrator of health services, wrote Smallwood in January 1956 with suggestions for increased bed capacity, including renovating the military hospital (for 50 beds) and reopening the former Merchant Navy Hospital on Water Street (75 beds). Other suggestions included dedicating 20 pediatric beds in the Gander hospital and ensuring adequate accommodations in a new hospital in Corner Brook. Some discussions about building a 400-bed children's hospital came up among government and health professionals in 1958, but no definite plans followed.

In 1960, the American army vacated Fort Pepperrell in Pleasantville. All of the buildings, including a hospital, were turned over to the Canadian and Newfoundland governments. The history of Fort Pepperrell and the building of the military hospital are described by Kelland in *History of the Janeway*:

> The building was a spacious one built entirely of concrete with the perimeter walls constructed of 18 to 24 inches of solid triple reinforced concrete. The building was 3 stories high in the north and east sections and 2 stories in the west and south. It was opened on June 11, 1943. The actual square footage was not mentioned but the hospital could accommodate roughly 147 inpatient beds and 132 emergency beds. There was a modern operating room, X-ray department and a spacious outpatient area.

Meeting minutes from the Easter Seals (known at the time as the Crippled Children's Society) of Newfoundland on March 15, 1961, record that the organization actively petitioned the government to convert the military hospital into a children's rehabilitation centre.

In April 1961, Dr. Ted Shapter, at the request of the NMA, chaired a committee to study possible uses for the vacant hospital. The committee, consisting of two pediatricians (Joy and Doug Simms), a general surgeon, an internist, a specialist in physical medicine and rehabilitation, and a hospital administrator, were instructed to inspect the physical building, review its plans, and meet and discuss its possible uses. The hospital's physical structure was deemed to be in excellent shape, but its equipment had been removed. From a practical point of view, the committee recommended that the building be used for one of five functions: a children's hospital, an orthopedic hospital, a convalescent hospital, a rehabilitation centre for children and convalescent hospital, or a total children's care centre.

The committee discussed each option but could not come to a consensus. Joy and Simms were convinced it should be a child health centre; others, a convalescent hospital. At a meeting on April 21, 1961, the NMA executive passed this resolution:

That the Executive of the Newfoundland Medical Association met on 21 April 1961 and recommended to the Minister of Health that after due consideration, their suggestions for the use of Pepperrell Hospital should be:

    1. That the hospital be a combined children's rehabilitation centre and convalescent hospital to the City hospitals.

    2. If funds were of no consequence, the hospital should form the nidus for the Children's Medical Centre and the surrounding buildings utilized for such purposes as retarded children's home, school, deaf and dumb school, blind school, occupational therapy, etc.

Although Joy and Simms were members of the committee, they opposed this recommendation. They, along with pediatrician John Collins, strongly supported the concept of a child health centre, but they did not have the backing of all of their colleagues. On March 3, 1961, pediatrician Tom Anderson wrote the NMA to support the proposal for a rehabilitation centre and to suggest that a pediatric wing be constructed at the General Hospital. In June 1961, a debate at the NMA annual meeting concluded with the decision that the military hospital should *not* be a child health centre.

Undeterred, Joy and four other pediatricians met several times to plan how to advance their dream. Without NMA support, they determined that their only way forward would be for Joy to become a Liberal member in the House of Assembly and Collins to be active in the Canadian Pediatric Society. If Joy could win over the premier and his government with active support from Collins and the Society, they would have a better chance of achieving their goal.

Collins became president of the Canadian Pediatric Society in 1961. The next year, Joy became the member for Harbour Main for the Liberal party under Smallwood. On April 19, 1962, in his maiden speech, Joy stated that he would like to see the American military hospital at Fort Pepperrell become a children's hospital. In a February 1962 letter, Collins promoted the same concept. The proposal received little support in the medical community and less among politicians and the general public. The total cost of the project was considered to be too high; two polio epidemics had swept through Newfoundland in the 1950s and rehabilitation sites for children and adults were deemed a priority; and most physicians felt that any child health centre should be close to the proposed Health Sciences Centre and Medical School.

Meanwhile, on July 25, 1962, Oscar Ewing (Easter Seals president) recommended that a strongly worded letter be sent to government to lobby for the use of the American military hospital as a rehabilitation centre. In November 1962, Easter Seals met with deputy health minister Leonard Miller, reporting that "there was every indication that [they] would get part of the hospital as a rehabilitation centre but as yet no definite commitment had been made by the Department of Health." And, sure enough, at the 1962 Newfoundland Rehabilitation Council's annual meeting, Smallwood endorsed the NMA's proposal that the hospital become a rehabilitation/convalescent hospital. He vetoed Joy's child health centre. In September 1963, Easter Seals submitted plans for a rehabilitation centre to the Public Works Department.

The Tide Turns

In 1962, a stand-alone child health centre at Fort Pepperrell seemed an unlikely prospect. In the next year, however, several events helped change Smallwood's mind.

An increase in the number of scurvy cases was recorded in 1963. More significantly, that year brought an epidemic of *Enteropathogenic E. coli* (EPEC), caused by a particular strain of *Escherichia coli*. EPEC causes gastroenteritis in infants. The number of reported cases of gastroenteritis doubled in 1963 over previous years; over half were caused by EPEC. One hundred infants died that year.

Considerable concern was expressed through the press about these deaths. The Department of Health introduced a radio and, where available, television educational program. EPEC was considered a public health problem which could be combatted by good infection control and nutrition practices such as thorough hand washing, breast feeding, and proper formula preparation.

Many pediatricians believed that public health initiatives were not enough. The chief pediatrician at the Royal Victoria Hospital in Montreal was quoted in the October 19, 1963, *Daily News* as saying that "overcrowded wards, lack of trained nurses and the absence of a children's medical centre are some of the reasons for Newfoundland's current gastroenteritis epidemic." The epidemic, he suggested, could be controlled if the province had better facilities.

That same month, Harry Medovy, professor and head of the Department of Pediatrics at the University of Manitoba, and A.F. Hardyment, associate clinical professor in the Department of Pediatrics of the University of British Columbia, with the support of the Canadian Pediatric Society, and at the invitation of Newfoundland's health minister, began to investigate the outbreak of infantile gastroenteritis in the province. They met with physicians and health officials in St. John's, Corner Brook, and Stephenville Crossing. Hospitals were inspected and several seriously ill infants examined. They submitted a written report to Smallwood and health minister James McGrath. It recognized significant advances in health care but highlighted areas in which health resources were inadequate: the shortage of health care personnel, and, although statistics on infectious diseases had been kept since the 1920s, very little information about handicapping conditions, such as cerebral palsy, spina bifida, and others, was available. Inadequate immunization practices—no universal immunization program for children had existed until the 1950s—a high incidence of malnutrition and dental caries, and the continuing prevalence of childhood diseases related to poor hygiene and sanitation were also issues.

Medovy and Hardyment's report made several recommendations: increase child health care personnel, obtain information about congenital malformations and handicapping conditions, establish pediatric wards to accommodate children to the age of 16 in all provincial hospitals, establish a perinatal mortality committee, increase the number of physicians and dentists in the province, establish distinct pediatric referral centres in Corner Brook and St. John's, and establish a child health centre in St. John's.

Before Medovy and Hardyment left the province, they met with Smallwood at his home on Roaches Line in October 1963, a meeting arranged by Joy and Collins. Medovy, who was highly respected across Canada, spoke passionately about the plight of Newfoundland children and the importance of creating a provincial pediatric centre. The availability of the military hospital, he said, was a wonderful opportunity for the government to create a world-class operation. Medovy obviously knew that Smallwood desperately wanted to bring Newfoundland's economy and health standards on par with those in the rest of Canada. Smallwood had been long skeptical of the idea of a free-standing children's hospital, but as Medovy spoke, he changed his mind.

Charles A. Janeway at the hospital opening, 1966.

At the end of the meeting Smallwood declared that a pediatric centre would be established in St. John's—and that it would be one of the best in the country. Smallwood had enormous influence and control and, with his blessing, Joy invited Charles A. Janeway to be a consultant to plan the centre. Janeway, a professor of pediatrics at Harvard Medical School and chief of medicine at the Boston Children's Hospital, endorsed the proposal to set up a pediatric child health centre in the vacant military hospital on his first visit on December 26, 1963.

Opposition Continues

In spite of Smallwood's support, opposition to the children's hospital continued. On January 29, 1964, the secretary of the General Hospital's medical advisory council, Dr. A.M. Taylor, wrote McGrath: "With reference to the recent publicity given to the establishment of a Children's Hospital in St. John's, the Medical Advisory Council of the General Hospital urges the Premier to give the most careful consideration to the many advantages which the General Hospital possesses for the establishment of such a unit as an adjunct to this Institution."

The letter detailed the advantages of having a children's hospital adjacent to the General Hospital, including those well-established programs which had been approved by the Royal College of Physicians and Surgeons of Canada. The General Hospital, which would have a close relationship with the proposed medical school, would need all the specialties, including pediatrics, to maintain its high reputation. Having the children's hospital at the General Hospital would also bring cost savings.

At the behest of Smallwood, Joy responded to Taylor's letter on February 17, 1964. He stated that the General Hospital building was unsuitable because of its age and limited space for beds, and that many services, such as laboratory and X-ray, were already overbooked. He argued that the establishment of a modern pediatric facility at the Pepperrell site would enhance the medical school and that, although costly, would greatly strengthen provincial pediatric medical care. Using the Pepperrell building for convalescent patient care would be "criminally wasteful." He outlined prevalent children's medical problems—infectious diseases, diabetes, asthma, and cystic fibrosis—and said that building a pediatric wing at the General Hospital would only perpetuate the already low standard of children's medical care.

The Deed Is Signed

The Speech from the Throne on March 6, 1964, confirmed Smallwood's decision to have a stand-alone children's hospital. Editorials in the *Daily News* and *Evening Telegram* on that day noted the controversy behind the choice but not the reasons or the cost of the facility.

In April, Joy, speaking in the House of Assembly during the Throne Speech debate, stated that "the development of the Pepperrell hospital into a children's hospital as the centre of children's health will prove to be one of the greatest advances in the medical history of Newfoundland." Newfoundland, he pointed out, had both the highest birth rate and the highest infant mortality rate in Canada. He blamed the latter on the low rates of immunization against common infectious diseases and suggested that the programming that would emerge from the establishment of a children's hospital would reduce this mortality rate. He did not mention the advances that had already been made by public health professionals—immunization was done by the public health physicians and nurses who would have very little to do with a central child health centre. Infant mortality rates decreased and immunization rates increased dramatically in the 1950s because of increasing prosperity and efforts within the public health system—clean water, better nutrition, and improved access to health care, as well as better immunization.

On May 6, 1964, Smallwood officially donated the Fort Pepperrell school (a 23-room concrete former high school), instead of the hospital, to Easter Seals. He stated that this building, in conjunction with the children's hospital, would be an important part of the child health centre. Easter Seals resolved to turn the school into a 53-bed facility.

On June 4, 1964, Smallwood introduced a bill with the government's proposal for the children's hospital at Fort Pepperrell, defending it on advice from Janeway and other prominent Canadian and British pediatricians. He detailed the size (300 beds) and cost ($3 to $4 million) of the project. A brand-new facility, he continued, would cost between $7 and $9 million. He credited Joy for his energy, vision, and hard work. "Vast improvements will be made in child health in Newfoundland and Labrador," Smallwood stated. "We will have one of the best [facilities] in Canada because we will spare no expense and no trouble to make it one of the best." More importantly, he added, the hospital would allow Newfoundland and Labrador to catch up with the rest of Canada.

General practitioner Noel Murphy, the Tory member for Humber East, agreed with using the Pepperrell building but wondered where physically and mentally handicapped children would be accommodated. He was also concerned that, because the Americans had stripped the building, it would be very costly to renovate.

Smallwood thanked Murphy and assured him that, while the Americans had taken some furniture and equipment from the hospital, what they had actually taken was greatly exaggerated. Engineers and architects had surveyed

Renovations under way at the vacated Fort Pepperrell military hospital, c. 1965. The Janeway in Pleasantville, c. 1970.

the building, he added, and estimated that refurbishing costs would be reasonable. Smallwood also indicated that the hospital would likely be operated by the Department of Health, not by a board.

James Greene, leader of the opposition, asked if the government was giving any consideration to building a school for the deaf, blind, and mute in the province. Smallwood responded that it was studying the "feasibility and practicality" of establishing such a school. The premier, when asked by Murphy if there would be a school for mentally disabled children, stated that the government had set aside $600,000 from the sale of the Newfoundland Savings Bank to aid that sector of the population.

On August 26, 1965, Collins and Joy presented a brief before the Brain Commission about why the province still had the highest infant mortality rate. They stated that "the proposed children's medical centre at Pleasantville would serve as a focal point to draw together fragmented children's health services and provide a nucleus for a province-wide network of facilities"—a provincial referral centre for sick children and a teaching facility to train future physicians and nurses who would practice province-wide.

Fly in the Ointment

After the new child health centre was approved in the House of Assembly in June 1964, public debates and editorials slowed down, although obvious dissatisfaction remained among many in the medical profession. NMA physicians would not be dissuaded that pediatric beds should be housed in general hospitals, and they were concerned about the cost of renovating the military hospital. Many still felt that the military hospital should have been turned into a convalescence and rehabilitation hospital.

In 1966 the federal government introduced Medicare. The program was immediately accepted by Newfoundland, and the provincial government received a grant of $7 million. Though it became a hot topic of discussion for government, physicians, and the public, the advent of Medicare did not halt dissention for the child health centre. At the NMA's annual meeting in June 1965, Joy made a motion, seconded by Collins: "Be it resolved that [NMA] strongly support the concept of a distinct Child Health Program for Newfoundland." It was defeated.

Joy, upset at the rejection, phoned Smallwood at home at 7 a.m. the next day. Smallwood invited Joy and his wife, Flo, to lunch. After listening to Joy, he said, "Cliff, I don't care what those doctors think. This province is going to have a pediatric child health centre in Pepperrell, and that's that."

The debate fell quiet until the release of two commission reports in early 1966. In January 1966, the Brain Commission's report strongly supported a child health centre at Fort Pepperrell:

> It is recommended that the Pepperrell Children's Hospital should become an Institute of Child Health for the Province. Specific recommendations are made with regard to the establishment in the hospital of units concerned with cardiac surgery, neurology and neurosurgery, metabolic biochemical and chromosome work, genetic studies, child psychiatry and the care of the newborn.

In 1965, J. Arthur MacFarlane, dean emeritus of the University of Toronto's Faculty of Medicine, was appointed by Memorial University to report on the feasibility of establishing a medical school. MacFarlane's report, released on February 15, 1966, supported the establishment of a medical school and the construction of a 300-bed teaching hospital but was critical of the decision to create a stand-alone child health centre. MacFarlane agreed with the NMA's recommendation to use the building on the site as a rehabilitation centre: the

300-bed venue would be too large for a children's hospital and the location would isolate children from the mainstream of medical care in the City of St. John's as well as the teaching facilities for physicians. MacFarlane suggested that the university hospital, which was in the planning stages, include pediatric beds.

The MacFarlane report was criticized by Smallwood and Joy. In a speech in the legislature, Joy quoted medical reasons for the establishment of a child health centre at Pepperrell, as well as the support he had obtained from the Canadian Pediatric Society and elsewhere.

An editorial in the *Evening Telegram* on February 21, 1966, titled "Fly in the Ointment," commented on MacFarlane's stance, particularly in light of Brain's support of the children's hospital. MacFarlane's report, it noted, would have little effect on the future of the child health centre because the decision had already been made to go ahead with the centre. The editorial did, however, echo some of MacFarlane's concerns that the centre would likely face many problems, such as having the children's hospital separate from the university, and it suggested that the idea of a rehabilitation centre at the site be re-examined.

Joy, responding critically to the report, pointed out that MacFarlane's committee members met only with physicians opposed to the proposal. He justified the number of beds and said that the appointment of Professor A. Victor Neale, a pediatrician from Bristol, England, as a consultant to oversee the project would overcome all difficulties:

> 40% of the population is under 16 and ... the existing hospital facilities for children and the organization of these institutions are primitive and dangerous to children healed therein. Failure to develop our children's hospital into a children's university hospital would perpetuate our present inadequacies.

On February 25, 1966, in the House of Assembly, Smallwood expressed his surprise to find a summary of the MacFarlane Commission report published in the media—he had understood that it was confidential:

The newspaper comment shows two things: (1) certain local doctors disagreed with the establishment of the children's hospital at Pepperrell, and (2) the authors of the report agreed with the local doctors and expressed the hope that the government would change its mind and decide not to proceed with the plan. As a result I intend to do something that I did not intend to do, I am going to table in the House, perhaps tomorrow, a list of the government's reasons why we decided to build the hospital at Fort Pepperrell. Then I will leave it to any impartial observer to decide whether or not it was right.

Smallwood released a list of 14 reasons for a children's hospital, stating that "the government are intensely proud, not only of the children's hospital, but of having put it at Fort Pepperrell and having done so on the weight of evidence that has been absolutely overwhelming."

In the March 11, 1966, session of the House of Assembly McGrath tabled an NMA report concerning the Pepperrell hospital. Its last paragraph clearly

---

Smallwood's 14 Points for a Children's Hospital

1. 50 per cent of the population was under 16 years of age

2. the province's high infant mortality and incidence of malnutrition

3. the practice of pediatrics could not possibly develop properly within a general hospital in Newfoundland

4. the high incidence of such pediatric diseases as gastroenteritis

5. plans for a pediatric hospital at Pepperrell were already under way

6. consultants from outside the province, including Dr. Charles A. Janeway, supported a child health centre at Pepperrell

7. the Brain Commission had enthusiastically endorsed the concept

8. the number of beds needed, based on a formula used by Britain's National Health Service, justified 350 beds

9. as a provincial referral centre for pediatrics, it would liaise closely with cottage hospitals

10. it would be a training site for nurses, doctors, and social workers

11. it would provide an efficient centre for diagnosing and treating congenital heart disease and establish a unit of cardiovascular surgery

12. it would create, in liaison with maternity hospitals, a newborn medicine program

13. it would be a provincial genetic referral centre

14. it would establish a pediatric mental health centre

indicated that it "not only approve[s] but recommend[s] the very action that the government have taken with regards to the Children's Hospital." In other words, after the government decided to go ahead and renovate the Pepperrell hospital into a child health centre, the NMA had had a change of heart.

The child health centre, officially opened on August 9, 1966, was named the Dr. Charles A. Janeway Child Health Centre in honour of the American pediatrician who had strongly supported its establishment at that location and offered early encouragement to Joy and Collins.

"Janeway" was not the province's first choice for a name. The provincial government wished to preserve the close bond it had developed with the American armed services in World War II and asked the Kennedy family for permission to name the hospital the Caroline Kennedy Pediatric Health Centre, after the daughter of US president John Kennedy. The Kennedys declined. Some St. John's physicians suggested the Pepperrell Children's Health Centre. But Smallwood, with Joy's support, settled on naming it after Janeway. Janeway was not asked for permission and was surprised to find the hospital had been named after him.

The New Janeway and the Consolidation of Health Care Facilities

When the Janeway opened in 1966, it joined three general hospitals and a psychiatric hospital to become the fifth acute-care hospital operating in St. John's. In 1968 the Children's Rehabilitation Centre moved into the Fort Pepperrell school, making six health care centres spread across the capital city, leading government members to raise concerns about the efficiency of service delivery and the cost of maintaining so many structures. And so began decades of study, discussion, and debate about how to best deliver efficient, effective health care for the region.

The St. John's Hospital Advisory Council, later the St. John's Hospital Council, was established in September 1968—though it was largely inactive for several years—to help coordinate services and avoid duplication in city hospitals. In May 1978 the council commissioned Toronto consulting firm McKinsey and Company to study the development of the individual hospitals

The Children's Rehabilitation Centre, in the former Fort Pepperrell school.

and their ill-defined roles. The report *Provision of Clinical Services and Programs: A Study to Determine Future Requirements*, released in 1979, offered nine conclusions and recommendations—none of which involved closing the facilities. It recommended that "birth care," provided by three hospitals (St. Clare's Mercy Hospital, the Grace Hospital, and the Janeway), be consolidated in the Janeway because of its Neonatal Intensive Care Unit (NICU), its mandate to serve all children of the province, and its board of directors, made up of members from across the province. It also recommended establishing a single adult and child rehabilitation service, without closing the Children's Rehabilitation Centre. All laboratories should stay open, it concluded, but their efficiency needed to be increased.

Five years later, in February 1984, the *Report of the Royal Commission on Hospital and Nursing Home Costs* recommended that "the St. John's Hospital Council be appropriately funded and charged with the responsibility of developing a comprehensive plan for the delivery of health care services in St. John's." It suggested keeping the same number of hospital beds and limiting major construction or renovations to two sites.

In October 1985 the St. John's Hospital Council released *A Plan to Rationalize Hospital Services in St. John's—Benefits and Cost Implications*, a report by Ernst & Whinney which recommended that the Grace, the Janeway, and the Children's Rehabilitation Centre be rebuilt in close proximity to St. Clare's at an estimated cost of $143,155,000. The Janeway board of directors' medical advisory committee favoured this plan, which they considered a serious plan to modernize and improve the efficiency of the acute-care hospitals in St. John's. It was dubbed "Option 7" by the Council. Another, "Option 10," proposed that the Janeway, the Children's Rehabilitation Centre, and the Grace's Obstetrical and Neonatal Unit relocate to the Health Sciences Centre on Prince Philip Drive.

Option 10 was more popular with the provincial government due to the readily available space for expansion, the tertiary-care services already in place at the Health Sciences Centre, its proximity to the medical school, and, more importantly, the lower cost. Newfoundland and Labrador faced major financial setbacks in the early 1990s: a cod moratorium was declared in 1992, its federal government transfer payments had been reduced, and a national and international recession had begun. Not surprisingly, the government favoured Option 10.

The government wrote a letter in the spring of 1990 to the governing boards of acute-care hospitals in St. John's in which it proposed closing the Grace Hospital and moving its obstetrical and neonatal services to the Health Sciences Centre adjacent to the General Hospital, the School of Medicine, and other specialized services. It further proposed that the Janeway Child Health Centre and the Children's Rehabilitation Centre be relocated to a new facility to be constructed on that site. The projected estimated savings would cover the capital cost of relocation and redevelopment of the services on the Health Sciences site. At the time, this was considered to be about $120 million over five years. The proposal was designed to take advantage of better synergies of services through a centralized arrangement, especially neonatalogy, obstetrics, and other pediatric-related medical services. Existing programs and initiatives between the discipline of pediatrics and the medical school would also be supported and enhanced. The government moved quickly to make the proposal a reality. In early June 1990 a meeting was convened between the minister and senior officials of the Department of Health and the boards of all St. John's hospitals to discuss and advance the proposed restructuring of hospital services in St. John's. The Janeway board chair, John Baker, and executive director, Rick Nurse, took part.

In March 1991, the Janeway's board of directors, as well as its medical advisory committee, agreed to merge the Janeway and the Children's Rehabilitation Centre. The board of the rehabilitation centre, however, did not support this.

Before 1966, the Department of Health operated and oversaw all government facilities. Starting with the opening of the Janeway, however, the minister of health (under the Hospital Act) appointed an independent board of trustees, or health board, to govern each health centre. In its 1992 budget speech, the provincial government announced that it intended to review the Hospital Act and the number of operational health boards. Lucy Dobbin, a private health care consultant and retired executive director of the General Hospital, was commissioned to conduct the review. The guiding concept: consolidating the boards would improve the quality of service by improving coordination of acute and long-term-care services, more effectively using scarce human and fiscal resources, and providing better opportunities for overall cost reduction.

In August 1992, the Janeway's medical advisory committee declared its support for a separate provincial pediatrics board. A special committee drawn from the Janeway's medical advisory committee and hospital board met in late 1992 and early 1993 to discuss major concerns with the restructuring process. The committee—executive director George Tilley, board chair John Baker, medical advisory committee chair Austin Rick Cooper, and board member Wayne Ludlow—strongly supported a separate board for child health, including rehabilitation and perinatal services. The committee also met with Dobbin. Baker submitted a lengthy letter to the minister of health in support of a separate child health board.

Dobbin's report, submitted in February 1993, recommended a merger of the Janeway and the Children's Rehabilitation Centre and consolidation of the boards of all acute-care institutions in St. John's and Bell Island, including the Janeway.

Baker met with the health minister in April 1993 and again advocated for a separate child health board and an independent child health centre. In September 1993, Tilley reported that the health minister intended to recommend to Cabinet the establishment of two hospital boards in St. John's—one for pediatric services, the other for adult services. In November 1993, Baker again wrote the minister to reinforce the Janeway's proposal for a separate pediatric board.

The government officially accepted the Dobbin report in February 1994. This elicited a series of major changes in health care organization in Newfoundland and Labrador.

A single board, the Health Care Corporation of St. John's (HCCSJ), would oversee the acute-care facilities in St. John's and Bell Island, including the merged Janeway and Children's Rehabilitation Centre. Two board members would represent child health; a pediatric advisory committee was not mentioned. Unhappy with the decision, members of the Janeway medical advisory committee (Cooper, David Price, and Albert J. Davis) met with health minister Hubert Kitchen, who suggested that, although there would not be a separate pediatric board, an advisory group could be set up to advise the HCCSJ on pediatric health issues. This group was never appointed.

The new HCCSJ board, including two members from the old Janeway board, Nancy Cook and Ed Kelley, held its first official meeting on July 16, 1994. Sister Elizabeth Davis, appointed CEO of the HCCSJ in September, spoke to the Janeway medical advisory committee in October about the new board and introduced the concept of program management. Program management would mean restructuring the traditional health care departments; clinical departments would be transformed into interdisciplinary patient-based care units. Davis answered many questions about how the Janeway would fit into that model.

That year, the HCCSJ began its consolidation of acute-care services. Although services were still offered in each St. John's hospital, under the new system they would fall under a single administrative department. For example, four acute-care facilities had pharmacies but were considered to be one department. Emergency medicine (excluding the Janeway), diagnostic imaging, and laboratory medicine were also reorganized this way.

In May 1994 a new HCCSJ medical advisory committee was set up under the chairmanship of Ron Whelan. Pediatricians Cooper and Davis represented child health. In April 1995 the medical staff of the acute-care hospitals in St. John's were consolidated into one organization under the HCCSJ.

In July 1995 the provincial government announced that the Pleasantville Janeway would close; two months later, a focus group under chair Davis, with members Cooper, M. Pardy, Mary Baker, and Cindy Tedstone, was set up to discuss the relocation.

In October 1995, the HCCSJ decided to close the Children's Rehabilitation Centre and move it into the Janeway until the new child health centre was built. A transfer committee, with equal representation from the Children's Rehabilitation Centre and the Janeway, was formed to oversee clinical matters, administration, and human resources. The rehabilitation facilities moved into space made available on the first two floors of the Janeway and in the Janeway Apartments. A portable trailer was purchased for play therapy. The Children's Rehabilitation Centre was officially closed in October 1996, after 28 years of operation.

Program management was officially introduced in the HCCSJ in January and February 1996. The Children's and Women's Health Program incorporated child care, as well as all aspects of obstetrics, including labour and delivery, provided by the Janeway and the Grace.

The mandate of the Children's and Women's Health Program, according to an official statement issued on October 10, 2001, was to provide primary, secondary, tertiary, and rehabilitation services to children from birth to 16 years (later 18 years) on an ambulatory, in-patient, and outpatient basis, and ambulatory and in-patient services to women in obstetrics and gynecology, including tertiary care.

The attitude toward creating free-standing pediatric hospitals (see The Evolution of Free-Standing Child Health Centres) has evolved considerably. Before 1970, the trend was toward creating totally independent facilities; after that date, children's hospitals tended to be associated with adult health care facilities and medical schools. In the 1960s, when the Janeway opened, the concept of a free-standing child health centre was a good one, and the hospital thrived for decades. But several factors drove the need for a new centre.

The NICU, an integral part of the Janeway which cared for babies under 30 days old, needed to be located in the same site as obstetrics. No other hospital had a functioning NICU, although some babies, particularly newborns who required surgery, could be treated in an Intensive Care Unit (ICU), which served children older than 30 days. As expertise grew, the management of sick newborns expanded dramatically and all ventilated newborns had to be admitted to the Janeway—those born at the Grace or outside St. John's had to be transferred to the Janeway, often at a very critical time in their life. Delivering all babies at the Janeway was not a viable option as it had no backup care for high-risk mothers and the cost was prohibitive.

In the new Janeway, the delivery suites would be adjacent to the NICU, offering advantages for parents, infants, and neonatologists, and likely lowering the mortality and morbidity in this group of infants.

Due to the high cost of maintaining the old building, the government determined it would be cost neutral to build a new Janeway at the Health Sciences Centre site and close the Grace. Having the children's hospital in close proximity to adult facilities would allow the hospitals to share diagnostic equipment and laboratory services and consolidate food services. Medical professionals would also notice the advantages: subspecialists such as cardiologists, infectious disease specialists, endocrinologists, rheumatologists, and neurologists would find it much easier to exchange ideas with their colleagues and keep up to date at one central location. Physicians who worked with the medical school would find it much easier to teach and do research in close proximity to the university.

In June 2001 the Janeway moved from the Pleasantville site into a new hospital built adjacent to the Health Sciences Centre specifically to accommodate children's and women's health. The goal was to merge hospital space and eliminate duplication by consolidating services: administration, laboratory medicine, housekeeping, security, accounting, diagnostic imaging, maintenance, and public relations.

The staff of the old Janeway recognized other advantages: moving adjacent to the medical school and the adult Health Sciences Centre, having better access to emerging technologies, particularly in diagnostic imaging and laboratory medicine, and more contact with adult health care workers to exchange ideas.

Many of the new Janeway's services are organized differently than they were at the old hospital. Laboratory medicine and dietary services are part of

The Janeway, 2001.

the Health Sciences Centre; emergency medicine falls under the umbrella of children's and women's health and is situated on the main floor of the Janeway. Child Psychiatry is under Mental Health and Addictions—not Children and Women's Health—although it is situated on the fourth floor of the Janeway building. The Diagnostic Imaging Program at the Janeway has a pediatric sub-division but also offers services to adults, including computerized tomography (CT) scans, Magnetic Resonance Imaging (MRI), and prenatal ultrasounds. Delivery-room suites are adjacent to the NICU, but the post-natal ward is in the Health Sciences building. Pediatric wards, the pediatric ICU and all pediatric clinics, including rehabilitation and the NICU, are situated in the Janeway and are part of the Child and Women's Health Program. The Janeway also houses offices for clinicians, a surgical day care, and a medical day-care unit. Although the Janeway is no longer a free-standing hospital, it offers the same clinical services as before, with the advantages of being adjacent to the medical school and the adult hospital.

Although Newfoundland and Labrador has a relatively small population of 500,000, and a low birth rate of approximately 5,000 per year, the province's geography and isolation require it to maintain a modern tertiary-care hospital that can offer the same quality care that other Canadian centres provide.

The Evolution of Free-Standing Children's Hospitals

The Hospital for Sick Children, which opened in Toronto in 1875, was the first major free-standing pediatric hospital in Canada. Children's hospitals in other cities soon followed.

Free-standing pediatric hospitals were designed to address the lack of pediatric care in general hospitals, the high proportion of children in the population, the emergence of pediatrics as a discipline separate from obstetrics and adult medicine, and, related to that, the demand for specific pediatric teaching in medical schools. Many advances made in pediatric care, especially in neonatology and surgery, demanded special equipment and expertise. Free-standing pediatric hospitals had the ability to raise significant amounts of money to equip their centres.

Segregating children's health care from adult facilities did carry some disadvantages, including high costs, isolation from other disciplines, and the duplication of expensive diagnostic equipment (especially in diagnostic imaging). Non-medical services such as food catering, housekeeping, and tendering of medications and medical devices were also duplicated. In many cases, children's hospitals were relatively inaccessible to medical and nursing schools—the schools were generally located next to a teaching general hospital, but the children's hospitals were sometimes several kilometres away. This led to difficulty in research collaboration with medical schools and universities.

In 1970, the children's hospital Saint-Justine UHC in Montreal merged with a maternal hospital, a pioneering move that would be adopted by other Canadian institutions. In 2017, the trend is still toward creating pediatric hospitals as a part of larger health sciences centres, or for older free-standing children's hospitals to merge with obstetrical hospitals or adult health sciences centres. Sixteen pediatric health centres are in operation in Canada in 2017; only two are free-standing hospitals. Three have merged with maternal health facilities, four with adult health care centres, and the remainder are pediatric programs within larger medical centres.

The Janeway has done just that. Formal and informal evidence point to good outcomes in pediatric care, not only at the Janeway but also in the province as a whole. Infant mortality, once very high, is now consistent with the national average. Outcomes for newborns are on par with other Canadian institutions, according to the Vermont Oxford Neonatal Outcome Survey. Informal discussions with the Canadian Association of Pediatric Health Care Centres, the support of the Janeway Foundation, and high satisfaction rates from parents and referring physicians all point to the facility's success. Eastern Health tracks outcome statistics and, for some specialties and diseases, the Janeway measures up to national standards.

On the other hand, the high incidence of genetic disorders, maternal obesity, drug usage, smoking, and increasing maternal age may be leading to worsening newborn health, but these factors are beyond the hospital's control.

Since the new Janeway opened, significant increases have been made in academic research, particularly collaborative research with other centres. Safety standards have been improved, including the implementation of fall prevention initiatives and a "surgical pause"—everything in the operating room is double-checked before the procedure starts and high-risk medications are independently double-checked. Medicine reconciliation, a process of taking and maintaining an accurate medication history, helps avoid adverse drug reactions.

Efforts are ongoing to improve family-centred care, implement quality assurance initiatives, and monitor the workloads of staff and salaried physicians. No plans to change the direction of the Janeway exist; however, everyone engaged with the hospital continues to look for ways to improve services and facilities. The Janeway is accountable to Eastern Health, the provincial government, and the people of Newfoundland and Labrador. A well-trained, dedicated staff and highly trained health care workers together offer the best in quality care.

Clifton Joy

Pediatrician Clifton Joy, the founder of the Janeway, was born in 1922 in Port au Port, a small community in western Newfoundland. He attended school in Stephenville until grade 10, and then St. Bonaventure's College in St. John's for the final year of school. Joy's parents wished to prepare him for the seminary and priesthood, but he had other ideas. He attended St. Francis Xavier University in Nova Scotia for premedical studies, and entered Dalhousie Medical School in 1943. After completing his internship in 1948, he became a medical health officer in St. John's. After one year in that position he took on a family practice in St. George's, Newfoundland.

Clifton Joy.

Over the course of his youth, training, and work in the medical professional, Joy developed a deep understanding of the plight of Newfoundland children. He fully appreciated the hardships families faced, the poor medical care that was available, and the high infant mortality.

Joy decided to become a pediatrician in 1951 and trained at the Montreal Children's Hospital and the Children's Medical Centre in Boston. In 1954 he moved back to Newfoundland and set up a private practice in St. John's.

In 1957 he became chair of a special study group for the NMA to examine hospital facilities for children in the province. The group found that the hospital facilities for children in Newfoundland were inadequate; one of the recommendations was to build a 350-bed children's hospital in St. John's. It took several years but Joy—against a lot of opposition—finally received the support of Premier Smallwood to convert the American military hospital in Pleasantville to become a child health centre.

When the Janeway opened, Joy was active in seeing patients as well in his role as acting Chief of Medicine (Pediatrics). He was well liked by the staff, parents, and children and was always approachable. Several physicians commented that he was a very good bedside teacher and was always available to discuss issues with interns and resident physicians. Joy had a keen interest in allergic diseases, especially asthma, and he always had busy offices and clinics.

Joy was always sociable. In the 1980s he would go to the Aquarena swimming pool in St. John's and, according to his son, spent more time talking to different people there than swimming. He was an avid hiker and walker and would walk for hours, even when he was older. He was an active member of the Bally Haly Golf Club.

He had four children with his wife, Flo, who was always supportive of him and was very proud when the Janeway was opened. Clifton Joy was an excellent pediatrician who loved his family and enjoyed his many friends. His legacy is that of a man with a dream—perhaps an impossible one—who worked tirelessly to make it come true. The Janeway stands in tribute to his dedication and passion.

PART II
CLINICAL DEPARTMENTS

PEDIATRIC MEDICINE

Department of Medicine

The Janeway's Department of Medicine (the official name for the pediatric medicine department) was organized in 1966 under the direction of Dr. Joy. The department welcomed non-surgical and non-psychiatric patients, such as children with asthma or leukemia. Pediatricians, some of whom were also trained as subspecialists, admitted patients to the ward, attended outpatient clinics, and acted as consultants to other disciplines. In 1966, six pediatricians were on the call schedule—Joy, Rufus Dominic, Douglas Simms, John Collins, Kevin Linegar, and Norah Elphinstone Browne—and were also consulting specialists in areas including internal medicine, dermatology, and adult psychiatry. Two additional pediatricians were on the consulting staff and did not do call; all had private practices in addition to their work at the Janeway.

In 1955, a child health program was implemented in the province. The first of its kind in Canada, this government program covered the cost of taking children under age 12 to emergency or outpatient departments and paid for their hospital care. By making medical care more accessible, the program indirectly increased the number of hospital admissions of children. The start of the Medical Care Plan (MCP) in 1969 provided free medical care for residents of Newfoundland and Labrador and further increased the demand for child health services.

From 1966, pediatric residents and rotating interns provided 24-hour coverage for the Department of Medicine. Residents were employed by the hospital, while rotating interns came from Dalhousie University, the General Hospital, and, later, the medical school at Memorial University.

The Janeway had several medical wards. Ward 1B (isolation ward for infectious diseases) accepted transfers from the Fever Hospital and welcomed its first patients on August 2, 1966. Other medical patients were admitted to 2A (children who did not have contagious diseases), 2B (toddlers who did not have infections), and 1A (children with respiratory problems, including croup, bronchiolitis, and asthma). Ward 3E was later opened as a combined surgical and medical ward for neonates (babies in the first four weeks of life). Critically ill children were admitted to the ICU and treated by the pediatrician responsible for their care.

Derek Matthew, 1976.

Surgeons also admitted children to ICU. Many of those patients who were admitted to the wards in the 1960s and 1970s would be managed as outpatients in 2017.

The pediatrician who admitted a child was responsible for his or her care throughout the child's stay, and again if the child was readmitted. A patient was only signed over to another pediatrician if the admitting doctor was leaving town or on leave.

In the early 1960s and 1970s, some specialty areas were covered by physicians who treated adults. Neurologists J.C. Jacob and A. Max House, for example, treated both children and adults. General practitioners did not admit patients to the hospital but worked in the emergency department and walk-in clinic. General practitioner Peg Cox also worked in the Child Development clinic. In the planning of the hospital it was expected that family practitioners would have a more active role than they did in reality.

In 1966, the Department of Medicine had only two sub-departments: neurology and cardiology. Because the Janeway did not have a critical mass of general pediatricians, subspecialty pediatricians covered general pediatrics as required. Pediatrician Derek Matthew was hired as a neonatologist at the Janeway and the Grace hospitals in 1975 and, in time, other subspecialists were hired to focus on child development, pediatric intensive care, neurology, hematology-oncology, and other areas.

Fifty Years Later

In 2017, 48 pediatricians work at the Janeway. Fourteen do general pediatric call; others are on call lists for child protection, hematology-oncology, neonatology, critical care, neurology, or diabetes. Some of the pediatricians who cover general pediatrics are also subspecialists or have special interests, such as respiratory concerns, diabetes, child protection, "normal" newborns, gastroenterology, child development, or administration.

Remuneration for services has changed. Before 1990, pediatricians were paid on a fee-for-service basis and did not receive a stipend for being on call. In 2017, the majority of pediatricians receive a salary from Eastern Health, the regional health authority, through MCP. Some services are paid via sessional payments (a fee for a fixed period of time, usually a half-day clinic or a full-day coverage of a service such as neonatology). An additional stipend is paid for some "essential" call schedules, such as general pediatrics.

The days of a patient being assigned to one pediatrician throughout his or her hospital stay and future visits are gone. In today's system, pediatricians who do general pediatric coverage work for a week at a time, about one week in six, with different pediatricians covering at night. General pediatricians have other duties that keep them busy, such as outpatient clinics, research, administration, and teaching. If a child is admitted to the pediatric intensive care unit (PICU) directly from the emergency department and is later transferred to a ward, the pediatrician on service assumes that child's care. Children who have a medical problem such as asthma, and who are not admitted to PICU, go first to emergency. From there they are admitted to hospital by the pediatrician on call. While some subspecialties such as hematology-oncology admit patients directly, most children are admitted under the general pediatrician on call. These call arrangements allow pediatricians to protect time for their private practices and academic activities.

In the early days of the Janeway, pediatricians on call did not have back-up from neonatologists or other subspecialists, except those in cardiology and hematology-oncology. Anesthetists helped with ventilation in the PICU, but general pediatricians were directly responsible for the care of these sick children.

Pediatricians on call in 2017 are backed up by neonatologists, intensivists,

Lisa Follett's Story

Lisa, the only child of Gloria and Doug Follett, was a smart, healthy, happy, mature young girl. She loved school, was a hard worker, and had plenty of friends. Athletic, kind, and compassionate, Lisa was concerned about the children in Africa and gave her weekly allowance to the poor box in her church.

In July 1986, when Lisa was nine years old, she was diagnosed with idiopathic thrombocytopenia purpura (ITP) (*idiopathic*, cause unknown; *thrombocytopenia*, lack of platelets; *purpura*, bruising). Most children diagnosed with this disease have an acute form, and either get better on their own or respond well to treatment.

Lisa did not respond to treatment but improved spontaneously after four months. The family hoped that that was the end of their ordeal; however, she relapsed four months later. This time she responded to treatment with intravenous gamma globulin—for a short while.

After several relapses, Lisa's physician, Kaiser Ali, requested that surgeon Abdalla Hanna remove her spleen. Splenectomy was known to often help in cases when ITP does not respond to conventional therapy. Lisa improved after surgery, for a while, but relapsed again in August 1989. Ali, with the approval of the hospital ethics committee, gave her intravenous Rhogam, a blood product used to prevent Rh disease in newborns.

Lisa seemed to be responding to Rhogam treatment until February 1990, when the disease invaded her red blood cells. She became anemic. This was a rare complication, and Lisa was referred to the Izaak Walton Killam (IWK) Health Centre in Halifax. Doctors there were puzzled and tried different treatments, to no avail. Lisa returned to the Janeway with no answers and, despite aggressive treatment, her ITP and hemolytic anemia worsened. She also had increased pressure on her brain and became very weak. Her bone marrow was no longer functioning. Her case was presented to a visiting expert from Harvard Medical School in August 1990. He was familiar with the condition but pointed out that, although appropriate treatments had been given, her disease was pro-

and subspecialists, as well as anesthetists, surgeons, and pediatric psychiatrists. Twenty-six residents usually work at the Janeway at any one time, but the rotating internship has either disappeared or been incorporated into the disciplines of family practice, anesthesia, and psychiatry. Pediatricians work gressive and she would not recover.

Over the next few weeks, Lisa's condition gradually worsened as her bone marrow shut down. On October 29, 1990, at the age of 13, Lisa died peacefully with Gloria and Doug at her side.

Lisa was fully aware of what was happening as her condition worsened, and she was worried about her parents. She told her doctor that she prayed to God to get better, but unless she could have her old life back, to play sports and be herself, she would accept her death. She even made Christmas presents in September, a few weeks before her passing, for her family. In those last weeks, Lisa wrote a poem about her illness.

Lisa's poem
If it's not today, it'll be tomorrow.
When my wishes come true
To run and play sports,
Like I always used to do.
I will always have faith in God
And never give up hope,
But until that time comes,
I will do everything but mope.
I try not to let it get me down,
I like to wear a smile and not a frown.
And when it's all over,
I'll be feeling happy and not blue,
I'll be waiting then,
For all my new wishes to come true.

Lisa Follett.

Lisa was a remarkable person who affected everyone she met—her parents, family, friends, and the caregivers at the Janeway, who still remember her.

closely with colleagues in other disciplines, nurses, and allied health professionals. When a child is admitted to hospital, parents are invited to stay and ample room and services are available for them. Parents are also expected to be involved in their child's care.

The role of pediatricians has changed over the past 50 years in light of the

Jacob Whelan's Story

Jacob Whelan was born at the Janeway on January 1, 2007, to parents Joyce and Kevin. When Jacob was about two weeks old, they, noticing that his fingers were red and swollen, brought him to the Janeway. Jacob was treated for an infection but, despite being treated by several specialists, he continued to get worse. Soon his skin, bones, and joints were inflamed. One of the nurses commented that he looked like a child dipped in acid. Most difficult for the parents, Jacob was obviously in a lot of pain and could not be comforted.

Jacob was given powerful anti-inflammatory drugs, which did not help much. He was transferred to the Hospital for Sick Children (SickKids) in Toronto, but doctors there could not help either. Jacob was sent home without diagnosis or treatment.

Through those difficult days, Jacob's parents rarely left his side and they were always polite and thankful to the doctors and nurses who looked after their son. They knew that, despite the attention and care he received, he might not get better.

Janeway rheumatologist Paul Dancey, noting the inability of Jacob's immune system to control inflammation, contacted physician scientist Raphaela Goldback-Mansky at the National Institute of Health in the US. Goldback-Mansky believed the condition that Jacob was suffering had never before been diagnosed. She arranged genetic testing, which confirmed a previously undetected genetic anomaly. Jacob's body was unable to synthesize a protein that controls interleukin-1, an inflammation stimulator; without that protein, his body suffered widespread inflammation.

After further consultation with Goldback-Mansky, on October 8, 2007, Dancey agreed to try Anakinra, an interleukin-1 receptor antagonist for rheumatoid arthritis. The doctors were not sure that the drug, which was not known to have serious side effects, would work for Jacob, but decided it was worth a try. Joyce evolution of the incidence and treatment of pediatric diseases. In 1963, 15,443 children were born in the province; in 2017, the annual birth rate was around 5,000. Public awareness about environmental issues, vaccines, smoking cessation, seat-belt legislation, breast feeding, and better nutrition have helped lower the morbidity and mortality of children in Newfoundland and Labrador.

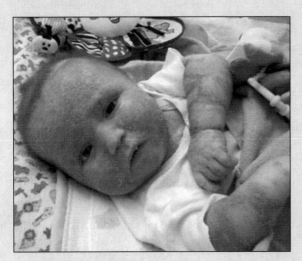 

Jacob Whelan in 2007 and in 2015.

and Kevin gave their consent.

After 48 hours of treatment with Anakinra, Jacob's rash had improved and he was no longer in pain. After two weeks, he was behaving like any other 10-month-old child. Joyce, Kevin, and their daughter, Emily, were ecstatic. Dancey and his team were relieved that they had found a treatment for Jacob.

As of 2017, Jacob is a happy 10-year-old living with his mother, father, and sister. Symptom-free since October 2007, he is an active boy and a delight to his parents.

Since Jacob's diagnosis, at least nine other children in the world have been diagnosed with a deficiency of interleukin-1 receptor antagonist. Without Dancey's persistence, the diagnosis and treatment would never have been discovered.

Sophisticated treatment in clinics, the Emergency Department, and medical and surgical day care unitss has resulted in less reliance on in-patient services. Overall, the high standard of care at the Janeway is comparable to that at other Canadian pediatric teaching hospitals.

Neonatology

The prevailing trend among health care providers in the first half of the 20th century was to take a hands-off approach to sick neonates. The death rate for neonates in North America was quite high in that era, and higher in Newfoundland and Labrador than elsewhere in Canada.

The 1950s brought many innovations and research on sick and premature infants and, by the end of the century, neonatal mortality had decreased in Canada from 45 per 1,000 live births in 1926 to approximately 3 per 1,000 live births in 2006.

Neonatology is a fairly new pediatric subspecialty. Before 1950, little medical treatment was available for sick neonates. The administration of oxygen, introduced in 1900 to treat premature babies with respiratory distress, was accompanied by serious adverse effects such as retrolental fibroplasia (the development of abnormal tissue behind the eye, which can lead to blindness). Exchange transfusions for erythroblastosis fetalis or Rh disease in the 1940s, and the introduction of antibiotics in the 1950s, were successful. The introduction of incubators in the late 1800s and a better understanding of thermal stability in the 1930s lowered the mortality rates for premature babies.

Prematurity, a major cause of neonatal death in North America, was poorly understood before 1950. The general belief was that premature babies who were initially stable deteriorated if handled too much in routine procedures such as weighing, bathing, or inserting feeding tubes. That hands-off approach was certainly in play in Newfoundland—an intern in my medical school class in obstetrics at St. Clare's Mercy Hospital in 1969 was told by the attending physician "to do nothing" for a sick premature baby, as the outcome was "in God's hands."

By 1966, the neonatal mortality in Canada stood at 20 per 1,000 live births. Many babies died of prematurity and Respiratory Distress Syndrome (RDS, seen in premature babies and caused by a lack of surfactant, a substance which makes it easier to breathe). The infant son of President John Kennedy, Patrick Bouvier Kennedy, born August 7, 1963, died of RDS at 36 hours of age, despite the best care. In 2017 RDS is a treatable and preventable disease and infrequently causes neonatal death.

In 1966, Newfoundland and Labrador's birth rate was 12,000 births per year. Two obstetrics units operated in St. John's at St. Clare's and the Grace hospitals. Surgery was done on full-term neonates, but premature babies were only given comfort care—they were not ventilated or given intravenous fluids. Several advances were adopted in the late 1960s, including a technique for giving intravenous fluids with "butterfly needles" (very small needles with plastic wings to facilitate holding the needle during insertion) and augmenting feeding using oral tubes. Premature babies with RDS were given oxygen and sodium bicarbonate following pH monitoring, but no attempts were made to ventilate them and there was no way of transporting them to the Janeway.

Basic neonatal medical services were available at the Janeway, St. Clare's, Grace, and other larger regional hospitals in the province, including exchange transfusions for erythroblastosis, silver nitrate drops to prevent ophthalmia neonatorum, oxygen for apnea and respiratory distress, Vitamin K to prevent hemorrhagic disease, and incubators to keep babies warm. Nasogastric feeding and some intravenous fluids were used. In 1966, no provincial hospital, not even the Janeway, had a neonatal intensivist (a pediatrician with advanced training in neonatology) or pediatrician trained in neonatology on staff or even respirators capable of ventilating neonates.

The Janeway was aware of these deficiencies. In 1967, Joan Dawe, a nursing graduate from St. Clare's, went to Washington to train in neonatology. By 1969, sick neonates were being sent to the Janeway from other hospitals. They were often hypothermic upon arrival because of inadequate warmth and oxygen en route. Pediatricians, nurses, the Janeway administration, and the provincial government were all concerned and encouraged other nurses to travel out of the province to take five-month courses in neonatology on full salary.

In 1969 the Janeway started a post-basic course in neonatal intensive care and recovery nursing and nurses Marilyn Pardy, Maisie Adery, Elizabeth Gran-

The Uptown Hospitals

For decades, all obstetrical care in St. John's was performed at "the uptown hospitals": Grace General Hospital, which opened in 1926, and St. Clare's Mercy Hospital, which opened in 1928. This did not change until St. Clare's closed its obstetrical unit in 1992 and the Grace closed its in 2000.

Before the obstetrical unit opened at the new Janeway, the uptown hospitals took high-risk obstetrical cases referred from the rest of the province. Each hospital had an intermediate level nursery and a well-baby nursery staffed by pediatricians: Helen McKilligin had neonatology experience at a staff level, and Austin Rick Cooper, William Sprague, and Poh Gin Kwa had neonatal experience gained through their pediatric residencies. Flo Downey, head nurse at the Grace, had taken a course in neonatal nursing at the Grace Hospital in Halifax and was trained in managing sick neonates. Together, these individuals did their best to modernize the management of neonates. The arrival of neonatologists Derek Matthew (1976) and Wayne Andrews (1978) brought more improvements.

Because three city hospitals were involved with neonate care after 1966, scarce resources had to be split three ways. Inevitably, neonates who were sick or became sick would have to be transferred to the Janeway in order to benefit from its higher level of resources. Although most neonates responded well after transfer, others suffered adverse consequences. Moving the neonate also meant that he or she was separated from the mother, which medical staff wanted to avoid if at all possible. Some transfers were delayed because the severity of the neonate's condition was not initially recognized, or doctors felt that the neonate might improve with treatment.

Medical staff did not stay overnight on site at the uptown hospitals, which often led to delays in obtaining the obstetrician, pediatrician, and anesthetist on call for emergency deliveries. At the Janeway residents stayed overnight, and delays could be reduced.

Communication between the hospitals in the 1970s was sometimes a problem, as there were no regular obstetric or perinatal rounds. Newly trained neonatologists, pediatricians, and neonatal nurses found it difficult to introduce new concepts of neonatal care in an adult hospital environment.

dy, and Marion Pratt were the first to earn certificates, in January 1970.

The infant mortality rate (the number of deaths in the first year of life) in Newfoundland and Labrador was at 22.9 per 1,000 live births in 1971—one of the highest, if not the highest, in Canada. The national average at that time was 17.5 infant deaths per 1,000 live births. Pediatrician Albert J. Davis, who came to the Janeway in 1969 from Corner Brook, brought a proposal to improve the neonatal transport system to chief of pediatrics John Darte. He received Darte's full support. Davis next approached Donald Kelland, executive director of the Janeway, and received his backing. Davis next met with Department of Health

---

Visiting St. Anthony
By Albert J. Davis

I distinctly remember most of our visits to arrange neonatal transport from communities and cottage hospitals to the Janeway, but the one that I remember most clearly was a visit to St. Anthony in 1974.

Brian Ryan and I had the opportunity to go on one of the airlift flights to Labrador to bring back a woman who was having a difficult pregnancy. It was January, and the plane landed on a big frozen lake; it was quite exciting to experience that. As soon as the plane landed, a swarm of snowmobiles sped up to the aircraft and I wondered if some of them would be able to stop! The patient was put on the plane and flown back to St. Anthony.

Albert J. Davis.

In St. Anthony, the plane landed on the harbour, across deep snow and ice. As the woman was being brought from the plane, one of the individuals who had been carrying the stretcher sank into the snow. The stretcher turned on its side and the poor woman cried out in discomfort. I only give that detail to indicate some of the potential hazards which would occur with transport of any kind.

deputy minister Ed Roberts, and the government pledged to finance the number of incubators required.

Davis, along with Brian Ryan, the Janeway's director of respiratory therapy, identified the appropriate neonatal transport incubators and accessories for the acute management of neonates during transfer to the Janeway. The technical staff who maintained the government emergency aircrafts modified each aircraft to accommodate the neonatal transport incubators and medical staff required to look after the neonate during transport.

Pediatricians with the Janeway team travelled across the province to help set up transport systems and to teach neonatal care. Once the transport equipment became available and was distributed to the regional hospitals, and the training had been completed, local physicians and nurses were responsible for transporting the neonates to the Janeway. This transport service officially started in 1971. Davis writes about one of his more memorable trips in the sidebar "Visiting St. Anthony."

Although this transport infrastructure marked a considerable improvement in service, the transportation of neonates from across the province was still rife with problems. Physicians and nurses from referring hospitals often did not have the necessary skills to accompany the transport.

In 1979 the Janeway was given the responsibility of transporting all neonates in the province. Its transport team consisted of a pediatric resident (until 1990), a nurse with at least one year of neonatology experience, and a respiratory therapist. Nurses, under the leadership of Ramona Strong, and respiratory therapists Brian Ryan and Arthur Osborne played a major role in the safe transport of many sick neonates.

Challenges remained in the care of neonates. Many specialists, such as plastic surgeons and neurosurgeons, were based at the Health Sciences Centre, across town from the Janeway. Little space—no chapel or quiet room—was available at the Janeway for parents and families. As well, the ICU was shared by neonates and children over one month old; this would not change until the hospital moved to the Health Sciences Centre site in 2001.

Other pediatric centres in North America were developing NICUs in the 1960s and 1970s and many produced clinical research that greatly enhanced

The Neonatal Transport Team
By Charlene Pike, RN

Due to the increasing number of sick children being transported to the Janeway, in 1971 the hospital initiated a province-wide effort to organize and improve neonatal transports. Pediatrician Albert J. Davis was instrumental in successfully lobbying for the purchase of transport incubators, and one was placed in each major health centre across the province. Davis and Brian Ryan, a Janeway respiratory therapist, travelled to these centres to instruct on the use of the incubators and on other neonatal topics.

Neonatal transports carried a considerable amount of equipment, including a transport incubator, a Holter IV pump, a head box, an oxygen analyzer, and a "fishing tackle box" stocked with resuscitative equipment and supplies (e.g., IV solutions and syringes) thought to be necessary during transport.

In the mid-1970s the province obtained the services of neonatologists, who became responsible for directing the transport requests. Registered nurses with a minimum of one year of ICU experience were placed on a 24-hour call rotation for transport duty. Depending on the condition of the neonate, team members included a nurse and a respiratory therapist and/or resident.

By 1976 the neonatal transport team was doing an average of 150 transports per year. Babies were being delivered at most hospitals across the province, including Labrador. The two respiratory therapists on staff at the Janeway worked Monday through Friday, 8 a.m. to 4 p.m., and provided 24-hour coverage for transport call.

The resident physician was the pediatric resident who happened to be on call. This resident was the team leader, even though he or she may have had little or no neonatal experience.

In 1987 Joel Alpert, professor and chair of pediatrics at the Boston University School of Medicine, reviewed the Janeway's Ambulatory Education Program and suggested the establishment of "a team of skillful professionals to carry out transport functions which does not include residents and would avoid interrupting planned activities with this unpredictable event which depletes an already small resident staff."

In April 1990, medical residents declared that taking part in multiple neonatal transports offered little by way of educational value and that the transports and on-call time interfered with their ongoing residency training programs. They recommended that another system of neonatal transport be developed. In November 1990 residents sent another letter to the Janeway's medical advisory committee reiterating their suggestions. They strongly suggested a change in the number of residents on call each night. At the time, two residents were in the hospital at night, one for ward call and one for ICU call. Another resident was on call from home for neonatal transport. The residents suggested that only two be on call each night, one for wards and one for ICU. In the event of a neonatal transport, the resident on call for the wards would go, leaving one resident in-house.

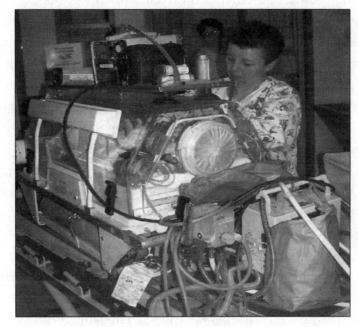

Nurse Agatha Howlett with transport incubator, c. 2001.

This was not totally acceptable to the hospital administration and attending staff but was accepted as an interim solution.

In July 1990, Wayne Andrews, chair of the medical advisory committee, sent a letter to Peter Roberts, president of the Newfoundland Medical Association (NMA), requesting approval in principle for the establishment of a non-physician neonatal transport team. This letter included the 1986 report of William Feldman, a professor of pediatrics from the University of Ottawa, who felt that "urgent attention must be paid to the problem of sacrificing the residents' educational program for the Neonatal Transport services' needs."

Andrews asked for approval from the NMA to transfer the neonatal transport resident functions to the nurse and respiratory therapist. This began the tedious process of gaining approval from the NMA for Medical-Nursing Shared Procedures and the Association of Registered Nurses of Newfoundland and Labrador for these procedures.

The first course for the non-physician neonatal transport team began on February 25, 1991.

neonate care. Equipment and technologies were being developed. Ohio Infant Warmer Systems, neonatal thermal regulation systems which provided precise manual and server control of the neonate's environment, were introduced in 1973. The same year, the Janeway acquired several Baby Bird ventilators to facilitate the ventilation of neonates. It also purchased equipment that allowed the laboratory to test minute quantities of blood; it would have been impossible to ventilate a neonate without a blood gas analyzer, which measured oxygen, pH, and carbon dioxide. By then, medical staff had a good understanding of acid-base balance, parenteral nutrition, infection control, and diagnostic imaging. These technological advances allowed the Janeway to treat many sick neonates, including premature neonates, that would not have survived without ventilation and parenteral nutrition.

Pediatric cardiologist Clifton Way took a sabbatical from the Janeway in 1975 for echocardiogram (cardiac ultrasound machine) training. Cardiac surgeon Gary Cornel operated on patients at the Janeway between 1974 and 1990. Between March 31, 1974, and May 1, 1975, 121 neonates under seven days of age were admitted to the neonatal unit, and 59 to ICU. By 1976 the neonatal transport team averaged 150 transports a year. With this expansion of services, particularly the intensive care of neonates, a lack of space and expertise became a concern.

Davis asked the Janeway's medical advisory committee in 1975 for additional resources for neonatal intensive care. Other physicians made similar submissions. Eight beds in Ward 3E were dedicated to that purpose, and in 1982 a new ICU with much more space to accommodate surgical, medical, and neonatal care was opened.

In 1976, the perinatal program, which follows the progress of high-risk neonates, was introduced under pediatrician Ann Johnson, based on a similar program in Halifax. It had two arms: a travelling clinic follow-up program for high-risk patients discharged from NICU, and a provincial educational program run by a nurse educator. The educational program in 2017 has a neonatal and obstetrical nurse educator, Clare Bessell, who coordinates obstetrical issues with the maternal-fetal obstetrician; Susan White coordinates the breast-feeding program, the Neonatal Resuscitation Program (NRP), and the Acute Care of At Risk Newborns (ACORN) program. These programs, still

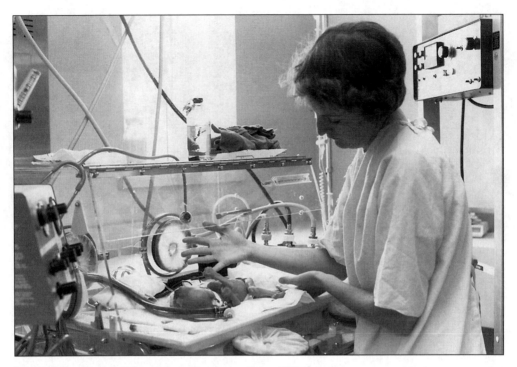

Nurse Mary Baker, ICU, with a premature baby, 1977.

operational in 2017, have been important in improving fetal, neonatal, and post-neonatal health. The arrival of neonatologists Derek Matthew in 1976 and Wayne Andrews in 1978 greatly enhanced the care of sick neonates.

In 1976, the Grace, St. Clare's, and the Janeway all expressed resistance to unifying their obstetric and neonatal services. This position was counter to that of many pediatricians who thought that merging the units would bring major benefits by allowing mothers closer contact with their sick babies. St. Clare's and the Grace both wanted to maintain their general-hospital status with the obstetrical and newborn services. The Janeway had developed a tertiary-care system—along with the other supportive disciplines, such as anesthesia and surgery—that Janeway neonatologists and pediatricians felt was an essential part of its mandate.

In 1978, Wayne Andrews, a neonatologist with expertise in nutrition, arrived at the Janeway; he played a major role in the care of neonates at the Grace and St. Clare's.

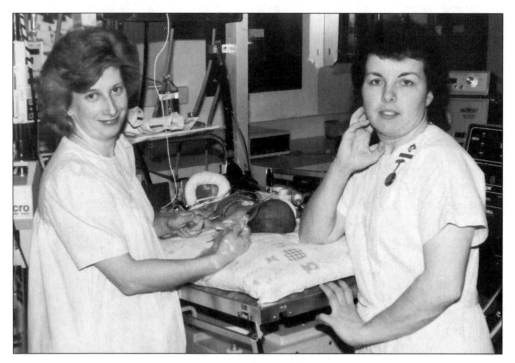

Nurses Michelle Murdock and Agatha Howlett, c. 1980, in neonatology.

In 1980, the provincial government put forward a plan to close the Grace and Janeway hospitals and concentrate obstetrics and pediatrics in a newly expanded St. Clare's. This proposal, referred to as "Option 1" by the government, introduced the idea of unification and coordination of perinatal services and opened a discussion of the benefits of amalgamation. After considerable outline planning, the whole idea was dropped for economic reasons.

Perinatologist James Goodwin, appointed in 1984, was a strong advocate for the unification of perinatal services under one roof and, along with neonatologist Don Reid in 1984, he convinced the Grace and St. Clare's hospitals to co-operate in the creation of a provincial perinatal centre at the Grace. A fetal diagnostic unit, to identify fetuses at risk, was established. As a result, more high-risk pregnancies were transferred to St. John's, and fewer sick neonates had to be collected from outlying areas by a transport team to make the hazardous journey to St. John's. In-town transport increased from the Grace and St. Clare's to the Janeway.

Renovations were made in 1985 and 1986 to the delivery suite and the neo-natal unit at the Grace to incorporate birthing rooms. The neonatal nursery was moved to the fourth floor, adjacent to the delivery room, easing the movement of patients between the delivery room and nursery; this had the welcome side effect of improving communication between obstetricians and pediatricians. Moving an unstable neonate directly from the delivery room to NICU at the Grace was ideal, but if this was not possible, moving the neonate into an environment where he or she could be rapidly warmed and stabilized before transport was the next best option. A second NICU in St. John's was impractical (duplication of services and a lack of demand, personnel, and finances).

When the new Janeway opened in 2001, obstetrics and neonatology were finally on one site and the need for in-town transports disappeared. Its NICU is a modern, well-equipped unit with a resuscitation room adjacent to the high-risk obstetrical delivery suite, which allows for resuscitation, insertion of lines, ventilation, and comprehensive care for sick neonates immediately after birth. A large unit where neonates could be ventilated for extended periods and several step-down units where they could be nursed after they became stabilized are also present. NICU has an adequate number of incubators, ventilators, overhead heaters, monitors, and intravenous pumps; it is close to the operating room for ease of transportation.

At one time, a pediatrician would be called to attend high-risk deliveries and resuscitate neonates. At night, pediatricians would be called in from home, as were the obstetrician and anesthetist for a Caesarean section or high-risk delivery. The new neonatal unit after 2001 had a neonatal resuscitation team, whose members—a nurse and a respiratory therapist—were trained in neonatal resuscitations. The team attended all high-risk deliveries and were always available in-house. Since 2001, a pediatric resident or nurse practitioner, neonatologist, anesthetist, and obstetrician have remained in the hospital overnight, improving the quality of care. Better training, the availability of sophisticated monitoring, especially of ultrasound equipment, and the development of fetal maternal medicine have also improved outcomes.

The Janeway's neonatologists and supporting staff have been involved with two national and international initiatives: Canadian Neonatal Network (CNN) and Vermont Oxford Network (VON). CNN, founded in 2004, is a consortium of NICUs that looks at the outcomes of all neonates admitted to participating NICUs in Canada who are 48 hours old or older. The Janeway has been an active participant in CNN since its beginning.

VON, founded in 1988, is comprised of teams of neonatal intensive-care professionals who represent NICUs around the world. Their stated mission is "to improve the quality and safety of medical care for newborn infants and their families through a coordinated program of research, education, and quality improvement projects." The Janeway has been an active member of VON since 1995 and submits data on a regular basis, allowing the hospital to compare outcomes with other NICU centres worldwide. Information on neonates weighing between 500 and 1,500 grams are collected, including mortality, length of stay, whether breast feeding occurred after discharge, and the presence of necrotizing enterocolitis, bacterial septicemia, blindness, or chronic lung disease.

Comparing the Janeway's outcomes with those from other institutions allows the hospital to pinpoint problems and make appropriate changes. Participation in these networks has greatly enhanced the care of neonates in NICU and the hospital's outcomes are comparable with other units in Canada and those in other countries.

The Janeway's neonatologists, under the leadership of Khalid Aziz and Wayne Andrews, have introduced and implemented evidence-based medicine. All aspects of care are routinely reviewed to ensure that good scientific evidence justifies all decisions made. Clinical practice guidelines are posted in the units.

The provincial perinatal program has been actively involved with the ACORN program, which connects peripheral hospitals that deliver newborns. Aziz has been actively involved with ACORN nationally and was responsible for instituting it in Newfoundland and Labrador's regional hospitals. ACORN and the NRP, initiated by the American Academy of Pediatrics, have greatly improved the care of sick neonates in the province outside the Janeway; those that need to be transported receive appropriate care from their local neonatal health care providers.

Brook-Lynn Moss's Story

Brook-Lynn Moss was delivered by Caesarean section on October 14, 2004, at Western Memorial Hospital in Corner Brook. Her parents, Melanie and Stephen, were excited—Brook-Lynn would be their fourth child, and everything was expected to go well. The pregnancy had gone smoothly, and all pre-Caesarean checkups were normal.

After the delivery the baby cried, but one hour later she was having trouble breathing and the parents were told by the pediatrician that she had a "wet lung" and was not responding. She did not improve and they were told she was not breathing well. The pediatrician told Melanie that they had done everything they could, but the baby was not doing well and had to be transferred to the Janeway. The family saw Brook-Lynn shortly after the pediatrician's visit and she looked blue, despite receiving oxygen through a ventilator. The Janeway transport team flew out from St. John's and the transport nurse, Agatha Howlett, quickly assessed the baby. She thought that the baby had persistent fetal circulation, a condition in which the blood supply to the lung is diminished. Howell spoke with Aziz, who suggested trying nitric oxide inhalation, a new therapy which had never been tried by the transport team. The team had some with them, however, and gave it to Brook-Lynn.

After nitric oxide was administered, Brook-Lynn improved considerably, and turned pink, and was well enough to be transported to St. John's. She initially had a difficult time at the Janeway NICU. She required ventilation and medications, but she slowly improved. After 25 days she was discharged. She still had some lingering problems, but these eventually were resolved.

Through Brook-Lynn's rocky course at the Janeway, the family never gave up hope—as another parent said, "As long as there is breath there is hope."

Brook-Lynn benefitted from the Janeway transport and the nitric oxide therapy and intensive care she received at NICU. In 2017 Brook-Lynn is an active 12-year-old who is doing well in school and, like her siblings and parents, believes that a person should live life the best one can and enjoy every day with zeal and purpose.

Neonatal care at the Janeway in 2017 is modern, up-to-date, and evidence-based. Its outcomes are comparable to or better than those from similar units in Canada.

A Wild Baby Chase
By Michael Jeavons, Pediatric Resident 1975–1976

It would have been about 4 p.m. in January or February 1976. I was first on call and responsible for any neonatal transports. A call came in from the Burin Hospital that they had a premature neonate who needed to be picked up. The routine was that the first on-call resident and one of the ICU nurses would go out in the ambulance to pick up the baby. Since the baby was coming from Burin, their ambulance would come as far as Goobies and we would meet them at the gas station there and exchange an empty transport incubator for the one with the baby. We went to the emergency department entrance and were met by the ambulance driver, who commented, "Better bring your winter coat, b'y; there's a storm coming in."

We stopped at the gas station just outside St. John's city limits to fill up before setting out on the Trans-Canada. In those days, St. John's city ambulances had radios that barely worked within city limits and not at all outside them. The wind was getting stronger and the snow heavier, and when we reached the barrens, the full force of the wind became evident. It was blowing so hard that the sides of the ambulance were blowing in and out, making a sound like an oil drum on a hot day. It was hard for the driver to hold the vehicle on the road and the visibility was dreadful, but there seemed to be no other traffic and the only issue was whether we would be blown off the road. In those days the Trans-Canada was a two-lane road and as much of it was raised above the level of the barrens there was a drop-off either side with no guardrail. On a couple of occasions the windshield became so iced up that one of the ambulance attendants had to get out to scrape it and de-ice the windshield wipers. I remember that when he got out he had to hold on to the ambulance to stop from being blown away as the road was so slippery and the wind so strong that he was in danger of ending up in the ditch.

The trip was slow and nerve-wracking and took several hours. Finally, we reached the gas station at Goobies and staggered across the parking lot to the office. We were greeted with the question, "Didn't they tell you, b'y? The weather's too bad in Burin and they couldn't leave." We were told that this news had reached the Janeway just after we left and they had been unable to reach us by radio but had called every gas station between St. John's and Goobies. Unfortunately, they called the one where we had stopped just after we had left. The RCMP had closed the highway because of the conditions and had taken their patrol cars off the road—this was the reason we did not meet any traffic. After gassing up and getting a cup of coffee we got back in the ambulance and made the return trip to St. John's through the same kind of weather.

We finally got back to the hospital about 10 or 11 p.m. and I walked back into Emergency to be met by the words, "They just called from Burin; it's turned to rain and they're leaving now." My response could not be printed here but I made it very clear that the responsibility for the return trip belonged to the second on-call resident.

Critical Care

NICUs and PICUs were established in Canadian pediatric hospitals in the early 1960s. The Janeway hospital opened in 1966 with a combined NICU and PICU, which provided complicated post-operative care and ventilator support to children with respiratory failure and served patients with septic shock, severe trauma, diabetic ketoacidosis, status asthmatics, and a variety of less common, but serious, diagnoses. Although this combined ICU was adequate, very few premature neonates, and no cardiac surgery patients, came to the facility. The patients were looked after by pediatricians, surgeons, anesthetists, and the nurse in charge. Ramona Strong, the nurse in charge from August 1966 until 1980, was the binding force that held the place together.

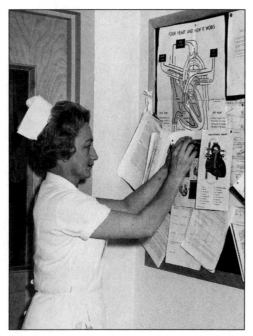

Ramona Strong, the first head nurse, ICU.

No neonatologists or intensivists were on staff in 1966 and the admitting physician, either a pediatrician or a surgeon, was usually the attending physician. Most ventilated patients were intubated and stabilized by anesthetists. Nurses who had special training in neonatology and intensive care, together with respiratory therapists and physicians, followed the care of these patients.

In 1967 the Janeway's first respiratory therapist, Brian Ryan, arrived; he was followed by Arthur Osborne, who dedicated most of his time to the ICU. Ryan and Osborne had a detailed knowledge of ventilators and their role expanded with the dramatic increase in neonatal and cardiac surgery.

The ICU, located on the third floor, was an open concept with 13 intensive-care beds, two recovery-room beds, and two isolation rooms (a double with two beds and a single), for a total of 18 beds, although up to 25 beds could be used if required. The unit was shared by medicine and surgery, including neonates in medicine and surgery.

In 1974, the unit was poorly lit, windowless, and drab. It provided adequate service but looked cold and inhospitable and offered little room for parents to sit with their children; it was also difficult to maintain patient confidentiality.

The hospital did not have special-care units. Post-op surgical patients who needed close observation but were not critically ill were kept in ICU.

Almost right away, bed distribution was a problem. In the early 1970s, neonatology rapidly expanded and cardiac surgery was established. It was impossible to practice good infection control. A lack of equipment and staff, particularly in nursing and respiratory therapy, were also issues. Elective cardiac surgeries sometimes had to be cancelled because of the lack of intensive-care beds required for their post-operative care. Some surgical patients who were retained longer than ideal because they had indwelling catheters or drains, who could have been looked after in a special observation unit on the ward, added to the overcrowding.

In the late 1970s, an extension was planned to house a new ICU on the third floor and a large teaching/conference room on the main floor. The new, larger, brightly lit ICU opened in December 1980 with two isolation rooms and 16 beds in the open area, as well as a quiet room for parents and an office for the neonatologist and nurse manager.

Although this was a definite improvement, significant problems were noted. Neonatologist Wayne Andrews and cardiac surgeon Gary Cornel sent detailed letters outlining their concerns to the Janeway's medical advisory committee in the summer of 1980.

Andrews felt that the new ICU, although likely to be overused, would have adequate space if non-critical constant-care patients, particularly urology patients, were admitted to a constant-care room instead. He recommended that nursing staff be divided into two separate functional sections, neonatology and medical/surgical, a well-accepted nursing pattern that had been shown to promote greater nursing expertise through educational programs and improved morale. He also suggested that the neonatal section of eight beds for intensive care should be physically separate from the older children; however, he admitted that that would be impossible given the space restrictions. Finally, Andrews suggested separate organizational hierarchies for the neonatal and medical/surgical services.

Cornel had five recommendations: a fixed allocation of bed space; a surgical special-care unit of about six beds on the ward to take non-critical constant-care patients and a similar special-care unit on the surgical ward for stable surgical neonates; a division of nurses into neonatal, surgical, and medical groups; the acquisition of better monitors and respirators to service neonates, and the purchase of infusion pumps, percutaneous blood gas analyzers, and ultrasonic blood pressure monitors; and the appointment of a medical director to oversee the ICU.

Some of the recommendations from both men were approved. Eight neonatal beds in the ICU were designated a "neonatal unit." The concept of constant-care units was approved. The concept of an ICU director was supported but did not become a reality until much later (in the meantime, the chair of the critical-care committee was designated ICU director). The concept of a separate NICU nursing team was approved; however, the neonatal unit remained a part of the ICU. These changes, along with improvements in technology and standards of clinical care, increased the ICU efficiency.

In 1992 Cornel resigned from the Janeway, although he returned several times a year to perform elective cardiac surgery. The number of births was determined to be too small to maintain a pediatric cardiac surgical service.

In the old Janeway, pediatric intensive-care patients were under an open system, that is, the physician who initially saw the patient continued to be the physician most responsible for that patient—although the intensivists did most, if not all, of the care.

Before 1988 none of the Janeway pediatricians had specialized training in pediatric intensive-care medicine, although the Janeway's medical advisory

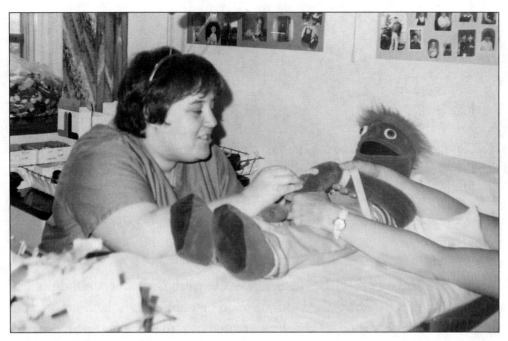

Debbie Reid, first intensivist.

committee and hospital board fully supported the need for these services. Very sick patients often could not be transported to larger centres on mainland Canada and it became imperative that the Janeway have intensivists and provide intensive care for all critically ill children in the province.

In 1988, pediatrician Debbie Reid, a graduate of Memorial's medical school and the residency program at the Janeway, took a leave of absence to train for two years in London, Ontario, as a pediatric intensivist. In July 1990 she was designated chief of the non-neonatal section of ICU. In 1995 a second pediatric intensivist, Jill Barter, arrived. Barter, also a Memorial University medical school graduate, completed pediatric and pediatric intensive-care training at Montreal Children's Hospital. Reid and Barter greatly enhanced the ICU's pediatric section with new treatment protocols, excellent teaching, and the introduction of better pumps and ventilators. They were supported by several skilled general pediatricians, including pediatric cardiologist Christina Templeton, who started at the Janeway in 2001.

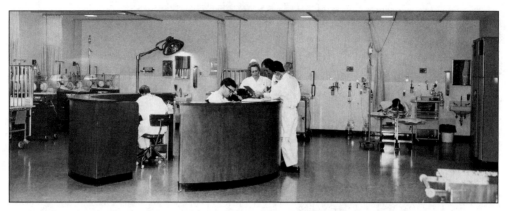

Dr. George Sharpe (seated) and Ramona Strong in the ICU, early 1970s.

At the New Janeway

The new Janeway, at the Health Sciences Centre, has separate units designated NICU and PICU. The PICU has four open beds and two isolation rooms for patients up to 18 years of age. The unit, situated next to the operating room and close to the respiratory therapy department, is spacious with windows looking outdoors. A waiting room for parents, a teaching and meeting room for house staff, three physician's offices, a storage room, and a utility room for cleaning used equipment are also part of the unit. Reid was chief of the PICU until Barter took over in 2009. In 2017, the unit is covered by three intensivists, a pediatric cardiologist with experience in critical-care medicine, and 20 nurses, many with ICU training. Senior pediatric residents are assigned to the unit 24 hours a day.

In addition to their duties in the PICU, intensivists consult other physicians in the emergency room and wards, offer advice to physicians across Newfoundland and Labrador, do clinical research, and are actively involved with Memorial University's teaching program at the graduate and undergraduate levels. Intensivists have been actively involved in running simulated programs in critical care for pediatricians, family physicians, residents, and medical students.

Pediatric intensivist Kristina Krmpotic came to the Janeway in 2014 and reviewed the population of patients who had visited PICU over the previous 24 years. She collected information, including patients' age at admission, diagnosis, length of stay, and, if they were ventilated, their duration of intubation. Her study showed that from September 1991 to August 31, 2015, 4,506 children

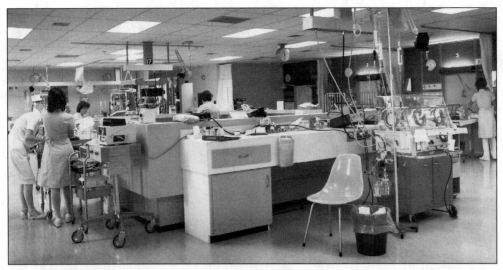

The renovated ICU, 1990.

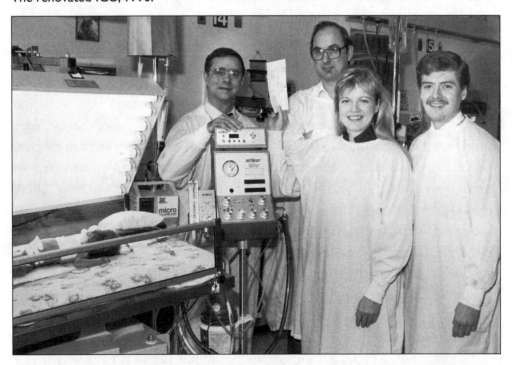

Dr. Don Reid (left) and Dr. Wayne Andrews (back) accepting a cheque for $10,886.25 from Angela Genge and Christopher Cook, representatives of the Medical Students' Society. The society raised the money at the 10th annual Monte Carlo Night in December 1984 to purchase a neonatal ventilator for the ICU.

were admitted to PICU. Of these, 850 were under one year of age, the largest age group by far. This was similar to the demographics of patients in similar institutions in Australia and New Zealand. The proportion of medical and surgical admissions to the Janeway's PICU (2001–2015) was comparable to that in a statistical report from the UK and Ireland (Macrae 2005).

The number of surgical admissions to the Janeway's PICU declined from 120 in 1992 to 57 in 2014. This can be attributed to the discontinuation of cardiac surgery after Cornel's departure.

The number of pediatric medical admissions has been between 100 or 120 in most years. The most common reasons for "medical admissions" have been respiratory insufficiency, cardiac insufficiency, and neurologic or toxic/metabolic trauma. The mortality rates, the number of intubated patients, and the number of intubated days has declined. However, the mean duration of intubation has not changed significantly.

Children and neonates with severe respiratory distress are often treated with Extracorporeal Membrane Oxygen (ECMO) in larger hospitals; this, however, is not available in the Janeway. ECMO is used to treat life-threatening refractory respiratory failure that is unresponsive to mechanical ventilation and is expected to resolve in a short time. Since 2011, a number of patients who would have been candidates for ECMO were treated in PICU with aggressive mechanical ventilation, and eventually did well. A visiting pediatric intensivist commented that the survival of these was remarkable and reflected the skill of the intensivists, nurses, and respiratory therapists.

Not surprisingly, much has changed in the Janeway ICU/PICU over the past 50 years. Some of these changes were external—the decrease in invasive infectious diseases like meningitis and meningococcal disease due to vaccines, in trauma patients because of safer cars and seat-belt legislation, and in spina bifida cases because of folic acid administration in the mother or the termination of affected fetuses. Reye's syndrome is no longer observed because of the discontinuation of acetylsalicylic acid for minor illnesses in children. The birth rate has declined significantly as well. Improved internal factors include the introduction of intensivists, the education of the nursing staff, better ventilators, parenteral nutrition, better monitoring devices, and more sophisticated

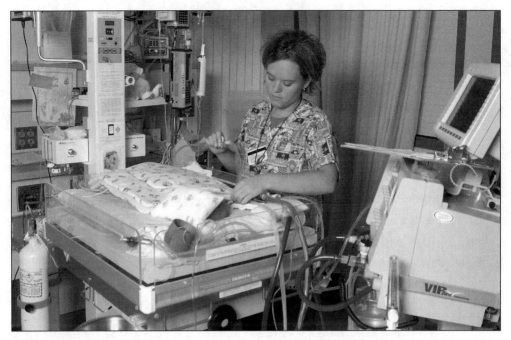

Nurse Jeaniel Hayes, PICU.

laboratory investigations and imaging.

In 2017, priorities include improving follow-up after PICU discharge, optimizing post-operative handover, using preprinted orders for common serious diagnoses, and formal and simulation teaching. Simulation teaching and learning creates new opportunities for the deliberate practice of new skills without involving real patients. Sleep studies that are now referred to centres on the mainland could be done in the PICU with appropriate funding, space, and physician training. In the future, sedation for children requiring it for certain procedures such as bone marrow aspirations could be done in PICU.

Adolescent Medicine

Adolescent patients (ages 12–16; up to 18 since 2005) have been treated at the Janeway in all disciplines since its 1966 opening. According to a 1984 report by pediatrician Delores Doherty, 22 to 25 per cent of the Janeway's medical and surgery patients fell into this age group at that time. This figure reaches as high as 40 to 50 per cent in psychiatry.

Adolescent medicine—and adolescence itself—has changed dramatically since 1966. Fifty years ago, infectious diseases contributed to adolescent illness, HIV was unknown, and type II diabetes was rare. Teen pregnancy rates were much higher in 1966 than they are in 2017 and birth control was just starting to become accessible.

High-school dropout rates are also much lower in 2017; adolescents stay in high school longer, and a higher percentage pursue university and college education. On the other hand, obesity and sedentary lifestyles have a profound influence on adolescent health in 2017. The incidence of eating disorders has increased dramatically and has become a major issue for physicians who focus on adolescent care.

Access to electronic devices, the Internet, social media, and video games has had a profound influence on the well-being of adolescents. Excessive use of these devices is negative—but certain programs are educational and beneficial, as is the sharing of information.

Starting in 1977, Doherty developed adolescent-specific services at the Janeway and devoted much of her practice to the care of this age group. In June 1984 she submitted "Obstacles to Adolescent Care at the Janeway: Definition and Proposed Remediation" to the Janeway's medical advisory committee. The report's key recommendations: designate a multidisciplinary team to organize an adolescent service, establish an adolescent in-patient ward for medical/surgical/orthopedic patients, reorganize the outpatient/emergency area to account for adolescent needs, and provide a separate unit for adolescent psychiatric patients. Doherty also recommended the creation of an adolescent service team (physician, nurse, and social worker) and a general adolescent walk-in clinic.

The committee supported Doherty's suggestions and an adolescent walk-in clinic was initiated, although funding and recruitment issues delayed some of the other objectives. Psychiatry, a separate entity, was not included in the initial service offerings.

Delores Doherty.

The adolescent ward, an 18-bed unit located on the third floor, opened in 1986. It served patients with eating disorders, as well as those with oncology, surgical, and other medical needs. Adolescent psychiatry patients were admitted to the psychiatry ward. Morale was high among the nurses, and adolescent patients considered it a special place. The ward closed in 1990 due to budget cuts and a shortage of nurses and because the surgeons wanted their adolescent patients to be admitted to a surgical ward.

Adolescent Medicine 1999–2016
By Joanne Simms

Before the 1999 arrival of Anna Dominic, a pediatrician trained in adolescent medicine at SickKids, adolescent eating-disorder patients were seen by a team which included a pediatrician, psychiatrist, dietician, and social worker. Dominic greatly expanded adolescent services at the Janeway and established the first fully functioning adolescent medicine clinic east of Montreal. The clinic provided a much-needed and long-awaited service to adolescents in need of a specialized approach to care.

As the number of referrals of adolescents to the Janeway for assessment of eating disorders and other health concerns continued to rise—a phenomenon that started in the late 1980s, and continues in 2017—Dominic lobbied for resources and supports for the adolescent population. Her expertise was sought by health professionals throughout Newfoundland and Labrador. When government funding was announced for nurse practitioners in 1999, doctors Dominic, Cooper, and Leigh Ann Newhook secured funding for a nurse practitioner specifically for adolescent medicine. Joanne Simms was hired in January 2001. Simms and Dominic led the adolescent medicine group and worked diligently to build an efficient team, knowing that the best approach for adolescents and their families would be the ability to access all resources and services needed from a coordinated team of professionals working to provide the best possible care.

In 2002, pediatrician Denise Hickey joined the adolescent medicine team and provided in-patient and outpatient support. In 2009, Colleen Crowther completed her adolescent medicine fellowship at McGill University and joined the team, which grew to include a full-time registered dietitian, social worker, and psychologist.

Over the years, the adolescent medicine team has forged relationships with other groups and programs. It has been actively involved in the planning, development, implementation, and evaluation of an Interprofessional Community Capacity Building Program, a government-funded program dedicated to coordinating and rationalizing services for patients with eating disorders, including the development and presentation of an intensive two-day training workshop for health professionals and educators in six communities throughout Newfoundland and Labrador. Information pertaining to this project and its evaluation have been presented locally, nationally, and internationally. Team members are also involved in education, leadership, and research activities in many capacities (as guest lecturers, board members, research team members, and policy/program consultants).

From 1999 to 2015, almost 12,000 patient visits to the adolescent medicine team have been recorded. Referrals for adolescent medicine are accepted around a wide variety of illnesses/issues, including eating disorders, pubertal growth and development concerns, psychosomatic complaints, organic chronic illness, psychosocial issues, anxiety, depression, adolescent gynecology, and gay, lesbian, bisexual, transgender, and queer issues.

The adolescent medicine team offers focused in-patient and outpatient treatment for adolescents with eating disorders. Since the fall of 1999, they have diagnosed 322 adolescents with eating disorders, and 222 in-patients have been admitted for this reason, totalling 7,000 in-patient days.

Working on the Adolescent Unit
By Margie Rossiter

The adolescent unit is a very dear place to me. Rose Blackwood was in charge in 1986 when I arrived, and each nurse did a month of team leading. I worked with Jill Withers, Judy Kelly, Charlene Daley, Cathy Collins, Lori Campbell, Linda Colbourne, Joyce Smith, and Rhonda Short.

I don't know when the unit closed or why, but the beds gradually closed down. It was a special place with a real team and family approach. I still remember the adolescents I looked after, some of whom went on to very successful careers in medicine and laboratory medicine.

By Jan Humber

The Janeway adolescent unit was my favourite place to work. Everyone worked there by choice and were devastated when the unit closed in 1990. I remember teamwork, commitment, camaraderie, and great morale. I always sensed that the staff on the unit were satisfied and happy.

We all understood the unique nature of the adolescent. You needed patience by the truckload, superb listening skills, and the ability to be non-judgmental. I often had to tap into my inner teenager to help me understand the nature of the patients I worked with.

I once read that adolescent medicine, like all of medicine, is whole-person based, not just organ-based, and the staff were very aware of this. We were a close-knit team, aware of the complexities of this age group. We took a family approach, but respected the patient's need for a confidential environment. We wanted our patients to be healthy, both physically and emotionally.

By Charlene Daley

Working in the adolescent unit in 1989 taught me much about their conditions and about life—things I could never learn from any textbook. In my opinion, the patients also learned from each other: the teen who overdosed on a Friday night for a lark might have been placed in a room with an oncology patient, showing the first teen the true value and fragile nature of life. I remember that all the nurses working in the unit were "put" there with little or no input, but as a group we thrived, and wanted to succeed, and did so, making the unit a great place for us and for our patients. Many of the teens were "frequent flyers" or long-term patients, and we got to know them and their families very well.

We did our best not only to treat the medical issues but also to meet the varied needs, developmental and psychosocial included, of each adolescent.

Reflections on Ward 3C
By Kenneth Jerrett

A significant part of my adolescence was spent in the adolescent ward of the Janeway. In addition to many short stays, I was there from April until October 1987, with only a brief respite in the middle. The adolescent ward was my home.

Facing adolescence while enduring chronic or acute illness, or trauma resulting from accident, can be especially difficult. We were old enough to at least partially understand our circumstances but not mature enough to fully accept them. In some ways we were the biggest collection of misfits to be found outside of a 1980s teen movie.

Despite all our problems we developed a sense of community. We shared our tastes in music and movies like teenagers anywhere. Instead of meeting at the mall, we met by the nursing station. Some days we had fun; other days we tried hard to ignore the screams of a burn victim or the hysterical sobs of a family watching their child's life slip away. Even in this tragic environment we found humour in many situations, and laughed almost every day. Some friendships lasted long after we all returned home.

Trying to handle a group of adolescents in such circumstances is not

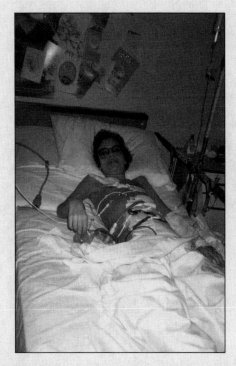 

Kenneth Jerrett.

easy. At that time, parents did not stay with their children overnight, except in the final stages of palliative care. The nurses of 3C often needed to assume the additional roles of mother, teacher, counsellor, friend, and referee. They let us be ourselves, never being too restrictive or pandering to our immaturity. We were always treated with patience and respect and with just enough irreverence to occasionally make the Janeway a fun place to be. Our little space, furnished with only an ancient bed and metal drawer, was made to feel like home.

For me, one incident best illustrates life on the adolescent ward. I was required to have abdominal dressings changed several times a day. It was a messy and tedious affair. The nurses and I would make it more fun by playing music and having a bandage changing sing-a-long.

One night I was being visited by an elderly relative from England. He embodied the stereotype of the English stiff upper lip, having spent five years in a prisoner-of-war camp in World War II after his airplane had been

Kenneth Jerrett.

shot down. During his visit, one of the more vivacious nurses of the unit came skipping in and announced: "Get the music on. It's time to change the dressing!" Upon seeing I had company, she turned crimson, meekly apologized, and backed out of the room.

Once the nurse left, my relative turned to me and, with a smile, said, "In all the times I've been in hospital I've never been so lucky as to have a nurse like that."

He was right. We were very lucky to have nurses like that.

While we all had the misfortune to require a stay at the Janeway, those of us who spent significant time on the adolescent ward were very lucky to receive such competent and compassionate care. We were part of a very special place.

Infectious Diseases

The incidence and prevalence of pediatric infectious diseases in Canada has decreased dramatically over the past century. No polio, typhoid, diphtheria, tetanus, or smallpox cases ever came to the Janeway, even back in 1966, because of universal immunization and, in the case of typhoid, the establishment of clean-water supplies and strict surveillance. New vaccines, adequate food and clean water, an improved economy, better education, public health initiatives, a greater emphasis on hygiene, and active treatment have eliminated many infectious diseases or have greatly diminished their morbidity and mortality.

Since the early 1950s, Newfoundland and Labrador has had an excellent public health system and in 2017 it has the highest immunization rate for children in Canada.

In 1966, several infectious diseases were problematic: children were being treated for tuberculosis at the sanatoriums in St. John's and Corner Brook until the Janeway opened. Measles, varicella (chicken pox), bacterial meningitis, epiglottitis, congenital rubella, viral and bacterial pneumonia, septicemia (blood infections), gastroenteritis, and neonatal sepsis were also common in the first few years. The incidence of these has declined significantly because of new vaccines and, in the case of group B streptococcal neonatal sepsis, surveillance, prophylaxis, and early treatment with antibiotics.

HIV/AIDS

HIV/AIDS was a major problem in pediatrics in North America in the last two decades of the 20th century. HIV/AIDS patients at the Janeway fell into one of two groups: those who had acquired it from their mothers, and those who had acquired it from infected blood products.

The infection was unknown until 1981, when *Morbidity and Mortality Week-ly*, the journal from the Centre for Disease Control in Atlanta, Georgia, report-ed on several sexually active gay men who has acquired *Pneumocystis carinni* pneumonia, an infection seen only in severely immune compromised people. The early years after the discovery were marked by fear and misunderstand-ing, which were slowly combatted as it was established that the condition was caused by a retrovirus, later named Human Immunodeficiency Virus (HIV).

In 1982, the Centre for Disease Control reported that the Acquired Immune Deficiency Syndrome (AIDS), as it was named, had been found in a number of Haitians and hemophiliacs. Those considered at the highest risk for HIV infection included children born to HIV-positive women, hemophiliacs, and blood recipients. In 1983 the cause of AIDS was discovered simultaneously by French scientist Luc Montagnier and Robert Gallo of the US National Institute of Health.

In 1987, the American Food and Drug Administration approved Zidovu-dine (AZT) for the treatment of HIV/AIDS, the first drug available to combat the disease.

HIV Infection from Blood Products

Hemophilia, an inherited disorder of blood coagulation, is characterized by a permanent tendency to spontaneous or traumatic hemorrhages. It is seen in males and, in most cases, is caused by a lack of clotting factor VIII. The in-cidence of factor VIII deficiency hemophilia is higher in Newfoundland and Labrador than the rest of the world, and all children with hemophilia born in the province are treated at the Janeway.

Hemophilia was a devastating and painful disease before modern treat-ments. Patients with severe cases bled into their joints, which was agonizingly painful. An injury to the head or an internal organ could be fatal. The severely affected generally became very debilitated and died at an early age.

In 1965, a product called cryoprecipitate became available for the treatment of hemophilia. In 1979, a dried concentrate of factor VIII became available and was widely circulated by the Canadian Red Cross. This product, brought in from the US, was derived by pooling blood from multiple paid blood donors.

The first hemophiliacs to develop AIDS were reported in the US in 1982 and in December of that year the Canadian National Hemophilia Foundation issued a medical bulletin warning of the increased risk of acquiring infection from contaminated factor VIII concentrate. Despite the perceived risks, a debate about whether HIV was transmitted through blood donations was ongoing, and steps were not taken to screen donors adequately in either the US or Canada. Heat-treated factor VIII concentrate, introduced in Canada in May 1985, was believed to lower the risk of HIV contamination. The enzyme-linked immunosorbent assay (ELISA test), which could detect the HIV virus, became available in 1985 and both donors and blood recipients were tested.

In Newfoundland and Labrador, 21 hemophilia patients tested positive for HIV between 1985 and 1989; no others were found after screening the blood supply for HIV began. Eight children with hemophilia who had received factor VIII concentrate from the Janeway became HIV positive. All developed AIDS and died, except one. All 12 adults with hemophilia who had been infected developed AIDS, and subsequently died.

Most of the factor VIII concentrate was brought in from a commercial source (Cutter Laboratories) in the US by the Canadian Red Cross and distributed by the Janeway to adults and children with hemophilia.

Vic Parsons in his book *Bad Blood: The Tragedy of the Canadian Tainted Blood Scandal* (Lester & Orpen Dennys, 2002) tells the story of Newfoundland and Labrador patient Justin Marche, who had received contaminated factor VIII concentrate. At age 16 he changed from a mild-mannered shy teenager into an unpredictable, violent, and obsessive young man, and eventually developed dementia from HIV encephalopathy. Justin died in January 1992, in his early 20s.

Mother to Child Transmission

Maternal to child transmission is the most common type of HIV transmission to children, and most children who acquire HIV this way usually present symptoms in the first five years of life. Before treatment became available, the chances of an infant born in North America to a HIV-positive mother acquiring HIV was around 20 per cent.

In November 1994, Edward M. Connor published a study in the *New England Journal of Medicine* that showed that giving AZT to HIV-positive women before and during labour and delivery and to the newborn for six weeks reduced the risk of maternal-infant HIV transmission by approximately two-thirds.

In the early 1990s, Newfoundland and Labrador had a high incidence of HIV infection. Of the 157 people diagnosed in the province as of December 31, 1994, 33 (20 per cent) were women, most of child-bearing age. In the early 1990s, Newfoundland and Labrador had approximately double the national incidence of HIV infection in women.

The Janeway's first case of HIV acquired from a mother was a four-month-old baby boy admitted on April 30, 1991, with respiratory distress. The mother stated that she was not at high risk for HIV. The baby was quite ill and was initially respirator-dependent. An antibody test for HIV was positive in the baby and the mother. He was subsequently weaned off the ventilator but died of cytomegalovirus pneumonia at 11 months of age. Four other infants were infected from their mothers: two in 1991, one in 1992, and one in 1994. All of these children died of AIDS. Although treatment was available, they already had advanced diseases when diagnosed.

Physicians, public health officials, and public health laboratories in the province were concerned about the high rate of incidence and, in particular, that the HIV-infection rate was so high in women of child-bearing age.

Sam Ratnam, director of the Public Health Laboratories and a member of the Advisory Committee on Infectious Diseases Committee (ACID), published an article in the *Canadian Medical Association Journal* (April 1, 1996) about HIV infection in women and the danger of transmitting this infection to their offspring. He anonymously tested blood that had been sent for prenatal screening for HIV in 1993 and 1994. Of approximately 15,000 samples, nine were HIV positive. Most of these were not tested nominally for HIV.

In the early years of HIV infection, health care providers were concerned about the issue of consent and HIV testing. Because the first patients to be diagnosed with AIDS were gay men, those who identified as either gay or bisexual feared discrimination. Privacy for anyone being screened was extremely important; routine HIV screening, including that of pregnant women, was not

Introduction of Vaccines in Newfoundland

1799: Smallpox (introduced in Trinity, Newfoundland, by physician John Clinch)

1920s: Bacillus Calmette-Guérin (BCG) for tuberculosis

1930: Diphtheria

1940: Tetanus toxoid

1943: Whole cell pertussis vaccine

1955: Polio

1963: Measles

1969: Mumps

1971: Rubella (in Measles, mumps, rubella [MMR] vaccine)

1977: Pneumococcal polysaccharide

1978: Meningococcal polysaccharide

1981: Hepatitis B, plasma

1986: Hepatitis B, recombinant

1997: Acellular pertussis

1985: Haemophilus polysaccharide

1990: Haemophilus conjugate

1995: Varicella

2005: Meningococcal conjugate

2006: Zoster vaccine

2006: Human papillomavirus

2006: Rotavirus

2010: Pneumococcal conjugate

Pediatric Infectious Disease Specialists

Austin Rick Cooper: 1974–present

Rudy Ozere: 1982–1992

Rob Morris: 1984–present

Natalie Bridger: 2012–present

Infection Control Officers, 1966–2001

Heidi Davis

Linda Foley

Peggy Bartlett

Marion Yetman

welcomed. This was an issue in Newfoundland and Labrador because of the high incidence of infection in pregnant women, most of whom were asymptomatic. With the introduction of AZT, it became critically important to identify and treat the offspring of any HIV-positive women. Although ACID recommended routine HIV testing for all pregnant women in May 1993, it was not implemented.

At the November 17, 1994, ACID meeting, Cooper advised that the incidence of prenatal HIV testing had increased but many high-risk pregnant women were still not being tested. While routine testing was not the norm across North America, it was becoming understood that increased screening was necessary for the good of both mother and child. Dr. Ian Bowmer, ACID committee chair, shared these concerns to the provincial health minister.

In February 1996, the ACID committee again recommended that routine prenatal screening include HIV testing, unless the laboratory was specifically directed not to do so. It was to be the physician's responsibility to ensure that his or her patients were aware of the test and had given consent. This controversial recommendation was eventually approved by the Newfoundland and Labrador Medical Association (NLMA) and the Department of Health, and by March 1997 routine HIV testing on prenatal blood samples began.

Newfoundland and Labrador was the first province in Canada to adopt such a measure. Most pregnant women had prenatal blood screening. If a pregnant woman showed up in the case room without having been screened, she was considered high risk, and tested, with consent. In 2017, many North American jurisdictions, but still not all, have implemented some form of routine HIV testing.

This provincial strategy was simple, but very controversial, and virtually eliminated HIV infection in newborn infants. Although HIV-positive mothers have since delivered babies in the province, because of prenatal testing and the ability to treat the newborn, and the mother before and during labour, no cases of HIV infection have been reported in infants born in the province since 1997. Lobbying for and implementing this strategy was a team effort by the Janeway (Cooper), the Public Health Laboratories (Ratnam), and the Department of Health (Faith Stratton).

Infectious Disease: The Future

Although many improvements have been made since 1966, challenges remain in the treatment of infectious diseases. The infection rates of tuberculosis, HIV, septicemias, and newborn sepsis are falling but are still present and problematic. Children with these diseases may become infected with bacterial organisms that are multidrug resistant.

Newfoundland and Labrador accepts a high number of immigrants and refugees. Some of these children have infectious disease that are not common here, such as malaria.

Sexually transmitted infections and infectious diseases seen in IV drug abusers are on the increase in Newfoundland and Labrador, and often affect adolescents.

The push to immunize all children and keep up to date with recommendations of the National Advisory Committee (the national body that recommends immunization schedules for Canada) is a constant challenge. As of 2017 Newfoundland and Labrador has the highest immunization rate in the country.

Implementing ongoing infection control practices, particularly handwashing, requires constant effort, at the Janeway and all health care institutions.

Could an epidemic of the deadly avian influenza strike? Will some infectious bacterial organisms become totally antibiotic-resistant? The increase in travel allows for the introduction of new pathogens, such as strains of influenza (e.g., H1N1), and the reintroduction of old pathogens (e.g., tuberculosis). The need for constant and up-to-date education about issues, trends, prevention, and treatment of infectious diseases for all health care practitioners and the general public is ongoing in the province.

Diabetes and Endocrinology

Type I diabetes mellitus is one of the most prevalent chronic diseases in childhood. It results in acute and sometimes life-threatening symptomatic hyperglycemia.

Newfoundland and Labrador has the highest incidence of childhood type I diabetes worldwide and the incidence is climbing. Between 1987 and 2010, it was 37.8 per 100,000 people. It is most prevalent on the Avalon and Northern peninsulas, where an average of 40.2 and 40.6 cases per 100,000 were reported per year. The incidence from 2007 to 2010 was 49.9 per 100,000 per year.

The relatively high rate of type I diabetes can be attributed to the unique genetic background of Newfoundlanders and Labradorians (because of the small number of founding families and isolation), the northern latitude, vitamin D deficiency, low breast-feeding rates, and high rates of Caesarean sections.

In the first 10 years of the Janeway, no specific diabetic program existed and children with type I diabetes were followed by pediatricians who may not have had support from other health care workers. Diabetic patients in Newfoundland would have been treated by physicians, pediatricians, internists, and family practitioners in their nearest health centre, not necessarily at the Janeway.

Diabetes was diagnosed in a central laboratory based on blood glucose levels; patients with diabetes were followed by measuring glucose in their urine. There were no meters (portable devices that give blood sugar results at the bedside) and blood tests required a large sample of blood and several hours to process.

In March 1971, Albert J. Davis initiated a weekly diabetic clinic attended by a pediatrician, social worker, dietitian, and nurse coordinator (Rita Dawe). This was the beginning of the diabetic program at the Janeway. Some pediatricians followed their patients in their own clinics.

Children with diabetes in that era required several injections a day of beef and pork insulin; urine glucose monitoring was also done five or six times a day to determine insulin requirements. In the early 1980s, this process was replaced with a blood glucose monitor, which meant that patients simply had to prick their fingers and the blood was tested immediately. This greatly improved management of the disease.

A common complication of type 1 diabetes is diabetic ketoacidosis, which occurs when high levels of blood acids called ketones are produced. Patients displaying symptoms often require admission to hospital.

In the late 1980s, insulin pumps were invented, and in 2000 the province started a pump program for children with type 1 diabetes. Initially this was for individuals younger than 18, but in 2010 this was extended to those up to 25. In 2014, approximately 70 per cent of patients under 25 with type 1 diabetes used insulin pumps.

Participants in the Janeway diabetic program continues to grow, and stands at about 300 in 2017. Similar programs are in place in Grand Falls-Windsor, Gander, St. Anthony, and Clarenville. The Janeway team also acts as consultants for other programs. The Janeway's 2017 team has two diabetic nurses, four physicians, a part-time psychologist, a part-time social worker, a dietician, and a part-time teacher.

The multidisciplinary team approach, modern drugs and equipment, thorough teaching of children and families, knowledge translation, and support from emergency and intensive-care physicians have greatly improved the quality of care received by patients with type 1 diabetes, even as incidence of the disease continues to rise.

Paula's Story
By Donna Haggerty

Our baby girl, Paula, was born in 1977. In February 1980, when I was working at the Health Sciences Centre in neurosurgery, Paula started wetting the bed every night and drinking bathtub water. She was diagnosed with Type 1 diabetes at almost three years of age. I was in complete shock.

I didn't know much about diabetes at the time, but I did know that my little girl needed insulin and would need to follow a special diet. Her first injection was given in emergency. She cried and so did her father and I. We were told she would be admitted for a hospital stay, but I refused: my little girl wasn't spending a night in the Janeway. We headed home to Torbay. Partway home I got scared. I asked my husband to turn around and we returned to the hospital. This was the beginning of a new reality for our family. We wanted only the best for Paula.

Two days later I was rocking Paula to sleep in her hospital room. She wasn't a good eater while in hospital. On this particular evening she was irritable and I was tired. When I finally saw her close her eyes and fall asleep, I was delighted. I decided to rock her for a while before leaving her for the evening.

Soon Dr. Chaker Hobeika came in, and I said, "Oh please don't wake her, she just went to sleep." He took one look at my sleeping princess and quickly took her out of my arms and alerted the nursing staff. Soon Paula started twitching and went into a seizure. Before I knew it, she had an IV, and was settling. This was my introduction to hypoglycemia.

Two weeks later she was discharged. My head was on bust—please, no new information!

Paula needed two needles a day. She cried with every injection. She would hide everywhere so I couldn't find her. She would say, "Please mommy, no needle … I'll be a good girl today." At that time, beef and pork insulin was used, and it needed to be refrigerated. Cold insulin is very painful when injected. We used 12.7-millimetre needles, which we also now know are very painful, as most of the injections are muscular (for a three-year-old little girl, I would say all the injections were muscular, into her tiny arms and legs).

Because glucose monitoring was not available, urine testing was ordered at least five or six times per day. We placed two drops of urine in a test tube along with 10 drops of water to see what colour it would turn: blue meant normal-to-low sugars; orange indicated high. Every time we checked the urine, we needed to colour in the appropriate area in her diary with the correct colour. We received our first glucose monitor about a year after Paula was diagnosed. I thought I was in heaven—it took just two minutes to know exactly how much sugar was in Paula's blood. But I was always afraid it was wrong: test strips were diluted with water prior to testing and the amount of water differed from person to person. This result determined how insulin was given and adjusted. No wonder everyone worried about complications.

Low blood sugars were scary. Glucagon, a hormone that raises the blood sugar, had to be given with a needle in the muscle in the early years. It had to be the hardest thing I have ever had to do. That needle was so big (I now have a 1 cubic centimetre syringe in the glucagon box for administration, which is much less stressful for the patient, and me).

Going to school was another challenge. Teachers just didn't get it. When Paula was in Grade 1, her teacher called and told me she thought Paula was low. I asked the teacher what Paula was doing, the teacher's response was, "I sat her outside to get some fresh air." I responded, "Can you go give her a juice box while she gets her fresh air and I'll be right there?"

I considered myself an over-protective parent. Knowing Paula's blood sugar levels at all times was very important to me. I worked so hard to keep the sugars within target and got so frustrated when they weren't. One day I called Paula and the first thing I said to her was, "What was your lunch-time sugar?" Her response was, "Mom, why is it always about my sugars? Why don't you ask me how I am or how my day is going?" That was an awakening for me: Paula is not a number; she's a beautiful girl with diabetes.

When Paula was 11 years old, I accepted a position at the Janeway as diabetes coordinator. I read everything I could get my hands on about diabetes, but at the end of the day I must admit that I learned all about the management of diabetes from right inside my own home and from the children I taught.

Every new meter, insulin, or delivery device (including pens) that arrived would make me so excited to bring it home to try it out on Paula for her review.

In 2000 insulin pump therapy was gaining great publicity. I learned all about it. It seemed like an amazing way to manage diabetes. I started my first pump in the Janeway in November 2000. I was so proud and couldn't wait to tell Paula all about it. To my shock, Paula made it very clear that enough was enough. She would *not* use a pump. She was using pens for her injections and doing just fine. No way was she going to have a pump hanging on her waist to show the world. I accepted her decision—she was 23 and old enough to make her own decisions.

Three years later, Paula informed me she and her boyfriend had made the decision that she would start pump therapy. In the next four years Paula and Stephen were married and wanted to start a family. Her obstetrician, however, gave them little hope of having a healthy baby, as her hemoglobin A1C levels were high, in the 7 per cent range (the A1C test shows how well the diabetes is controlled and provides an average of blood sugar control over two to three months; the normal range is between 4 and 5.6 per cent). We concluded that Paula could better manage her diabetes if she wore a sensor, though in 2007 sensors (a device that gives continuous blood sugar results) were painful and expensive, and transmitters were large. Paula and Stephen were determined to do whatever it took to have a healthy baby. She wore a sensor throughout her pregnancy and maintained A1Cs in the 6s. On July 17, 2007, they were blessed with a healthy baby boy, Ethan. Paula attributes her health to sensor therapy. On August 18, 2009, they had their second child, a healthy baby girl, Mary.

Today Paula is a healthy young mother in complete control of her diabetes and makes both her mom and dad very proud of her accomplishments in life.

Cardiology

When the Janeway opened in 1966, cardiology was a division of the Department of Medicine under the direction of cardiologist John Collins. In 1967, 590 electrocardiograms (EKGs) were performed. The first cardiac catherization (a procedure in which a sterile catheter is inserted in a vein and passed through the venous system into the heart; dye is then injected so that the structure of the heart can be visualized on X-ray) in Newfoundland and Labrador was done by Collins on July 31, 1967.

Cardiologist Clifton Way came to the Janeway in 1968 and by the end of that year he was doing most of the hospital's cardiology work. In 1970, a total of 534

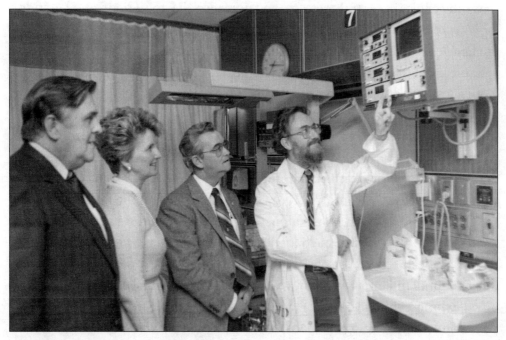

Cardiac surgeon Gary Cornel demonstrating new monitoring equipment, c. 1988.

Cardiologists

John Collins: 1966–1967
Clifton Way: 1968–1981
Shyma Virmani: 1977–2001
Geoffrey Sharratt: 1982–1993
Suryakant Shah: 1996–present
Christina Templeton: 2001–present
Heather Bremner: 2012–present

Nurse Coordinators

Theresa Clarke: 1981–1996
Charlene Daley: 1996–present

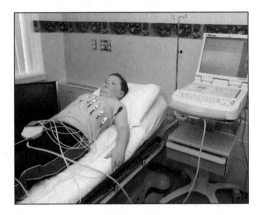

Child getting an EKG.

EKGs, 50 cardiac catherizations, 33 cardioangiograms, and 10 aortograms were done. Four years later, the busy department extended its program to include travelling clinics in central, western, and northern Newfoundland and Labrador.

Way took a sabbatical to study echocardiogram in 1978, and in January 1979 the first echocardiogram machine was installed, which made it much easier for a cardiologist to diagnose congenital heart disease. Before echocardiograms, cardiac catherizations were used to diagnose congenital heart defects; the introduction of echocardiograms greatly reduced the need for this procedure.

Cardiac surgeon Gary Cornel worked at the Janeway from 1972 to 1990, when he moved to Ottawa. By then, his case load had declined significantly, mainly due to the province's declining birth rate. He offered some elective services after that, but all cardiac surgery was discontinued at the Janeway by 1999.

Cardiology has always been a busy division at the Janeway, recording 4,679 child visits in 2015. Another 376 patients came to travelling clinics and 27 children went to a referral centre for possible surgery or another procedure not available in Newfoundland and Labrador. In 2017, this service consists of three cardiologists, who provide on-call service, a nurse practitioner, two cardiac sonographers, an EKG technologist, a receptionist, and a secretary. A spacious modern suite of rooms is dedicated to cardiology on the third floor of the hospital.

Cystic Fibrosis and Respirology

Cystic fibrosis, an inherited disorder, causes severe damage to the lungs and digestive system, which leads to malabsorption. It is the most common fatal genetic disease affecting Canadians under age 25; 1 in every 3,600 children born in Canada are diagnosed with cystic fibrosis.

Discovered by Dr. Dorothy Andersen in 1938, cystic fibrosis was once a hopeless condition, fatal in early infancy and childhood. Although there is still no cure, cystic fibrosis is today a chronic condition affecting more adults than children. In 1968, the median survival age for Canadians with cystic fibrosis was 14; in 2015 it was over 50. In Newfoundland and Labrador it is 50.9 years. In 2017 there are 81 cystic fibrosis patients (27 children and 54 adults) in Newfoundland and Labrador.

In 1972 Dr. Kevin Linegar and nurse coordinator Wendy Williams started the cystic fibrosis clinic at the Janeway, funded by the Canadian Cystic Fibrosis Foundation.

Damodar Vaze, cystic fibrosis coordinator, 2001.

Timely diagnosis and the aggressive use of intravenous, oral, and inhaled antibiotics have brought marked improvements in the treatment of this disease. Pancreatic enzyme replacement and better nutrition have improved outcomes. More importantly, a comprehensive multidisciplinary approach has led to improved survival and quality of life. A screening program for cystic fibrosis will be introduced for all newborns in the province in the near future.

Clifton Way, Damodar Vaze, Rob Morris,

Mary Noseworthy, Carolyn Cashin, and Mary Jane Smith were some of the pediatricians who supervised the care of cystic fibrosis patients throughout the history of the Janeway. Physiotherapists, social workers, and nurses are integral to the team. Adult cystic fibrosis patients are followed by adult respirologists. In 2017 the nurse coordinator for adult and child is Karen Doyle. Dr. Mary Jane Smith is the Janeway clinic director.

Neurology

The Janeway neurology department opened in 1966 under the direction of Dr. A. Max House; Dr. J.C. Jacob was appointed director in 1968. The department has had a senior technician and a secretary since 1966. Neurologists answered consults, admitted patients, held regular clinics, and did electroencephalograms (EEGs). In 1976, 1,228 examinations were done.

Jacob was an outstanding clinician who could make an accurate diagnosis on complicated patients before ultrasounds, CT scans, or MRIs were available. In addition to his work at the Janeway, his local private practice served adults. In 1984, Dr. Gabriel Ronen, the first fully trained pediatric neurologist at the Janeway, joined Jacob. Ronen, an assistant professor in the medical school, also had an active neurological practice.

In the new Janeway, the neurology department admits patients, runs regular clinics, and consults for pediatricians and surgeons. Members also teach medical students and resident physicians in pediatrics and neurology. CT scans and MRIs have enhanced the diagnosis of neurological conditions; however, the astute observations of a dedicated neurologist are still of paramount importance. The range of medications for seizure disorders have expanded and are often able to control the frequency and duration of seizures.

In 2017, the department has two certified pediatric neurologists, David Buckley and Muhammad Alam, as well as general pediatrician Laura Vivian. Nurse specialist Dianne McGrath teaches and screens patients; two EEG technologists, Karen Aubrey and Kevin Kean, and two secretaries, Germaine Barnes and Charlene Williams, round out the department.

Between April 2014 and March 2015, the department recorded 1,278 visits. The neurologists saw 725 patients and 553 EEGs, video EEGs, and electrophysiology studies (EPS) were performed.

Pediatric Nephrology

Pediatric nephrology at the Janeway specializes in the diagnosis and management of children with acute or chronic kidney disease. Nephrologists treat a variety of renal diseases, including glomerulonephritis, renal tubular acidosis, IgA nephropathy, polycystic kidney disease, nephrolithiasis, hypertension, proteinuria, and hematuria. They also provide comprehensive care for children with chronic kidney failure or acute kidney failure, children on hemodialysis or peritoneal dialysis, and transplant recipients.

The Janeway has never had a permanent pediatric nephrologist on staff. Children who present with kidney disease have been followed by general pediatricians, neonatologists, and internists. The Janeway's nephrology clinic, established in 1966, was attended by adult-focused nephrologists, including Michael Paul, Pat Parfrey, Brian Curtis, and David Churchill (Churchill was designated as an adult nephrologist with an interest in pediatrics in 1975). These doctors offered comprehensive consultations to in-patients and their families and held monthly children's clinics until 1998, when the service merged with the visiting Halifax pediatric nephrology clinics.

Attempts to recruit a full-time pediatric nephrologist to the Janeway were made but not considered a priority because of the province's small population, the availability of adult nephrologists, the ready availability of nephrologists from Halifax's IWK Hospital, the absence of a kidney transplant program, and the low birth rate.

Pediatric nephrologist John Crocker joined IWK in 1972; Philip Acott, also a pediatric nephrologist, started there in 1998. Crocker was readily available for phone consultations with Janeway medical staff, and his advice was invaluable. Patients under 12 years of age requiring long-term peritoneal or hemodialysis were referred to the nephrologists in Halifax. Patients with kidney fail-

Pediatric nephrologists Philip Acott and John Crocker.

ure or serious renal disease were also often sent to Halifax.

The IWK nephrology unit started by Crocker was fully equipped to handle all aspects of kidney disease and kidney failure. Staff dialyzed children of all ages and have done kidney transplants since the unit was established. The unit has an international reputation for excellence and its clinical care, teaching, and research are state of the art.

The Janeway's pediatric nephrology service has been a good model of collaborative care between two pediatric hospitals and would never have existed without the leadership, hard work, and excellent care provided by Crocker and Acott. Crocker retired in 2015. In 2017, Acott, James Tee, and Philip Wornell are the doctors on the IWK nephrology unit team.

Lydia Smith's Story
By Christina Smith

Lydia Danielle Smith was born on June 10, 1998, at 32 weeks gestation. Several weeks before, at an 18-week routine ultrasound, we were told that she was developing with one kidney—but that we shouldn't worry, as many people lived healthy lives with one functioning kidney. A precautionary follow-up ultrasound was scheduled closer to the delivery date to check on development. During a biweekly prenatal visit at 30 weeks, a requisition was sent for the follow-up ultrasound and, two weeks later, we went for a biophysical at the Grace General Hospital. Within minutes the ultrasound technician called for the doctor and it was explained that the baby had very little amniotic fluid surrounding her and that her one kidney was not functioning enough to sustain her in utero. It was decided that she would be delivered by emergency Caesarean section the following morning. Over the next 12 hours, her mother was given steroids to aid in lung development. It was explained to us that the chances of a baby in her condition surviving the delivery was 5 to 15 per cent.

Early the next morning, Lydia was born and doctors hurried to stabilize and assess her. She was transferred to the Janeway. Her kidney, lung, and heart functions were poor and, in the experience of the Janeway staff, it was very difficult to stay positive. As the first day progressed, Lydia faced many challenges. The chief of pediatrics, Dr. Austin Rick Cooper, requested that Dr. Philip Acott, a pediatric nephrologist from IWK, who was in town to speak at a Kidney Foundation event, be consulted on Lydia's condition. Acott suggested that, if the Janeway NICU could keep Lydia stable for one week, she could be transferred to IWK via air ambulance. He was cautiously optimistic that they could help her. It was a very difficult week for everyone, but at eight days old Lydia was transferred to Halifax.

Our entire family, including our two-year-old daughter, spent the next 16 months in Halifax. Lydia had many hurdles to overcome but, with the help of peritoneal dialysis, she developed into a strong, pleasant, and determined little girl. In October 1999, we moved back to Newfoundland. The staff at the Janeway worked diligently with the staff at IWK to maintain Lydia's good health. In fact, following Lydia's birth in June 1998, the IWK and the Janeway proceeded to hold quarterly nephrology clinics at the Janeway when a nephrologist—Acott or John Crocker— would travel to the Janeway to see children with potential kidney conditions.

In April 2000, Lydia developed an infection and needed to return to IWK. It was decided that she would undergo a kidney transplant. On October 4, 2000, at two years and four months, Lydia received a kidney from her mother and within six weeks was reunited with her family in Newfoundland. Once again, the Janeway took the lead, consulting with IWK as needed.

Lydia did well following the transplant. She started school and attended ballet

Lydia Smith.

class, but because of her immunosuppressant medication she developed many colds and infections. She often required oxygen. She frequently missed school, and nearly every little illness required hospitalization. In 2008, her lungs began to fail. In September 2008 Lydia was admitted to the Janeway and, following assessment and consultation with the respirology department at SickKids in Toronto, she was airlifted to SickKids for a lung transplant assessment. The Janeway staff worked tirelessly and spent many hours consulting with respirologists in Toronto.

On November 21, 2008, Lydia was placed on the lung transplant list and on December 2, just 11 days later, she received a double lung transplant. After one week in PICU and 10 days on the transplant unit, Lydia was given a day pass to leave the hospital to visit her family at their hotel. On December 24, Lydia was given a night pass and woke the following morning to find that Santa had found her and her two sisters (ages 8 and 12). On January 1, 2009, Lydia went ice-skating on an outdoor rink in downtown Toronto—an activity that was unthinkable just one month before.

On January 6 she was released from SickKids and February 21, 2009, we were on our way back home to Newfoundland. The Janeway staff developed a great working relationship with the lung transplant team at SickKids to keep Lydia healthy and never hesitated to consult as necessary. Every

Janeway staff member from housekeeping to blood collection, X-ray, outpatient clinic, medical day care, nursing staff, pulmonary-function technicians, doctors, and dietary and playroom staff have played a tremendous role in Lydia's life.

Returning to our home hospital, although sometimes stressful, was helped by the wonderful relationships the Janeway developed with the hospitals offering transplant programs. The team at the Janeway went above and beyond to ensure that Lydia's medical needs were always met. They consulted with the medical professionals at both IWK and SickKids and together they worked to bring Lydia to where she is today, a young woman of 18, a high school graduate, and a post-secondary education student.

We are very grateful to the incredible medical teams and their willingness to work together to put Lydia's medical needs first. We are grateful every day that we live in Canada where our medical system works as one unit to benefit all Canadians.

Medical Day Care

The Janeway's medical day-care unit, which provides pediatric day-care services, opened in November 1980. Its purpose was to accommodate oncology patients who needed clinical assessments for their chemotherapy, bone marrow aspirations, lumbar punctures, IV access, blood work, and other procedures. After a few months, other children were treated at the unit, including those who had significant allergic reactions and who needed immunizations. Patients who came to the unit were stable and, in the case of oncology patients, were receiving maintenance care that previously would have required admission. Doctors Kaiser Ali, Donald Hillman, and Albert J. Davis and administrator Donald Kelland, with the support of the medical and nursing staff and a grant of $13,600 from Imperial Oil, were instrumental in getting this unit started. Part of Ward 2A was renovated into the two four-bed rooms, procedure room, and supply room that became the medical day-care unit.

The opening of the unit offered convenience for patients and families—they no longer had to plan for an overnight stay in the hospital. The unit's nursing staff specialized in the care provided and they became familiar with patients who required multiple visits. Establishing the unit freed up needed in-patient beds, saved money, was more efficient for patients, and did not affect quality of care.

Over the years, the unit has been committed to providing continuing care to oncology patients. Non-oncology services have also been provided, such as colonic irrigations, immunization of high-risk children, administration of biological agents for rheumatoid arthritis and Crohn's disease, sedation for Auditory Brain Stem Response (ABR), hearing tests, testing for penicillin allergy, patient education, blood disorder management, Mantoux testing for tuberculosis, line-flushing for patients with permanent intravenous access, and administration of IV antibiotics.

The medical day-care unit in the new Janeway is, physically, an improvement over the old site, with its own area on the fourth floor. The new unit has two observational/treatment rooms, one with a single bed and the other with four beds. An ample waiting room, treatment room, examining room, storage area, meeting/conference room, and a nurse's desk complete the unit.

Medical day care is an integral part of the Janeway. It provides care to oncology patients and has adapted to the needs of non-oncology patients requiring "newer" treatments. In 2017, the unit operates from 8:30 a.m. to 4:30 p.m., Monday through Friday.

Hematology-Oncology

Rufus Dominic, a pediatrician with special training in hematology and on-cology, treated children with leukemia at the Janeway from its opening in 1966. Children with solid tumors were treated by pediatric surgeon Richard Kennedy, unless they had brain tumors, in which case they were directed to neurosurgeon Falah Maroun. Despite these services, the Janeway did not have an oncology unit as such—there was no oncology nurse, and medications and procedures were given on the ward and the clinics.

In 1968, Dr. John Darte, a professor of pediatrics at Memorial University, was appointed pediatrician-in-chief at the Janeway. He had extensive training and experience in pediatric oncology and was actively involved with oncolo-gy patients at the Janeway until his departure in 1975. After 1975, hematology patients, including leukemia patients, were treated by Dominic, and patients with solid tumors by Kennedy.

In July 1978, Kaiser Ali, a former Janeway resident, returned to the hospital after fellowship training in hematology and oncology at St. Jude's Hospital in Memphis, Tennessee. Ali assumed responsibility for most of the new oncology patients, including those with solid tumors. He was involved with hematolo-gy and the hemophilia program, particularly when patients became infected with HIV, and several research projects, and he had a geographic full-time ap-pointment at Memorial University's medical school. During his tenure at the Janeway and at Memorial, Ali was the only full-time hematologist-oncologist. Registered nurse Irene Walsh became the first nurse coordinator in 1981. Dom-inic, who also had a busy private general pediatric practice, continued to see hematology-oncology patients.

Ali took a leave of absence starting April 1, 1990, leaving the Janeway with-out a full-time hematologist-oncologist. A special arrangement was made with

Pediatric Hematologists and Oncologists
Rufus Dominic: 1966–1994
Kaiser Ali: 1979–1991
Lewis Ingram: 1991–1995
Lawrence Jardine: 1992–1999
Jack Hand: 1997–2012
Lynette Bowes: 2002–present
Lisa Goodyear: 2010–present
Paul Moorehead: 2013–present

Kennedy and David Price, who agreed to take on some of the solid tumor patients. Cooper and William Sprague assumed responsibility for the day-to-day running of the service. New leukemia patients were referred to IWK for confirmation of diagnosis and induction of therapy, then usually returned to the Janeway for therapy maintenance. This was a challenging period for families, patients, hospital staff, and pediatricians but, thanks to the support and co-operation of doctors Sheila Weitzman in Toronto and Alan Pysemany and Dorothy Barnard in Halifax, cancer care progressed without incident. Full-time hematologist-oncologist Lewis Ingram began at the Janeway in November 1991.

During his first year with the hospital, Ingram became involved with the Children's Cancer Group. That year, 1991, Ingram, nurse coordinator Jan Crocker, and secretary Pearl Vokey set up a research program at the Janeway's oncology department. This international pediatric oncology consortium, later renamed the Children's Oncology Group, is a large group of research centres in North America that treat children with cancer. Children who are enrolled in a Children's Oncology Group protocol receive the best up-to-date care with collaboration between experts in a number of centres; it is of paramount value to doctors who may be faced with rare or unusual cancers.

Hemophilia

Hemophilia is an inherited disease of blood coagulation. In the wake of the tainted blood scandal of the 1980s—when HIV- and hepatitis C-infected blood was given to transfusion recipients (see chapter on "Infectious Diseases")—

a Commission of Inquiry on the blood system in Canada (the Krever Inquiry) was established by the federal government in October 1993.

No formal registry of patients with hemophilia A (factor VIII deficiency) or hemophilia B (factor IX deficiency) existed in Newfoundland and Labrador when hematologist-oncologist Mary Frances Scully arrived in 1991. She was instructed by the clinical chief of medicine, Nigel Duguid, to work on a comprehensive-care hemophilia program. Scully organized the Hemophilia Program, which consisted of her, two nurses, a social worker, and a genetic counsellor who helped her identify, diagnose, counsel, and treat patients. Marilyn Pardy, director of the Women's and Child Health Program, designated a nurse to review old charts and identify patients with hemophilia lost to follow-up in the late 1990s. Pardy's list of patients became part of the national registry of hemophilia patients sponsored by the Association of Hematology Directors of Canada.

Scully and her team sent blood to the Genetic Hemophilia Laboratory in Kingston, where they identified a new hemophilia gene in patients from Twillingate, a gene now known as the "Twillingate gene." In 2002 Scully received a research grant to study the clinical impact of mild hemophilia A. She travelled to Twillingate and Corner Brook to assess patients and developed protocols for patient treatment. Patients with severe hemophilia were started on primary prophylaxis and a continuous infusion protocol was developed.

In 2002 Eastern Health designated Dr. Lynette Bowes as the Pediatric Hemophilia clinic director.

Rufus Dominic

Dr. Rufus Dominic was a medical pioneer and a pediatrician at the Janeway for 30 years, starting in 1966. He started a hematology-oncology and general pediatric practice and was the first pediatrician to practice hematology-oncology for children in the province.

Dominic was born in Botwood, Newfoundland and Labrador, and lived there as a child. He served in the Canadian Air Force during World War II and, after the war, attended St. Francis Xavier University in Antigonish, Nova Scotia, where he received a Bachelor of Science. He graduated from the National University in Galway, Ireland, with a Bachelor of Medicine and a Bachelor of Surgery in 1954. He practiced on Bell Island from 1954 until 1962, when he started specialty training in Toronto in general pediatrics and pediatric hematology-oncology. He started his practice at the Janeway and the nursery at St. Clare's in September 1966.

A remarkable physician who contributed significantly to the Janeway, the community, and Memorial's medical school, Dominic excelled at teaching the basics of primary pediatric care to pediatric residents, giving future family physicians tools they could use in their busy practices. He was a life-long learner himself and never stopped inquiring about new treatments and diagnostic tools.

Rufus Dominic.

He was quick to seek advice on a patient whose condition puzzled him. He worked long and busy hours and was the Janeway's only hematologist-oncologist for several years, but he never complained. He was an excellent practitioner of the art and science of medicine and not only saved lives but greatly improved the quality of life for the many children he treated.

Dominic was always friendly to colleagues, nurses, students, and all hospital staff. He was always respectful and available to the many community physicians by phone. We never remember him becoming angry or putting someone down—he was a gentleman in the true sense of the word. Even so, Dominic was not always fully appreciated for his outstanding achievements, perhaps because he was a quiet and humble person despite his many successes.

Family meant a lot to Rufus and Eleanor Dominic and they were blessed with children and grandchildren. Their daughter, Anna, became a pediatrician and in 2017 practices at the Janeway. He was active in his church and certainly believed in the phrase "Do onto other as they would do onto you." In his spare time he was an avid gardener and, after he retired, started wood working as a hobby. To quote one of his patients after he died in November 2013, "Dr. Dominic was a legend in his time."

Sean Goudie's Story

Sean Goudie, age 11, died at the Janeway on December 21, 1988. Sean had been diagnosed in early 1988 with acute lymphoblastic leukemia. He had tolerated chemotherapy well and, after his cancer went into remission, he seldom missed an opportunity to comfort his family by demonstrating how well he felt—he would run, rather than walk, to deliver the papers on his newspaper route if he knew people were watching; he always whistled as soon as he got up in the morning. Sean's younger sister, Stephanie, was found to be a perfect bone marrow match, which gave Sean a normal life expectancy.

A judicial inquiry into the cause of death determined that Sean had died from an injection of Leucovorin, an antidote for Methotrexate, a drug used to treat leukemia both orally and directly into the spinal canal. He had received more Methotrexate in his spinal canal that day than was recommended by hospital protocol. Dr. Archie Blyer, an expert witness from the University of Texas, stated that the overdose of Methotrexate would not have caused the severe cerebral edema which lead to death, but the dose of Leucovorin given intrathecally would have.

The inquiry made specific observations and recommendations about the inappropriate delegation of medical authority that may have led to the Sean's untimely death. The hospital has changed its protocol accordingly to prevent any similar incidents. An article outlining this case with specific recommendations, "Intrathecal Leucovorin after Intrathecal Methotrexate Overdose," was published in 1996 in the *Journal of Pediatric Hematology/Oncology* (vol. 18, no. 3). It was written by Lawrence F. Jardine, Lewis C. Ingram, and W. Archie Bleyer.

This was an unspeakable tragedy for an 11-year-old boy whose cancer was in remission. Medication errors will always be possible; however, by paying meticulous attention to protocols and training staff about drug toxicities, protocols, and procedures for dealing with drug errors, future episodes will become very rare.

Children's Oncology Group

The Children's Oncology Group (COG) is a conglomerate of 240 institutions with 5,000 members who pool their knowledge, research, and resources. The world's largest organization devoted to childhood and adolescent cancer research, COG is a clinical trials group and generally has about 100 clinical trials open at any one time. All three hematologist-oncologists at the Janeway are COG members and have access to its broad database of international research, support, and experts.

In the early 1950s, acute leukemia was treated with Methotrexate and/or steroids and had a median survival rate of six months. In the mid-1950s, with the addition of purine antagonists with steroids, the median survival increased to one year; in 2017, 80 per cent survive beyond five year (considered long-term survival). The cure rates for all types of cancers has improved from 10 to 60 per cent from 1950 to 2017. This improvement can be attributed to ongoing cancer research, which the Janeway is involved in.

In 1991, Ingram applied to have the Janeway become an affiliate of IWK and the first patient was entered in the COG database in December 1991. IWK became an associate member of COG in 1969 and a full member in 1980.

Physicians and Surgeons Who Treated Oncology Patients
Richard Kennedy, solid tumors, 1966
Rufus Dominic, leukemia, 1966–1994
David Price, solid tumors, 1989–present
Kaiser Ali, leukemia and solid tumors, 1979–1991
Austin Rick Cooper, leukemia, 1990
William Sprague, leukemia, 1990
Lewis Ingram, leukemia, 1991
Jack Hand, leukemia and solid tumors, 1997–2012
Falah Maroun, brain tumors, 1999–present
Lawrence Jardine, leukemia and solid tumors, 1992–1999
Lynette Bowes, leukemia and solid tumors, 2002–present
Lisa Goodyear, leukemia and solid tumors, 2010–present
Paul Moorehead, leukemia and solid tumors, 2013–present

Adele Fifield's Story
By Adele Fifield

I was 13 years old when I saw ortho-pedic surgeon David Peddle on April 6, 1979, because I had pain and swelling in my left leg. After viewing my test results, Peddle wanted to admit me to the Jan-eway that day. We agreed that I would be admitted the next day—April 6 is my brother's birthday and I wanted to be at his celebration.

I underwent a series of tests (X-rays, CT scan, etc.). My parents were told my diagnosis of osteogenic sarcoma, a ma-lignant bone cancer on Good Friday, April 13, and I was given the news the next Monday. Dr. Peddle amputated my left leg the next day (April 17). I met Dr. Rufus

Adele Fifield.

Dominic shortly after my amputation and I had my first Adriamycin chemo before being discharged from the hospital on April 27.

April 1979 to March 1981: Over two years, I had 35 rounds of che-mo. During the first six months, I alternated between Adriamycin and Meth-otrexate, with 10 days to three weeks between them. For the remaining time, I had Methotrexate every three weeks. The original plan was for a two-year treatment plan, but it was a struggle to find places to insert my two IVs. During one treatment, the anesthetist wanted to put one IV in my forehead—instead, Dominic consulted with others, including with SickKids in Toronto, and he learned that I had already had more treatments than SickKids administered in similar cases. That day I got the unexpected and wonderful new that there would be no more treatments at all.

April 1981 to February 1989: Dominic followed me with 24 checkups beginning April 1981 until a few months before I moved to Ontario in 1989 (even though I was no longer a "child," he had kindly continued to follow me until I finished university in Newfoundland and Labrador).

June 26, 1989: Date of first prosthesis. I always remember the date I walked out of the prosthetic centre with my first artificial leg; it was my mom's birthday.

May 1989 to February 2008: I joined the War Amps Child Amputee Program in 1980 as a child amputee member, began attending its seminars in 1981, and became a Junior Counsellor. In 1988, while working toward my Education degree from Memorial University I spent the summer working with the War Amps in Ottawa. Early in 1989, in the last year of my program, the War Amps offered me a job. I worked there for 19 years in various roles, and spoke at over 100 child amputee seminars across the country. I was director of the National Amputee Centre of the War Amps when I left the organization in 2008. I still believe in the tremendous good that the War

Adele Fifield.

Amps brings; I moved on simply to stretch myself professionally. During my time there I was nominated for and received the Order of Ontario for my work with amputees and veterans—it was a tremendous honour, although I felt uncomfortable about it as I believe there are countless individuals equally deserving.

2008 to 2017: Since 2008 I have been the chief executive officer of the Canadian Association of Radiologists. When I decided to seek a new role, I wanted to still contribute in some way to society. Medical imaging is a critical part of most health care, including in my own, so the job is a good role for me.

Child Protection

Most jurisdictions in Canada and the United States introduced long-overdue legislation to protect children from abuse and maltreatment in the 1960s. In 1972, the province of Newfoundland introduced the Child Welfare Act, which greatly enhanced the identification, reporting, and prosecution of individuals who abuse children. The Act stipulates that individuals who suspect child abuse, by law, must report it to a proper authority.

Child abuse may be physical, psychological, or sexual. Nutritional neglect, medical neglect, or failure to provide the necessities of life, including education, are all considered child abuse.

In 1966, no formal mechanism was in place to deal with cases of child abuse and neglect that were referred to the Janeway or diagnosed in the emergency department. In 1973, Dr. Gordon Gosse, director of ambulatory services, drew up a proposal for the management of cases of child abuse and neglect for patients and presented it to the Janeway's medical advisory committee in May 1973. Finally, in January 1976, Austin Rick Cooper was appointed as the liaison between the Janeway and Child Welfare, social workers, and other physicians; he was to be involved, directly or indirectly, in all cases of child abuse seen at the Janeway.

The Child Protection Advisory Team, consisting of Cooper, the Janeway's director of social work Frances O'Flaherty, and several social workers, was created soon thereafter. In 1977, hospital bylaws officially stated the mandate for the Child Protection Advisory Team and outlined the role of its chair. In 1977, the team submitted the Janeway child abuse reporting form to the medical advisory committee, which approved and adopted it for use in the hospital.

Sometimes the Child Protection Advisory Team would be referred patients by other physicians or emergency room nurses directly. The pediatrician

Social Workers, Child Protection Coordinating Committee	
Janeway	**Department of Social Services**
Frances O'Flaherty	Stead Crawford
Clarke Dale	Kim Jordan
Natalie Benson	Donna Ronen
Wanda O'Keefe	Andrew Edwards
Joan Fuller	
Paula Rogers	

on call would evaluate the patient and consult with social workers; if social workers thought that physical, sexual, or nutritional abuse was taking place, the pediatrician on the Child Protection Advisory Team would then report the case to the director of Child Welfare. Depending on the case, the patient could be referred to a social worker or pediatrician for further care.

Implementing this team involved educating the Janeway staff on the requirement to report all cases of suspected child abuse, even if the attending physician did not agree. The Child Welfare Act clearly stated that anyone who suspected child abuse—physician, nurse, teacher, or neighbour—had a legal obligation to report it to the Janeway team or to a child welfare worker.

The primary goal was to protect the child at risk. Referrals to the police were made where appropriate. Most cases of reported child abuse and neglect in the late 1970s were physical. Sexual abuse was managed differently; in that a designated family practitioner met with older children and adolescents in the emergency room, and appropriate investigations were done, usually at the General Hospital.

The Child Protection Advisory Team met regularly. Dr. Marcia Smith replaced Cooper as chair in 1981 and in 1985 Dr. Rob Morris took over. The committee functioned well, with good relationships between the hospital, Child Welfare, and the police.

Between September 1, 1985, and August 7, 1986, 54 patients from six weeks to 16 years of age, were evaluated by the team. This number greatly increased in 1989 when the Mount Cashel orphanage sexual abuse scandal erupted; 282

Pediatricians with Child Protection

Kim Blake	Rob Morris
Austin Rick Cooper	Julita Muzychka
Joseph Curtis	Jennifer O'Dea
Delores Doherty	Thodore Rosales
Anna Dominic	Marcia Smith
Denise Hickey	Shamim Tejpar
Maeve Kelly	Cathy Vardy
Sandra Luscombe	

medicals were done for suspected cases of sexual abuse that year, but not all were deemed to be so.

In 1990, pediatricians Delores Doherty and Rob Morris said that they could not cope with their case load.

The medical advisory committee noted their concern in September 1992 about the lack of a full-time pediatrician on the call schedule for child protection cases. Two problems were identified: a shortage of pediatricians to provide the coverage and no physician coordinator to act as a liaison with other agencies and physicians in the province. A half-time Child Protection Specialist position was approved and in early 1993, Morris was hired as the child protection liaison pediatrician, a role he still holds in 2017.

In 1998, the Child Youth and Family Services Act updated the old Child Welfare Act. Child Youth and Family Services provided 24-hour coverage for child protection, except for cases of an assault by a "stranger," which were referred to the police. The Janeway Family Centre was created in 2006, incorporating the old Anderson Centre (a centre for counselling children, adolescents, and families about mental health issues), and was staffed by psychologists, social workers, occupational therapists, and an administrative assistant.

While changes have been made in the management and administration of child protection issues since 1976, the Child Protection Advisory Team, composed of representatives from the Janeway, Child Youth and Family Services, and the Department of Justice, continues to offer support and care to children in need.

Child Development Rehabilitation Division

The Development and Rehabilitation Division is staffed by a manager, developmental pediatricians, general pediatricians, psychologists, speech language pathologists, a nurse coordinator, an occupational therapist, a social worker, and clerical staff. Because of its broad reach, it is closely linked to the neurology, audiology, genetics, children's rehabilitation, and diagnostic imaging departments. Links are also maintained with public health nurses, schools, family physicians, community pediatricians, and Child, Youth and Family Services.

All referrals to the program go through a central intake system. All patients must be screened and school and parent questionnaires submitted before the patient comes to one of three clinics: communication/developmental, cleft palate and craniofacial, and learning/behavioural. Referrals are accepted from public health nurses, schools, family physicians, and pediatricians.

The communication/developmental clinic, the first to be established, was started in 1968 by Norah Elphinstone Browne in a small office in the Janeway's outpatient department. Two years later, she moved to Building 615, adjacent to the main hospital. The clinic, then as in 2017, serves children up to six years of age with developmental delays, speech language concerns, hearing impairment, and other related conditions. Children with Down's syndrome, once treated in this clinic, are now referred to the Children's Rehabilitation department.

The well-organized cleft palate and craniofacial clinic serves children with craniofacial abnormalities from birth through adulthood. It offers services from dentistry, orthodontics, general surgery, and plastic surgery. Travelling clinics are held regularly during the spring, summer, and fall.

Physicians, Child Development Program:
Norah Elphinstone Browne (director, 1968–1975)
Damodar Vaze
Poh Gin Kwa
M. El Bardeesy
Margaret Cox
Marcia Smith (director, 1975–1985)
Delores Doherty (director, 1987–1992)
* Cathy Vardy (director, 1992–present)
Keith Golden
Victoria Crosbie
Sandra Luscombe
Susan Moore
Austin Rick Cooper
George Robbins
Ken Henderson
* Tina Doyle
* Lana Soper

* Completed fellowship training in Child Development

The learning/behavioural clinic serves children six years and up with learning problems, which may or may not be complicated by behaviour concerns. Many of these patients have Attention Deficit Hyperactivity Disorder or cognitive delays. Psychoeducational assessments are done privately or by the school board. Autism Diagnostic Observation Schedule assessments are conducted by a team consisting of a developmental pediatrician, speech language pathologist, and nurse specialist.

The Children's Rehabilitation Centre merged with the Janeway site in Pleasantville in 1996. At the time, the provincial government was reorganizing St. John's hospital services under a program-based model. Departments such as nursing or social work were replaced by programs which included Child and Women's Health, Mental Health, and Addictions. The Child Development Unit of the Janeway and the Children's Rehabilitation Centre were merged into a division of the Child Health Program of the Health Care Corporation of St. John's in 1996.

Although administratively under one division, Child Development and the Children's Rehabilitation have maintained their autonomy. In August 2014, the Child Development Program team included a nurse coordinator, development pediatricians, general pediatricians, psychologists, secretaries, a receptionist, a social worker, an occupational therapist, and a speech language pathologist.

What began in 1968 as a small communications and development clinic has become a large multidisciplinary group, the Child Development Neuromotor Rehabilitation Division of Child and Women's Health, with over 88 full- and part-time staff and 12 physicians. The number of patients annually has increased dramatically: In 2012 to 2013, program members saw 9,006 clients, including new clients and rechecks. The total attendance days for the Rehabilitation Division was 17,875; for Development and Rehabilitation, 26,881.

The neuromotor clinics are described under the neurology section.

Guiding Principles of the Child Development Program

The Child Development Program operates with the belief that all children have the right to be treated in accordance with their developmental age and stage. This attitude prevails in all interactions with children and adolescents in this health care program.

The Child Development Program team believes that all children have the right to work toward their maximum potential. Developmental disorders in childhood and adolescence may compromise this. Intervention that clarifies and defines the problems and then initiates a treatment plan/approach will move the individual toward his/her optimal functioning within family and community.

Developmental disabilities in childhood and adolescence place considerable stress on the family and community. Since the child does not function in isolation, the Child Development Program team believes that effective intervention is best accomplished by interdisciplinary teams of health and community personnel working with the family to provide support and community education.

The goals of this program are to enhance the implementation of a developmentally appropriate approach to all children and adolescents at the Janeway and in the community; to demonstrate a model of interdisciplinary intervention for assessment and treatment of children and adolescents with developmental disorders; and to facilitate appropriate use of community resources by fostering interactions between the Child Development Program and relevant agencies on behalf of children and adolescents with developmental concerns.

Norah Elphinstone Browne

Dr. Norah Christine (Elphinstone, Renouf) Browne dedicated her life to the care of sick, developmentally delayed, and hearing impaired children for almost 50 years.

She was born Norah Elphinstone, daughter of Maurice (an Anglican minister) and Christine Elphinstone. She grew up in a village in Yorkshire, England, and became acquainted with social and humanitarian issues at an early age. She trained at King's College, England, as a physician and obtained her diploma in child health in 1947. She trained for another six years in pediatrics and respiratory medicine in the UK. She moved to Newfoundland in February 1961 as clinical director of the west coast sanatorium, until January 1963.

Norah Elphinstone Browne.

After further pediatric training at Montreal Children's Hospital she moved to St. John's in May 1963 as a pediatrician. Very early on she developed special skills in the care of cognitively and hearing impaired children. During the 1960s, she voluntarily evaluated disadvantaged preschool children attending a Head Start Project at St. John Bosco School in St. John's.

As a general pediatrician in private practice she was highly regarded by her patients and their families. She made house calls at any time and would assist families beyond her role as a pediatrician. One mother described the doctor coming to her home late at night to see her sick daughter. Hospitalization was required and, as the mother did not have transportation, Elphinstone Browne took the child to hospital in her own vehicle. She made every effort to treat her pediatric patients with excellent medical care, compassion, and dedication. She was much loved by the children and their families in her practice, some of whom wrote letters of appreciation to her many years later.

In 1966, when the Janeway opened, she started a Communication and Development Clinic and accepted referrals from across the province. She also initiated a comprehensive Cleft Lip and Palate Clinic, which involved the co-operation of several specialist physicians and therapists for lengthy periods of follow-up. Having reduced hearing herself, she took a special interest in deaf children and was a consultant for many years at the Newfoundland School for the Deaf.

She was the recipient of several prestigious awards, including an Honorary Doctor of Laws and the National Therese Casgrain Award (1987) and Citizen of the Year (named by the St. John's Jaycees, 1987). The Canadian Hard of Hearing Association of Newfoundland and Labrador initiated the Dr. Norah Browne Bursary in her honour, as she was the founding president of the association.

Elphinstone Browne had a great interest in choral singing and was a member of the "Newfoundland Sings" choir, which recorded local music. She wrote music and poetry and published a booklet, "Carols and Stories," in 1991. As a parishioner of St. Michael's Parish in St. John's she generously gave her time, talent, and services to the church and the community.

She was married to St. John's lawyer Rex Renouf. After his death, she married William Browne, a judge, politician, and author. She maintained a close relationship with her stepchildren and step-grandchildren over the years.

Norah Elphinstone Browne spurned publicity and dedicated her life to the disadvantaged children who were least likely to attract the attention of the medical and lay community. She evidently took more than average care with the children and parents she encountered. This province has greatly benefitted from this humanitarian pediatrician and pioneer in child health.

Genetics

Genetics is a relatively new medical specialty. In 1953 Watson and Crick defined the structure of DNA; the DNA code was determined in 1965 and molecular genetics was developed in 1977. When the Janeway opened in 1966, knowledge about genetic concepts was limited and pediatricians had little training in the field.

Memorial University's medical school made genetics a priority from the 1960s and recruited clinicians, epidemiologists, and laboratory scientists in the discipline. Memorial's focus on genetics was well known and, because of the high incidence of genetic diseases in the province, the medical school recruited several prominent faculty members within a few years of its opening. Early faculty members who were involved with genetics include Dr. George Fodor and Dr. Colton in epidemiology; Dr. Richard Middleton, microbiology genetics; Dr. Bruce Sells, molecular biology; Dr. Clive Mellor, psychiatric (populations) genetics; and Dr. George Fraser, a clinician who trained in genetics and came to Memorial in 1971. The first dean of Memorial's medical school, Dr. Ian Rusted, made every attempt to form a research team. He consulted several well-known experts nationally and internationally as he strove to establish a centre of excellence for clinical laboratory and research genetics.

Every visiting geneticist who came to Memorial agreed with Rusted that the school provided a unique opportunity to contribute to the Canadian research scene. Equally important was the relevance of this research to the people and families of Newfoundland and Labrador.

In the early 1970s the Janeway became actively involved with Memorial in developing clinical and laboratory research in genetics. In the 1970s and 1980s clinical geneticists were affiliated with clinical departments in the hospital depending on their backgrounds, and several "pediatric" geneticists practiced at

Penny Allderdice.

the Janeway and had appointments in the discipline of pediatrics in the medical school. They also had cross-appointments in community medicine.

Penny Allderdice, a research scientist in cytogenetics, who came to Memorial and the Janeway in 1973, established a clinical laboratory and completed significant research until her retirement in 1997. In 1999, the discipline of genetics was formally established at Memorial's medical school.

The cytogenetics laboratory at the Janeway was the only one in the province until 2001. Since then it has come under Laboratory Medicine Eastern Health in the Health Sciences Centre, and provides a much-needed service to the community and university

Allderdice taught genetics to medical students, interns, and residents, met with families to discuss their genetic issues, published in prestigious medical journals, and received several competitive research grants. One of the first significant genetic studies in Newfoundland and Labrador used cytogenetics to identify the cause of severe disabilities among Sandy Point residents: a pericentric inversion on chromosome 3, a condition later coined the Allderdice Syndrome.

Clarke Fraser, a distinguished geneticist and scientist who founded the Department of Genetics at McGill in 1952, moved to St. John's with his wife, research scientist Marilyn Preus. Fraser was active at the Janeway from 1982 until 1985. Theodore Rosales, a pediatrician trained in genetics and a national expert in fetal alcohol syndrome, also came to the Janeway in 1982. Elizabeth Ives, a clinical geneticist and researcher, came to Memorial and the Janeway in 1988 and started a provincial genetics program. The Newfoundland and Labrador Medical Genetic Program had clinicians, genetic counsellors, a cytogenetics laboratory, and eventually a molecular genetics laboratory. Most of the program was housed at the Janeway until 2001, when it became a discipline in the medical school.

A molecular biology laboratory was established at the Janeway in July 1993 under the directorship of Dr. Peter Bridge and moved to the Health Sciences Centre in 2000. That same year, a diagnostic genetic service, which included cytogenetics, molecular genetics, and biogenetics, was established at the Health Sciences Centre. In 2017, this is an Eastern Health laboratory service and includes neonatal, pediatric, and high-risk obstetric consults and preconceptual and genetic counselling, as well as metabolic genetics in adults and children. The service also consults on endocrine tumor syndromes, hereditary cardiac genetics, hereditary cancer genetics, infertility, and neurology.

Elizabeth Ives, chief of genetics, 1988–1998.

SURGERY

The Janeway's original department of surgery was subdivided into general pediatric surgery, orthopedics, and eyes, ears, nose, and throat (EENT). General pediatric surgery was an umbrella covering neurosurgery, trauma, and cardiac surgery. In 1968, EENT was divided into ophthalmology and ears, nose, and throat (ENT). Plastic surgery and urology were not specific divisions but would also have been included under general pediatric surgery.

The department of surgery opened on November 14, 1966, and the first surgical operation was performed three days later. Three wards were dedicated to surgery—3A (orthopedics), 3F (toddler), and 3D—as well as beds in ICU. The ICU was shared with the medicine and neonatology departments. In 1966, 140 beds were available for surgery: 16 intensive care, 36 orthopedics, and 88 all others.

Three operating rooms were available mornings and afternoons, although during certain times staff shortages meant that only two operating rooms were available. An increase in operations was recorded despite cutbacks.

Since 1966, pediatric surgery outcomes, and the quality of patient care, have improved due to parenteral nutrition (the administration of liquid nutrition into a vein through an intravenous catheter), the opening of surgical day care in 1976, the expanded role of nursing in pediatric surgery, the appointment of surgical assistants and associates, the development of NICUs and PICUs, and the expansion of outpatient surgery options. As well, more young women take folic acid through pregnancy, which prevents spina bifida. Seat belts and infant care seats have been legislated in automobiles, and public awareness about reducing speed and drinking and driving has grown. A better system for transporting sick and injured children was implemented, and diagnostic imaging (such as MRIs and CT scans) is now used more often in fetal medicine. Pediatric anesthesia has also advanced.

Senior surgeons continued to educate medical students, house staff, physicians, and nurses. A close relationship developed between the department of surgery at the Janeway and Memorial's medical school, and Royal College-certified fellowship programs in pediatric surgery in Canada were established.

Adequate compensation for surgeons, nurses, and allied health workers in child health also had a positive effect on surgical outcomes, as did the establishment of casualty officers in the emergency room, and the overall strong support of the pediatric medicine department, especially cardiology, for pediatric cardiac surgery.

General and General Pediatric Surgeons
* Richard Kennedy: 1965–1996
Abdalla Hanna: 1966–1996
George Battcock: 1966–1990
Angus Neary: 1966–1990
P.J. Horan: 1966–1981
* Javed Akhtar: 1989–present
* David Price: 1989–present
* Andre Hodder: 2010–present
J.E.L. Price: 1966–1967
P.J. Whelen: 1966–1970

* General pediatric surgeon

General Pediatric Surgery

In the first half of the 20th century, surgical procedures performed on children in Newfoundland and Labrador consisted of tonsillectomies, adenoidectomies, hernias, appendectomies, trauma surgery, and other, less invasive, procedures. The first major attempts to treat anomalies was done by Nigel Rusted in 1950 when he operated on children with cleft palates. Rusted had spent time at SickKids and, under the mentorship of Arthur LeMessurier, learned the LeMessurier procedure for the repair of cleft lips and palates.

Richard Kennedy, a fully trained pediatric surgeon, returned to St. John's from Montreal to practice surgery at St. Clare's in 1959. In 1962, a new wing at St. Clare's, which included obstetrics, pediatrics, and emergency services, was opened. One ward (7 West) in it was designated a pediatric ward under the supervision of Sister St. Clare; its nurses were trained to care for children and infants. The hospital had trained anesthetists and a fully equipped operating room to treat children; however, no pediatric intensive care was practiced. Kennedy operated on children with solid tumors, tracheoesophageal fistulas, diaphragmatic hernias, abnormalities of the urinary tract, and serious trauma. The results were considered on par with those of other Canadian hospitals, although no interns or residents were present and the surgeons were totally dependent on the nurses.

In anticipation of the Janeway's opening, Kennedy was appointed its chief of surgery in December 1965. Kennedy was a member of the scheduling committee set up to direct the development of the Janeway under chair A. Victor Neale, an academic pediatrician. The scheduling committee met regularly for over a year and was phased out when the hospital opened. Kennedy consulted pediatric hospitals in the US and Canada regarding the organization of surgery in a pediatric hospital. Two consultants, Hugh Lynn, a pediatric surgeon at the

Mayo Clinic, and Harvey Beardmore, chief of general surgery and director of the training program in pediatric surgery at Montreal Children's Hospital, helped.

General pediatric surgery was well established from the day the Janeway opened and the standard of care was equal to that in other academic centres in Canada. An active teaching program with resident interns and medical students was in place, with bedside teaching rounds, weekly surgical grand rounds, lectures, and case presentations.

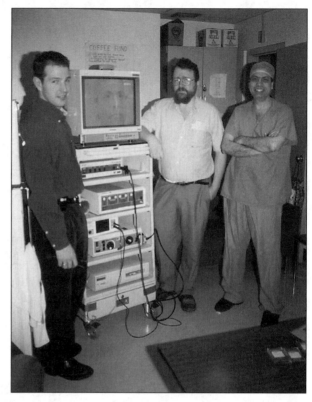

Sales representative Todd Grooves, David Price and Javed Akhtar with the first laproscopic "lower," 1999.

Initially Kennedy was the Janeway's only fully trained pediatric surgeon, although he had the support of several general surgeons who took an interest in pediatrics. If a complicated case came along, especially newborn congenital anomalies, such as a tracheaesophageal fistula (an opening between the trachea and esophagus), Kennedy became involved. With the high birth rate in the province, this responsibility meant that Kennedy was almost constantly on call.

Kennedy made several attempts to bring a trained pediatric surgeon to the Janeway. He urged a surgical resident, Rogelio Lacuesta, to train with Beardmore in the Montreal Children's Hospital. Lacuesta had spent two years at the Janeway as a resident and Kennedy was impressed with his skills. Unfortunately, Lacuesta sought advice from Dr. James Littlefield, chair of surgery at

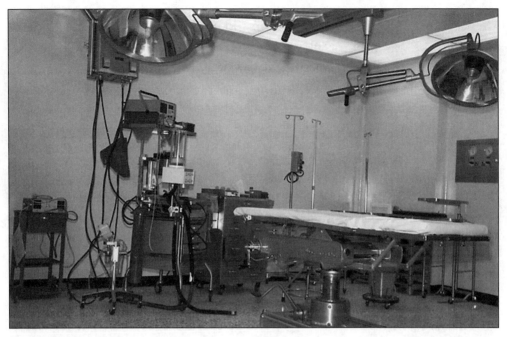

The operating room, c. 1970.

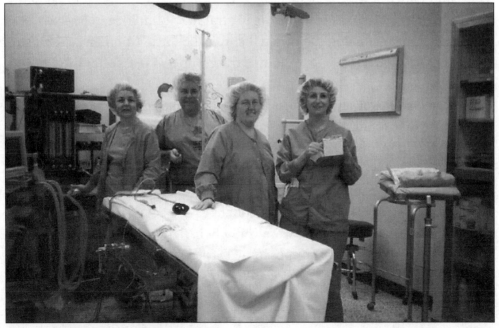

The operating room, c. 1990.

Memorial, who suggested that St. John's did not need a new pediatric surgeon (although she was given privilege at the Janeway, Littlefield's wife, Phyllis Ingram, a trained pediatric surgeon, never practiced surgery there). Kennedy pleaded with Lacuesta to go to Montreal and train anyway, but he opted to go to Grand Falls as a general surgeon instead.

Kennedy tried to persuade another Memorial University pediatric resident, Kevin Hoddinott, to go to the Surgery Department at SickKids, but he decided to study vascular surgery instead.

Kennedy was successful in recruiting Memorial University surgical resident David Price. Price trained under Sigmund Ein at SickKids and returned to Newfoundland as a fully trained pediatric surgeon in 1989. Javed Akhtar came to the Janeway in 1989 and Andre Hodder in 2010; both were trained pediatric surgeons. Akhtar had trained in Ireland; Hodder in Vancouver. In 2017, the Janeway has three general pediatric surgeons: Price, Akhtar, and Hodder.

The surgeons who practiced general pediatric surgery were Richard Kennedy (1966–1996), Angus Neary (1966–1990), and George Battcock (1966–1990). Neary and Battcock were general surgeons with a special interest in pediatric surgery. Battcock also was responsible for trauma. John Price (1966–1969) was responsible for organizing the original surgical clinics. Another general surgeon, Abdalla Hanna (1968–1999), joined the group two years after the Janeway opened.

In 1966 a plan was advanced to have Janeway-based general practitioners responsible for admitting patients, completing their histories and physicals, and assisting surgeons in the operating room. One suggestion was to have general practitioners oversee 10 to 15 surgical beds. These practitioners, however, did not admit any patients to the Janeway and, except in the emergency department, none was involved at the hospital.

General pediatric surgeons were initially assigned to look after all fractures, but this was vigorously opposed by David Landells, chief of orthopedic surgery. In the April 28, 1967, surgical business meeting, it was decided that fractures would be handled by orthopedic, not pediatric, surgeons.

The recruitment and retention of surgical residents was a difficult task for general pediatric surgeons. It had been generally accepted that in teaching

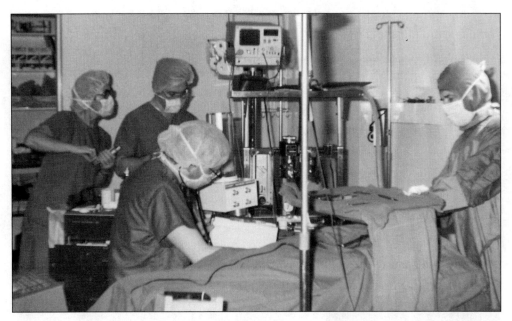

David Price readying the operating room when he was a surgical fellow with Richard Kennedy.

RIGHT: Richard Kennedy.

hospitals an adequate number of residents/interns would be available. Initially the Janeway recruited its own residents, except in orthopedics, for which residents were brought in from McGill and the Mayo Clinic (1969–1975). Some interns also came from Dalhousie University. In March 1973 Memorial assumed the administration of residents, and because the Janeway was a major teaching hospital, the general pediatric surgery department was dependent on the medical school to supply residents.

In April 1973, the residents and interns signed a contract without consulting clinical surgeons working in St. John's. Resident training in Canada was changing in the 1970s and the Royal College insisted that the resident's primary responsibility was to be educated—not a service provider. The num-

TABLE 3: Surgery Statistics

Year	Admissions/ Discharges	Operations	Clinic Visits
1968	3124	2874	7667
1978	3272	6248	14,747
1988	2247	5341	
2003		3983	
2008		4264	

ber of surgical residents was limited by available government funding and the on-call hours was reduced. All of this meant a shortage of residents, which in turn increased the pressure and workload for surgeons at the Janeway.

From June 1973 until the early 1980s, the surgical service had clinical clerks (fourth-year medical students) on the wards. After that it became optional for students to study pediatric surgery.

Kennedy, frustrated by the workload, wrote the medical advisory committee in July 1981 to request a surgical assistant. Five years later, he could finally recruit two fully funded surgical assistants who managed day-to-day admissions, discharges, and minor surgical procedures and assisted in the operating room. These assistants, often international medical school graduates, stayed at the Janeway for two to three years, and many went on to study in Canadian residency programs.

In 1990, the discipline of pediatrics at Memorial's medical school and the Royal College mandated that all pediatric residents rotate through general pediatric surgery. With the presence of surgical residents, pediatric residents, surgical assistants, and some elective residents from family practice and other disciplines, pediatric surgery has been well covered by the junior staff.

Over the years, the Janeway's general pediatric surgery service has provided an excellent teaching program to surgical residents, pediatric residents, family practice residents, and clinical clerks from the medical school.

Michael Healey's Story

Seven-year-old Michael Healey was playing with his friends at the start of his summer vacation in 1963. Next to his home on Water Street west, a construction company was digging up the street and laying new sewer pipes. The company had stacked a pile of concrete culverts 12 feet long and 36 inches in diameter on the side of the road. Michael, the tallest of the boys, accepted a dare to climb up on the pipes. When he reached the top of the pile, the concrete pipes came apart, Michael lost his balance, and he was caught underneath one of the pipes. Several adults quickly came to the rescue but were unable to lift the heavy pipe off his abdomen. Two men were finally able to roll the pipe off his body.

Michael was brought to St. Clare's in a taxi driven by Harry Lewis and accompanied by his uncle Leo Healey and a friend of the family, Eileen Moyst (Reddy). Eileen thought Michael was dead before they arrived at St. Clare's, where pediatric surgeon Richard Kennedy met them.

Michael's prognosis was grave and the type of crush injury he had sustained was often fatal. Kennedy and anesthetist Charles Henderson took Michael to the operating room and opened his abdomen. Considerable damage had been done, particularly to his liver, which was bleeding profusely. Henderson administered fluids and blood and Kennedy tried to suture the liver, but Michael's blood pressure kept dropping.

Kennedy eventually managed to stop the bleeding and Michael survived the operation. More surgery and a long convalescence followed. Michael received excellent care from the nurses and, after many months, he made a full recovery.

Michael and his family are extremely grateful to the excellent care provided by Kennedy and the nursing team of 7 West. Michael, now a father and retired auto mechanic, still has vivid memories of the ordeal and his long convalescence.

Neurosurgery

Neurosurgery—surgery performed on the nervous system, particularly the brain and spinal cord—was part of the sub-department of general pediatric surgery when the Janeway opened in 1966. The division primarily admitted children with brain tumors, head trauma, spina bifida, and hydrocephalus. Larry Sutherland and Falah Maroun were the Janeway's first neurosurgeons.

The number of children under age 16 has declined in the province from 200,000 in 1966 to 80,000 in 2017. Thus, while the incidence of brain tumors per 100,000 children has remained relatively stable (about three per 100,000), the actual number of cases has declined. In the Janeway's first 22 years, 132 brain tumors were operated on. There appears to be, however, a higher number of supratentorial lesions and a higher incidence of familial brain tumors in the 21st century.

Hydrocephalus and shunting procedures accounted for most pediatric neurosurgery in the Janeway's early years because of the higher incidence of spina bifida and brain hemorrhages in newborns. A child with spina bifida (a limited defect in the spinal column characterized by the absence of vertebral arches) requires early closure of the lesion and treatment of the resultant hydrocephalus (excessive accumulation of cerebrospinal fluid on the brain). They also require extensive rehabilitation with physiotherapy and occupational therapy. Between 1967 and 1990, the Janeway admitted 274 cases of spina bifida to its surgical unit. The incidence of spina bifida has dropped dramatically in the past 20 years to less than one per year, attributed to the introduction of folic acid as a maternal supplement and the use of routine ultrasound in pregnancy, which allows late abortions for fetuses diagnosed with the condition.

Head injuries and major trauma are still prevalent but dramatically reduced after 1982 with the introduction of seat-belt legislation.

The introduction of CT scanning in 1982 and MRI in 1992 has facilitated the diagnosis of intracranial lesions, hemorrhage trauma, hydrocephalus, and increased intracranial pressure.

Between 1966 and 1986, 820 neurosurgical procedures were completed on 393 Janeway patients.

Neurosurgeons
Larry Sutherland: 1966–1978
Falah Maroun: 1966–present
Neville Russel: 1973–1980
Gerald Murray: 1991–1997
A. Badejo: 1983–1987
Andre Engelbrecht: 2000–present

These numbers have fallen significantly. For example, between April 2010 and March 2011 only 17 neurosurgical procedures took place at the Janeway.

Plastic Surgery

Pediatric plastic surgery offers treatment for acquired and congenital problems of the head and neck, trunk, and upper extremities, including the effects of burns, cleft lips and palates, and injuries. Before the Janeway opened, surgeons Nigel Rusted and Richard Kennedy were repairing cleft lips and palates. Previous to their practices opening, children with these conditions were sent to hospitals outside the province.

Kenneth Anderson developed a comprehensive microscopic surgery program in St. John's, which greatly improved the outcomes in pediatric surgery, as well as in urology, neurosurgery, and cardiovascular surgery.

Plastic Surgeons

Kenneth Anderson: 1975–1982
David Jewer: 1987–present
Donald Fitzpatrick: 2002–present
Arthur Rideout: 1997–present
Joy Cluett: 2005–present
Shane Seal: 2010–present

Cardiac Surgery

Cardiovascular surgery on adults in Canada began at the Toronto General Hospital with pioneering surgeon Gordon Murray in 1929. Surgeon W.T. Mustard directed a program at SickKids in the late 1940s and did the first cardiac procedures in the early 1960s after the heart-lung pump was introduced in Canada in the late 1950s. The Janeway's first open-heart surgical procedure was done on July 27, 1970, by cardiac surgeon Cecil Couves. Open-heart surgery involves surgery on the internal structures, which is made possible by bypassing the blood artificially.

Heart disease in children is diagnosed by a cardiologist who examines the patient through a thorough history and physical examination, an EKG, an echocardiogram, and sometimes diagnostic cardiac catheterization. A case of congenital heart disease would be discussed with the cardiac surgeon before a decision about whether to proceed with surgery is made.

Cardiovascular Surgeons
Cecil Couves: 1974–1980
James Littlefield: 1966–1974
Gary Cornel: 1974–1990

Early procedures at the Janeway were done by Couves, who worked in Edmonton before becoming a professor and chair of surgery at Memorial, where he was when the Janeway opened. Couves encouraged cardiac surgeon Gary Cornel to move to St. John's in 1974. Cornel had attended medical school at the Royal London Hospital and done post-graduate training in the Birmingham Children's Hospital and the Hospital for Sick Children, London. He had further training in Edmonton with Couves.

Most of the cardiac surgical procedures at the Janeway were done by Cornel between 1974 and 1991. He had excellent support from cardiologists Clifton

Way and Shyma Virmani, chief of surgery Richard Kennedy, chief of anesthesia Charlie Henderson, and chief of radiology Walter Heneghan.

One of the first open-heart procedures at the Janeway was filmed and became the subject of a documentary on CBC television's *Here and Now*.

In the late 1970s, as caseloads increased, serious weaknesses in operating room equipment and the ICU became obvious. Repeated requests for better equipment were largely unanswered and in 1981 Cornel decided that he would not perform any more major elective surgery and patients would have to be sent elsewhere. In 1981 Cornel spoke to the Janeway board of directors, chaired by Robert Wells, and the problems were rectified.

During the 1980s, the caseload for pediatric cardiac surgeons gradually declined, and although the results of the surgeries were satisfactory and a full range of operations for complex problems were performed, it became a challenge for them to maintain their skills. In 1990, after performing over 1,000 surgeries in Newfoundland, Cornel moved to the Children's Hospital of Eastern Ontario in Ottawa. A declining birth rate meant that the numbers of cardiac patients requiring surgery were not high enough to warrant his staying at the Janeway.

Cornel returned periodically for several years to offer a "blended" service: less severe surgeries were performed at the Janeway, the more severe in Ottawa. The last cardiac surgery case was in June 1999. During the years Cornel worked at the Janeway, he, with the help of dedicated colleagues, nurses, and technologists, offered a first-class cardiac surgery service.

Pediatric Urology

U rology has been a full service in pediatric surgery since 1966. Re-implantation of ureters for vesicoureteral reflux (the backward flow of urine from the bladder into the kidney) and bladder exstrophy repair were common procedures, and are still done today.

Richard Kennedy did urological procedures at St. Clare's before the Janeway opened; at the Janeway he was joined by urologist Gordon Winsor. Over the years, others joined the department, including urologist George Kiruluta, pediatric urologist John Pike, urologist Christopher French, and Javed Akhtar, a pediatric surgeon with special training in urology.

In 1974, Donald Dow and Gordon Winsor, two local pediatric urologists, with the help of the adult nephrologists at the General Hospital, developed a kidney transplant program plan for St. John's. A kidney perfusion chamber was purchased, but the plan stalled after that. Despite much discussion and negotiation, in 1980 it was decided that no kidney transplant program would be developed for Newfoundland. Children with kidney failure and who require a kidney transplant are referred to the IWK in Halifax.

Urologists: Active Staff
Richard Kennedy: 1966–1996
Gordon Winsor: 1969–1981
George Kiruluta: 1979–1985
John Pike: 1990–2000
Christopher French: 2000–2011
Javed Akhtar: 2000–present

Orthopedic Surgery

Orthopedic surgery was an active sub-department of the surgery department in 1966. Before then, most in-patient beds for orthopedics in the city were in a temporary building at the General Hospital, which had been a military hospital during World War II.

David Landells, c. 1990.

Orthopedic surgeons treat pediatric patients with trauma of the limbs, congenital anomalies of the musculoskeletal system, congenital dislocation of the hips, tumor, and Legg-Perthes disease (a condition that affects the hip where the femur [thigh bone] and pelvis meet in a ball and socket joint). Hand surgery is usually done by plastic surgeons.

The director of orthopedics was David G. Landells in 1966. Three other orthopedic surgeons, Deuter Cowan, Frank Duff, and Edward Shapter, covered the service while also fulfilling duties in other hospitals. A senior resident from the Mayo Clinic in Rochester, New York, rotated in the department until 1975. Residents also came from McGill University until Memorial University's medical school established residency programs and its residents in orthopedics rotated regularly in pediatric orthopedics at the Janeway after it opened.

In 1966, 18 beds at the Janeway were dedicated to orthopedics and plans were in place to expand to 36. A critical shortage of nurses, however, meant that it was difficult to operate a larger number of beds. By 1969, 517 admissions and 5,645 clinic visits had been made to orthopedics.

The orthopedic sub-department had a close relationship with the Chil-

Orthopedic Surgeons

Philip Morris: 1968–1976

Louis E. Lawton: 1982–1984

Neil Turner: 1968–1998

D. Dingle: 1971–1986

Earl Cowan: 1966–1989

Frank Duff: 1966–1980

Robert Deane: 1989–present (chief, 1991–present)

Vic Sahajpal: 2003–present

Heather Jackman: 2005–present

David Landells: 1966–1990 (chief)

David Parsons: 1990–1992

James R.A. Deans: 1974–1989

dren's Rehabilitation Centre, which opened in 1967. Surgery was performed at the Janeway, but clinics and in-patient services were provided by the Centre, which also had its own occupational therapy, physiotherapy, social work, and nursing departments.

Physiotherapy was an integral part of the orthopedic service from 1966. The first director of physiotherapy in 1967 was Barbara Ellis. In 1976 one physiotherapist was dedicated to orthopedics.

Orthopedic surgery has always been a busy service but, over the years, more surgery has been done on an outpatient basis. In 2010, 112 surgical procedures were done in orthopedics, or approximately 12 per cent of the total number of surgical procedures done at the Janeway that year.

In 2017 three orthopedic surgeons trained in pediatric orthopedic surgery, two "plaster" technicians, and physiotherapists make up the division. Orthopedic surgery continues to be active in the teaching program at all levels, particularly in the orthopedic residency programs at Memorial University.

Otolaryngology and Ophthalmology

In 1966, otolaryngology and ophthalmology was a combined department. Ophthalmologist Robert Lawton was the first head. In 1968, Max Edgecombe, headed up a separate otolaryngology department.

Ophthalmology

Ophthalmology at the Janeway was run by general ophthalmologists who had a special interest in pediatrics. Robert Lawton, Cyril Walsh, and Sean O'Leary had private practices in the city but made many contributions to the hospital. In 2003, the first full-time pediatric ophthalmologist, Donna Bautista, came to the Janeway. In 2012, a second pediatric ophthalmologist, Lori Bramwell, joined the department. Two orthoptists, who assess binocular vision and defects in the action of ocular muscles, are also on staff.

The first ophthalmology clinic was in the Janeway Apartments. The new Janeway has a dedicated ophthalmology clinic with examining rooms for ophthalmologists and orthoptists. The clinic is equipped with a RetCam for taking intraocular photos, tonometers for measuring pressure, a slit lamp for examining the anterior segment, indirect ophthalmoscopes for examining fundi, a fundus camera, and a corneal topography machine.

Ophthalmology treats children from birth to 18 years with conditions in-

Ophthalmologists

Cyril Walsh: 1966–1984
Robert Lawton: 1966–2005
Ganeshan Sayuchchiyadevan: 1986–1996
Sean O'Leary: 1992–2012
* Donna Bautista: 2003–present
* Lori Bramwell: 2012–present

* Certified Pediatric Ophthalmologist

cluding congenital anomalies, trauma including non-accidental trauma, infections, strabismus, and visual impairment. General ophthalmologists cover pediatrics in the evenings and weekends or whenever pediatric ophthalmologists are unavailable.

Patients with retinal detachments or cataracts associated with retinal pathology are referred to James Whelan, an ophthalmologist specializing in retinal disease at the Health Sciences Centre. Whelan also provides a second opinion regarding diagnosis and management of retinal diseases. Children are referred to SickKids for consultations with specialists in anterior segment, glaucoma, and oculoplastics—services not available for children in this province.

Otolaryngology (ENT)

ENT has always been a busy surgical service, particularly with tonsillectomies, adenoidectomies, and the insertion of grommets in the tympanic membranes to provide drainage to the middle ear. In the Janeway's early years, infections such as epiglottitis, tonsillar abscesses, mastoiditis, complications of otitis media, and sinusitis, as well as congenital anomalies of the nose, throat, and ears, were common.

In 1998 Tony Batten started cochlear implant (an electronic medical device that replaces the function of a damaged middle ear, sending sound signals to the brain) surgery, which has helped many children. In 2014 Jonathan Kavanagh joined the staff after he completed special training in pediatric ENT. In 2017, five otolaryngologists work at the Janeway; all also have private practices in the city.

Otolaryngologists
Max Edgecombe: 1966–2011
V.U. Yap: 1966–1973
E.T. Tjan: 1969–2010
Tom Smith: 1978–2004
Ken Burrage: 1988–present
Wayne Redmond: 1989–present
Tony Batten: 1998–present
Lorne Savoury: 2002–2008
Boyd Lee: 2003–2010
Chris Drover: 2006–present
Jamie Tibbo: 2010–present
Jonathan Kavanagh: 2014–present

Terry Peach's Story

Terry Peach spent most of the first four years of his life on the surgery floor at the Janeway under the care of Dr. Max Edgecombe. Born in Corner Brook, Terry, at four months of age, was diagnosed with severe croup and had a tracheostomy (a surgical procedure to create an opening through the neck) in August 1967. The tracheostomy tube used was too large and Terry was left with a damaged trachea. He was admitted to the Janeway for further treatment and observation. He had frequent bouts of pneumonia, probably from aspiration of oral secretions, and was not discharged until the spring of 1971.

Today, Terry is a respiratory therapist and owner of a respiratory therapy company. He does not remember much about his years in the hospital but Edgecombe and the nurses who looked after him remember him well. He was always a happy, pleasant child and a real favourite. His picture hung in the boardroom at the Janeway for many years and was on the cover of the hospital's annual report in 1969.

PEDIATRIC ANESTHESIA

I t was not until the 1940s that the need for physicians with specific knowledge and experience in children's anesthesia was recognized. Certain operations that were being attempted in that era, such as addressing congenital malformations in neonates, clearly required an individual with specific clinical experience and technical skills.

By the 1960s, sophisticated equipment was available for use on infants; new drugs, such as fluorinated inhalation agents, short-acting opioids, and rapidly acting muscle relaxants, had become available. More accurate monitoring devices gave a wide range of information. A better understanding of the physiological and pharmacological basis of anesthesia in children was developing, as were training protocols for anesthesiologists. In 1942, the Royal College of Physicians and Surgeons had approved certification of physicians as anesthesiologists; in 1966 anesthesiologists from the US and Canada formed sections on pediatric anesthesiology in their professional societies.

Anesthesiologist Charles Henderson brought modern pediatric anesthesia to the Janeway as its first chief of anesthesia in 1966. Henderson had previously worked with pediatric surgeon Richard Kennedy at St. Clare's. Henderson would have noticed a difference in the level of care provided to children in a pediatric hospital compared to that in an adult health centre. Before the Janeway opened, three city hospitals provided pediatric care, but children were placed on large wards and competed with adults for position and priority. Very little operating room equipment was dedicated to children and little dedicated space was available for them in recovery rooms. A group of nine private-practice anesthesiologists provided services to the three city hospitals. All nine had thus gained some experience working with children.

Before the Janeway opened, Henderson visited the Montreal Children's Hospital, the Children's Hospital in Halifax (the predecessor to IWK, which opened in 1970), and the Boston Children's Hospital. A great deal of information was collected and used to help develop a program of first-class anesthesia care for the Janeway. Henderson, as chief of the department, spent most of his time at the Janeway. He was joined by Raymond Duffy in 1966; other members of the anesthesiologist group offered part-time backup. This sharing of services went on until the Grace developed its own anesthesia group, followed by the General in 1973.

In 1969, Memorial's medical school appointed Cloid D. Green as its first professor and chair of anesthesia. Green developed a teaching program and recruited several faculty members to the medical school. One his recruits, Paul A. Redfern, came to the General in 1973, and when Henderson became a full-time faculty member in November 1973, Redfern joined him at the Janeway. Henderson became chair of anesthesia in 1977.

In 1966, open-drop ether (liquid ether is poured on a piece of gauze or sponge over the patient's mouth) was still being used, but was soon phased out. Most hospitals were becoming familiar with halothane (an inhalation anesthetic which has a pleasant odour and is not flammable), and the use of muscle relaxants had become well established. Accurate vaporizers had been developed which could be used with modern volatile agents such as halothane. A standard non-breathing circuit was modified to administer gaseous anesthesia to infants and young children.

The introduction of cardiovascular surgery at the Janeway in 1972 and the development of its neurosurgery department could not have happened without the participation and expertise of its anesthesiologists.

The development and refinement of intravenous and intra-arterial catheters in the 1970s and early 1980s has improved clinical care. Difficulty with obtaining and maintaining lines in the veins of small babies and young children was a problem before 1975, when steel needles were used. The introduction of peripherally inserted central catheters (PIC lines) and the surgical insertion of permanent intravenous catheters have greatly improved intravenous access.

Ventilators specifically applicable to children were developed from the early 1970s for operating room and ICU use. This led to the technique of controlled respiration using muscle relaxants, narcotics, and/or safer inhaled gases, which necessitated mandatory endotracheal intubation with a special tube extending from the anesthetic machine to below the vocal cords. Sophisticated monitors that recorded pulse rate, oxygen saturation, pulmonary function, blood pressure, and other statistics also greatly improved patient care.

ICU services were developed at the Janeway simultaneously with surgical services. When the hospital opened, the ICU was most often used for post-operative surgical and complicated accident cases. The administration of ICU developed along the committee system, with representation from the departments of medicine, surgery, and anesthesia. The technical aspects of intensive care were often left to anesthesiologists, at least until the 1970s when pediatricians began ventilating premature infants. In the new Janeway, the neonatal unit, PICU, and recovery room are separate units.

There were four Janeway operating rooms in 1966; in 2017, the operating rooms are shared, three for children and two for adult gynecology patients. In the early days, most patients under anesthesia had intravenous fluids, endotracheal intubation, and careful temperature control. Anesthesia-related mortality rates in Canadian child health care centres have been low. Janeway records do not attribute any child's death to anesthesia.

Establishing an ICU recovery area has allowed for better recovery from complicated surgical procedures. A better understanding of temperature control, fluid and electrolyte balance, pain control, antibiotic use, ventilation, and intravenous analgesia for certain medical procedures (bone marrow aspiration, lumbar punctures) all have improved the work of anesthesiologists.

Charles Henderson

When Dr. Charles Henderson died on June 10, 2014, at the age of 91, he left behind a tremendous legacy.

As the father of modern pediatric anesthesia in this province, he touched many lives with his work. He was chief of anesthesia at the Janeway from its opening in 1966 until he retired in 1989. He joined Memorial University's medical faculty in 1973 and eventually became professor and chair of the department of pediatrics. In 1995, after he retired, he was named professor emeritus.

Educated at Bishop Feild College in St. John's, Henderson excelled as a scholar and athlete and seemed bound for an auspicious career. He studied pre-medicine at Memorial University College and graduated from Dalhousie Medical School in 1945. As a student, and for a short time after graduation, he was an officer in the Canadian Army.

Charles Henderson.

After several years in general practice and anesthesia in Corner Brook, he did a two-year, post-graduate program at the Victoria General Hospital in Halifax before returning to St. John's in 1955, where he practiced until he retired. He was especially interested in pediatric anesthesia and was highly sought after for complicated cases long before the Janeway Children's Hospital opened. He would go on to recruit skilled anesthetists and well-trained nurses for the Janeway. He was also influential at Memorial University, and many of his students became distinguished anesthetists.

Henderson took excellent care of his patients and was always up to date with the many progressive changes that occurred in his field. Above all else, he was a compassionate man who treated his patients with diligence, respect, and kindness.

He had firm views about clinical and academic mattes, but even when he disagreed with his colleagues, he treated them with respect. As one senior pediatrician put it, "He had strong opinions but was usually right."

Henderson was a past president of the NLMA and represented the province on the Medical Council of Canada. He had a particular interest in preventing and dealing with substance abuse in physicians. He also held strong religious beliefs, and he served as an elder at St. Andrew's Presbyterian Church

(The Kirk) for many years.

Henderson was a devoted husband, father, grandfather, and great-grandfather—two of his three children became physicians.

Henderson took full advantage of the challenges that life and his career brought him, modernizing pediatric anesthesia and providing the best of patient care.

PSYCHIATRY

The Newfoundland Health Department opened the first provincial children's psychiatric practice at the Child Guidance Clinic and Day Care Centre in the King George V Institute on Water Street in 1962. This service was transferred to the Janeway on September 15, 1966, initially as an outpatient-only service. In January 1967, the hospital began an in-patient service and accepted patients up to age 16.

The Janeway's first director of psychiatry was Charles A. Boddie, a well-known psychiatrist in St. John's. Boddie also served on the hospital's medical advisory committee and was vice-president of the first executive committee at the Janeway.

Boddie worked alongside psychologists Kay Beattie and Elizabeth Daly, registered nurses Ivy Tilley and Doreen Cook, certified nursing assistant Elizabeth Bartlett, coordinator Margaret Dunne, and secretary Ramona Tansley. When the in-patient service opened, a teacher and two social workers were added. Psychiatry was a sub-department of medicine until 1985.

Psychiatry referrals were accepted from physicians for conditions including anxiety, behaviour problems, learning disorders, and infantile autism. A few children with psychosis were also treated. Treatment plans took a multidisciplinary approach and children attended outpatient clinics or day-care facilities, or were admitted to the in-patient unit. Everything was done to recognize the needs and individuality of each child, to promote relationships, and to broaden the child's sphere of experience and knowledge. Most in-patients and outpatients continued to attend school, where they were encouraged to form new attitudes toward learning. Their school work was assessed and their achievement levels established.

When Boddie resigned as head of psychiatry in July 1969, the in-patient unit closed because of the unavailability of psychiatrists. Children with serious psychiatric illness who needed overnight care were admitted to the pediatric medical wards, which created considerable stress for nursing staff with no psychiatric experience. In September, Dr. Raymond Danson was appointed acting director; he emphasized outpatient treatment.

In 1969, St. John's was experiencing a shortage of foster homes, and very few facilities existed for the care and training of children with cognitive disabilities. Many of these children were

C.A. Boddie, first chief of psychiatry.

institutionalized, and some ended up in juvenile correctional centres where the staff had little applicable experience. Exon House opened in St. John's 1969 (until 1988) as a centre to care for children and adults with cognitive disabilities. It was hoped that there would be an increased emphasis on day care and community services. The Children's Home on Water Street west also accepted children with cognitive disabilities between 1964 and 1983.

Danson, who left the Janeway at the end of the February 1970, was succeeded by Bernard G. Boothroyd-Brooks. The in-patient unit reopened in January 1971 with 13 beds and operated at full capacity. Boothroyd-Brooks resigned in 1974 and Uma Sreenivasan became director of psychiatry. The psychiatry department provided a full range of services from 1971 to the mid-1980s and had two major functions. First, treatment was provided for children up to 16 years. The multidisciplinary approach involved psychiatry, psychology, social work, and nursing. Ambulatory services, consultation by other medical specialists, child welfare, and in-patient services were involved. Referrals came from medical doctors but were also accepted directly from school, social workers, or parents, and no exclusion criteria were in place. Psychiatrists were available on a 24-hour basis for emergencies. In-patients were generally serious cases: children with psychosis, anorexia nervosa, unmanageable school behaviour problems, a mixture of serious physical and emotional problems, or children who had attempted suicide. In-patients also came from crisis situations where no other agency could offer relief.

The second important function of the department was to provide teaching and training for undergraduate medical students and graduate trainees in psychiatry, psychology students, social work interns, and student nurses. The school's post-graduate program for resident physicians is accredited by the Royal College of Physicians and Surgeons in Canada and by the Canadian and American Academies of Child Psychiatry.

The Adolescent Health Counselling Centre, a facility for adolescent out-patients, was established as a separate unit in 1985 and located on LeMarchant Road. In October 1989, the Janeway took over the centre's operation and relocated it to the Janeway Apartments.

Some psychiatric services were offered to adolescents by social workers and counsellors outside of St. John's in community health centres, but the Janeway alone had staff psychiatrists.

Pediatrician Delores Doherty submitted a detailed report on adolescent services at the Janeway, including psychiatry, in June 1984. She recommended a separate unit for adolescent psychiatric patients and proposed admitting pre-adolescent psychiatry patients into a new unit in the Janeway Apartments and having a separate unit on Ward 1C to accommodate six to eight adolescent in-patients and two to four day-care patients. Her goal was to ensure that the Janeway

Psychiatrists

Charles A. Boddie: 1966–1969
Raymond Danson: 1969–1970
Bernard Boothroyd-Brooks: 1970–1974
L. Belhan: 1970–1973
Uma Sreenivasan: 1974–1987
Hubert White: 1987–present
Ranjana Nagpurkar: 1983–1988
A. Gandhi: 1998
Kim St. John: 1989–present
Barbara Maddigan: 1995–2009

Rhonda Vardy: 1997–2001
Tina McWilliam-Burton: 1999–present
Murray Rex Bowring: 1999–1998
Christine Snelgrove: 2001–present
Anton Baksh: 2002–2006
Rajive Rajan: 2005–present
Weldon Bonnell: 2006–present
Leslie Wheeler: 2009–present
Chantelle Reid: 2008–present
Andrew Latos: 2012–present

would meet the developmental and emotional needs of adolescents and provide quality medical care.

In August 1984, consultant David Aldridge from the provincial Department of Health's Mental Health Services Division submitted his own proposal for provincial child mental health services and for the development of such a service within St. John's.

Sreenivasan was also active in expanding the role of psychiatry in the Janeway and province-wide. She proposed multidisciplinary department meetings at the hospital with nursing, social work, psychology, and psychiatrists and suggested that community-based child and adolescent mental health services be expanded.

In a proposal submitted to the Department of Health in 1985, Sreenivasan and her colleagues suggested adding to existing mental health services to create a comprehensive integrated service. They proposed that only 10 per cent of the required outpatient treatment was being provided, while more adolescents were admitted to the in-patient services than was recommended by Canadian guidelines. Certain groups did not receive adequate services, including preschool children and the victims of sexual and physical abuse.

Although most of these proposals and reports were accepted by psychiatrists, administration, and pediatricians, few changes were implemented. An adolescent unit opened at the Janeway in January 1985 for all services except psychiatry and, although extensive renovations were done to the in-patient psychiatric unit, the number of beds remained the same and no special accommodations were made for adolescents until the new Janeway opened in 2001.

Ranjana Nagpurkar was appointed director of psychiatry in 1987, Hubert White in 1988, and Kim St. John in 1989. White was the first Memorial University graduate to become an adolescent and child psychiatrist at the Janeway.

The new Janeway's psychiatry in-patient area has separate areas for adolescents and children. The unit, a high-risk, acute-care crisis intervention unit designed to provide safety, privacy, comfort, and infection control, has a locked entrance with a buzzer system for entry, secure windows, a central observation area, and private patient rooms. A separate constant observation area for aggressive patients is available. Large play areas for adolescents and younger children, a large dining room and living room, a fully equipped kitchen, a computer room, and a staff lunch room are all part of the unit.

The outpatient area has a comfortable waiting area for all patients. It boasts a school classroom, a large conference room, a dictating and examining room, and offices for physicians, psychologists, social workers, outpatient nurses, art therapists, secretaries, and psychiatric residents.

In April 2005, the Janeway began taking patients to age 18 (previous cut-off, 16). This change did not affect in-patient admissions but did increase the need for outpatient resources. Between 2005 and 2015, admissions to in-patient units were low and in-patient beds decreased from 13 to eight. Admission is considered a last resort; children under 11 are rarely admitted, as other interventions are used first. Day care is available but rarely used. The number of referrals for psychosis, depression, obsessive compulsive disorder, and anxiety has increased.

An operative external review in 2009 resulted in significant changes in 2010.

In 1998, intake services were started for two areas: in-patient and outpatient psychiatry, and Community Mental Health located in Janeway Apartments (Anderson Centre). Four years later, the Janeway's child and adolescent in-patient psychiatry services came under the umbrella of Eastern Health's Mental Health and Addiction Services division.

In 2008, intake was centralized for psychiatric services in Eastern Health, including the Janeway, with a full-time central intake coordinator. Since 2008 referrals have been around 200 per month. Referrals are assessed and assigned by priority: P1 (urgent, to be seen within a few weeks); P2 (semi-urgent); and P3 (approximately 13-month wait list; exceptions: Bridges and addiction programs). The Bridges Program offers mental health services for youth 13 to 18 years of age with a mental health crisis or issue who will benefit from focused intervention.

As of 2017, the Janeway provides the only high-risk crisis intervention, acute-care psychiatric service in Newfoundland and Labrador for children and adolescents. Other mental health resources available for them within Newfoundland and Labrador include the Janeway Family Centre located at the Miller Centre, the Bridges Program for older adolescents at St. Clare's, community mental health counsellors in several communities, addiction counselling in several centres, and private psychiatric clinics in St. John's, Corner Brook, Stephenville, Gander, and Grand Falls-Windsor. In November 2014, a youth treatment centre for adolescents (13–18 years) with complex mental health needs and addictions opened in Paradise. Prior to this, patients requiring long-term treatment were treated out of province.

In 2017 nine full- or part-time pediatric psychiatrists work at the Janeway; seven of these have faculty positions at the medical school. Sixteen full- or part-time nurses, most of whom have special training in psychiatry, three psychologists, three social workers, an occupational therapist, three teachers, an art therapist, a music therapist, five secretaries, and two receptionists round out the department.

The department continues to have a close relationship with Memorial's medical and nursing schools. It has been productive in research on social media and telepsychiatry. Telepsychiatry is a direct video link between a child psychiatrist at the Janeway and a patient at a different site such as Labrador City and saves the family the time and expense needed to visit the Janeway.

PSYCHIATRY OUTPATIENT STATISTICS
April 1, 2002, to March 31, 2014

New Patients
Consults 549
Emergencies 2,114
Urgent referral 2,216
Regular referral 1,503
Court referral 36

Rechecks 56,480

Day Patient Program
# of patients 74
# of visits 895

Referrals for Outpatient
Assessment Child & Adolescent Psychiatry
Janeway

1968 1006	1989 487	2005 558
1969 589	1990 544	2006 629
1977 202	1998 494	2007 775
1978 356	1999 423	2008 745
1979 432	2000 464	2009 383
1980 356	2001 452	2010 339
1981 392	2002 507	2011 318
1982 299	2003 406	2012 462
1984 400	2004 445	2013 435

DEPARTMENT OF DENTISTRY

The Janeway's department of dentistry opened on December 7, 1966, under tchief of dentistry Bruce L. Bowden, with David G. Brett-Williams as director of the division of orthodontics and a staff of 16 dentists. The department was equipped for general dentistry, orthodontics, and general anesthesia. Initially one referral clinic was held per week with a maximum of 10 patients.

Every effort was made to provide high-quality service and dental education to the many children who came to the hospital from across the province. Special attention was given to severely physically and mentally handicapped children and adults; facilities for their care were not available elsewhere in the province.

Clinics were increased to three per week in 1968 to accommodate the number of patients waiting to have dental work under general anesthesia. The former medical library adjacent to the dental suite was converted into a waiting room. By 1969, 456 patients had received dental work in the clinic.

Patients requiring extractions under general anesthesia were referred to the dental clinic by general practitioners or dentists throughout the province. Ramon V. Winsor was appointed chief of dentistry in 1970. With the assistance of dental assistant Cheryl Perks, clinics under Winsor were better organized with a better continuity of patient flow. Forty-seven in-patients and 960 out-patients were registered for extractions and 75 in-patients and 14 outpatients were given restorative treatment with fillings and prostheses that year. Many of these in-patients were handicapped children who required fillings and other restorative work under general anesthesia.

The orthodontic division became very active in 1970, particularly in treating neonates with cleft palates and children with speech problems. The oral surgery division, under the direction of James Miller, was also well established.

The workload continued to increase in 1971 when extractions were performed on 1,142 outpatients and 67 in-patients. In 1977, 1,648 extractions were performed and 249 patients (total) had restorative work, including porcelain jacket crowns, root canals, and partial and complete dentures. James Flynn was appointed as a second orthodontist in 1976.

In 1978, 21.4 per cent (1,374) fewer teeth were extracted than the previous year, permitting the staff to increase the volume of restorative dentistry by over 50 per cent. Chief of dentistry Paul O'Brien introduced several new programs in 1982, including a dental audit committee to monitor the quality of dental care. In 1985, after undertaking a two-year post-graduate program, Geoffrey Smith began practice at the Janeway as a pediatric dentist, or pedodontist. By 1990 the department of dentistry had a full-time pedodontist, a dentist on call at all times, and a staff hygienist.

The dental suite in the new Janeway was a vast improvement over the old. The old hospital dedicated two rooms and a small reception area for dentistry; the new hospital had two offices, a kitchen, scrub area, space for a dental hygienist, and a spacious reception and waiting area. Three rooms are assigned for dental work.

During procedures in the dental suite, patients may be sedated with nitrous oxide or oral midazolam; lengthier procedures may require general anesthesia in the operating room.

In 2013, Trang Nguyen replaced Smith as pediatric dentist. In 2017, Nguyen works with four general dentists. Several oral surgeons practicing in St. John's consult at the Janeway, usually on the in-patient service. Most cleft lip and palate work is done by Janeway plastic surgeons.

DIAGNOSTIC IMAGING

The department of radiology, initiated under Walter Heneghan when the Janeway opened in 1966, was located on the ground floor near the emergency department, outpatient clinics, and the cardiopulmonary unit.

Radiology performed standard X-rays on children, with special emphasis on cardiology investigations. Image-amplified fluoroscopy and angiography facilities, including cine (motion picture), were available beginning in 1966. A portable X-ray machine was also available and particularly helpful in the NICU and operating room. Several radiologists from the other city hospitals were appointed to the Janeway's associate and consulting staff. In 1970, Spencer Bridger, a full-time pediatric radiologist, joined the staff.

Upgrades continued and by 1974 its facilities were on par with, or better than, those found in any Canadian pediatric hospital of a similar size.

Chiefs of Radiology
Walter Heneghan: 1966–1992
Spencer Bridger: 1992–2001
Eilish Walsh: 2001–2011
Angela Pickles: 2011–present

Radiologists
Walter Heneghan: 1966–1992
G.S. Bapat: 1968–1969

M.B. Nogrady: 1967–1968
H.D. Wilson: 1968–1969
Spencer Bridger: 1970–2005
Benvon Cramer: 1984–2014 (professor and chair of radiology, MUN, 2001–2014)
Eilish Walsh: 1990–present
Angela Pickles: 2002–present
Stephanie Jackman: 2007–present
Marc Elliott: 2015–present

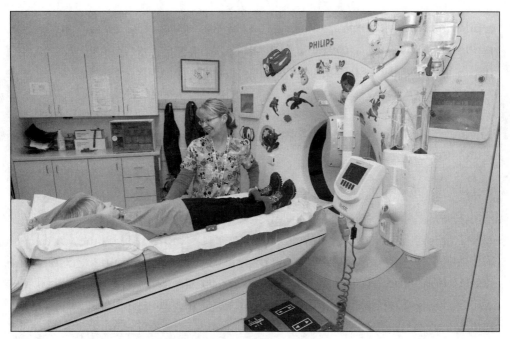

X-ray technologist Sharon Maynard giving a CT scan.

Nuclear medicine, a medical specialty that uses radioactive substances in the diagnosis and treatment of disease, was not available at the old Janeway, and patients requiring these techniques or treatments were referred to other hospitals. Nuclear medicine is available at the Health Sciences Centre, easily accessible by patients at the new Janeway.

In 1980, limited ultrasound diagnostic service was offered through equipment in the cardiology division. This equipment was heavily used and the need for a dedicated radiology ultrasound facility was apparent. Space was allocated for it, and the Janeway Auxiliary generously provided funds to buy the ultrasound equipment.

In 1981, the General Hospital acquired a CT scanner and the Janeway was allocated one half day per week of use, and emergencies as needed.

By the early 1980s, deteriorating radiology equipment, which had been purchased in 1966 and upgraded in 1974, was frequently breaking down, resulting in high maintenance costs and inconvenience to patients and staff. In 1984, the Janeway's board of directors approved the replacement of obsolete equipment in radiology rooms 1 and 2. Two new fluoroscopic units and an angiographic unit which incorporated 35-millimetre cine equipment, advanced TV recording apparatus, and biplane angiography, were purchased and installed in September 1985, as well as improved medical gas and anesthetic facilities.

Pediatric radiologist Benvon Cramer, hired in 1984, had ultrasound expertise. She made significant contributions to the advancement of this technology at the Janeway.

A new CT scanner at the Janeway was on the agenda of the St. John's Hospital Council in 1985 and 1986. The council approved, in 1986, that the next CT scanner for the city be at the Janeway site; however, the Department of Health placed a moratorium on the purchase of new CT scanners. The Janeway decided to raise the required funds on its own ($1.5 million, equipment; $500,000, construction of additional space; and $500,000 annually, operation), and approached the Janeway Children's Hospital Foundation for assistance. The Foundation made the CT scanner an objective for the 1988 Children's Miracle Network Telethon and over $1.4 million was pledged. A cost-sharing agreement was struck with the Department of Health, and this essential diagnostic service became a reality. The scanner was placed in service on December 11, 1989.

Regular improvements have been made to upgrade diagnostic imaging equipment and facilities to keep up with technology. The province, the Janeway Foundation, and the Janeway Auxiliary have been generous in the support of these initiatives.

Diagnostic Imaging since 2001
By Patricia Rose

The new Janeway gave us more space and newer equipment. Being part of the Health Sciences Centre has offered many benefits, such as the ability to avail of the services offered at their site. For example, if a patient at the old Janeway had to have a nuclear medicine scan, an ambulance would have to transport him or her to the Health Sciences Centre—but now the patient can be transported in a bed or wheelchair across a corridor. If we are having an issue with our CT machine, our patients can be sent across the hall. Our current facility has allowed us to provide better service to our patients.

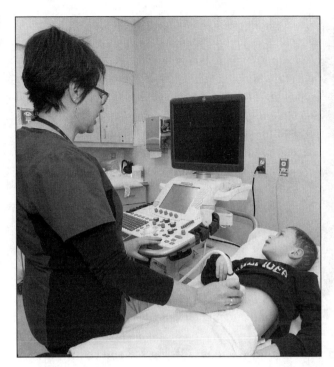

Spencer Bridger, chief of radiology, 1992–2001.

LEFT: Technologist Wendy Butt giving an abdominal ultrasound.

Since moving to our new home, we have installed our first MRI machine, which operates 16 hours a day. Another advancement is PACS (Picture Archiving Communication System), which enables us to capture, view, manage, store, retrieve, and communicate our images from X-ray (general radiography), CT, MRI, and ultrasound. If a patient is transported to Halifax but is being followed up in Labrador, for example, this system allows the remote medical teams to view the images obtained at the Janeway.

Technological advances have improved diagnostic imaging. A technologist at the old site would have to carry film cassettes to X-ray a patient. These cassettes weighed 2 to 3 pounds each; technologists often had to carry six to eight cassettes to the X-ray room and then to a darkroom for processing. In the darkroom, the film had to be removed by hand from each cassette and fed through a processor with chemicals to produce an image. The cassette was then reloaded with film to be used for another patient. Some orthopedic clinics had 50 to 60 patients in the morning and another 50 to 60 patients could go through another clinic running at the same time. At least 75 per cent of these patients

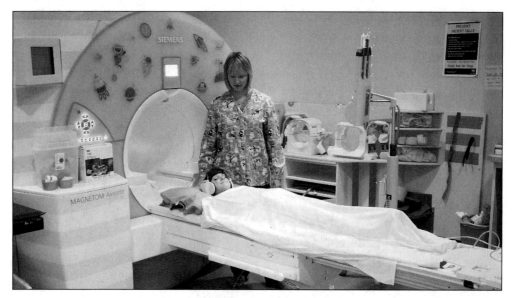

Technologist Glenda Devereaux giving a child an MRI.

would require X-rays, which meant a lot of heavy lifting for the technologist. We became a computerized department in 2001. Our cassettes were lighter and contained a computer chip which allowed the image to be displayed on a computer screen. The technologist could send these images to the radiologist for reporting with the click of a button.

In 2007, we stepped into the digital world. We became cassette-free in most areas of our department. The X-ray tables and wall buckys (a device used for table- or wall-mounted X-ray cassette and grid) have detectors which allow us to scan the patient while viewing the result on our computer screen. The images can then be sent to the radiologists with the push of a button. In 2017 our department is 80 per cent digital radiography and 20 per cent computerized radiography.

In an average month, the Janeway's diagnostic imaging department completes more than 3,500 examinations in general radiography, pediatric CT scans, and pediatric/obstetric ultrasounds. Our CT and MRI machines are used 16 hours a day, Monday to Friday. This allows us to accommodate all pediatric patients and many oncology patients at crucial times during treatments. Our ultrasound service strictly serves pediatric, obstetric, and women's health patients.

Deanne Hodder and Stephanie White, technologists working with PACS.

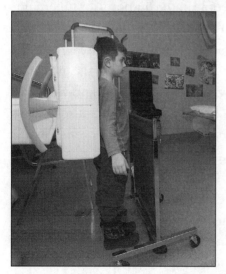

LEFT: Child getting a chest X-ray.

Pediatric patients are our number one priority. It is a pleasure and privilege to work every day with the greatest sector of our population, our children.

Our department is actively involved in the education of medical students, radiological technology students, and residents. Radiologists have been actively involved in surgery and medical rounds. Memorial University radiology residents rotate regularly through the department and elective rotations are offered to medical students and residents.

Janeway pediatricians, surgeons, and residents have been very appreciative of the excellent service provided to their patients by the radiology department. Radiologists make themselves readily available to physicians visiting the department for consultation; this has been the tradition since the Janeway's beginning.

Walter Heneghan
Director of Radiology (1966–1992)

Walter Heneghan, the Janeway's first radiologist, was active in the early planning of the hospital. The eldest of eight children, he was born in Louisburg, County Mayo, Ireland, in 1923. A year after graduating from the National University of Ireland in 1947 with a Bachelor of Medicine, Bachelor of Surgery, and a Bachelor of Obstetrics, he came to Newfoundland and began his practice in the St. Mary's Bay region.

Heneghan met public health worker Elizabeth

Walter Heneghan, 1966.

Lewis on board the *Christmas Seal* (a converted yacht that acted as a mobile clinic to screen people in the outports for tuberculosis). They married in 1953 and moved to Montreal, where he trained in radiology. Heneghan returned to St. John's in 1957 as a senior assistant radiologist at the General Hospital. He obtained his fellowship in radiology from the Royal College.

Heneghan was a brilliant diagnostician who had a thorough knowledge of anatomy, pathology, and clinical medicine. Through hard work and perseverance, he helped secure up-to-date equipment needed for a Children's Health Centre, especially the CT scanner purchased and installed in 1989.

He was a very educated man who loved the classics (as well as the TV show Jeopardy!) and was fond of quizzing his seven children about quotes from Shakespeare. He was fluent in Latin and Greek and was working on translating Homer's *Odyssey* from its original Greek in the months before his death in 1992.

Years later, Heneghan's daughter, Maggie, took her daughter Anna to the Janeway for a series of scans. It was in the early days of her multiple sclerosis diagnosis and, after one long day of tests, Maggie asked a technician about the photo of her father the hospital had on display. After all of Anna's tests and work-ups and scans, Maggie brought her tired daughter to see the photo of the grandfather she never met. "In a sense I entrusted Anna's care to him," Maggie recalls. "And it is the legacy of the Janeway that made such a step possible."

EMERGENCY DEPARTMENT

In 1966, the Janeway's emergency department was staffed by permanent nurses, overseen by head nurse Sheila Porter, and a rotation of interns and residents. Patients were assessed by these junior physicians, and pediatricians or surgeons on call would be consulted as required—no permanent medical staff were assigned to the department. In 1967, 12,144 children came through the department. The level of supervision of the house staff, the evidence-based guidelines for management, and the treatment of sick children brought to the department would not be considered adequate by 2017 standards.

In Canada, pediatric emergency departments did not exist until 1945. By 1957, only five centres had facilities specifically dedicated to pediatric emergency care, each with similar levels of care to the Janeway. New graduates in pediatrics and family practice worked in the department while they were establishing private practices. By the mid-1970s, full-time staff were hired as emergency medicine physicians and, by the end of the decade, the concept of modern pediatric emergency medicine had emerged.

The Janeway had emergency physicians (casualty officers) working in the department on a 24-hour basis by 1972. These physicians had varying amounts of pediatric training and they participated in the teaching and supervision of interns and residents rotating through the department.

The original emergency department consisted of one examining room with two curtained cubicles, a nursing-medical staff desk that divided the emergency and poison-control programs, a trauma room with an adjoining utility/sterilizer room, a small waiting room, and a three-bed observation room. If the

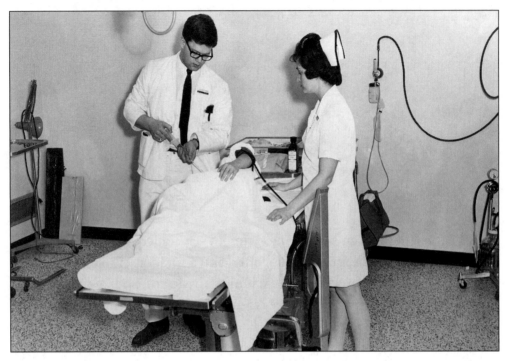

Pediatric resident George Sharpe and nurse Claudia Drodge treat an overdose patient the emergency department, 1972.

emergency department became quite busy on nights or weekends, staff would ask the pediatrician on call to help—often an unpopular request.

Children who came during the day without an appointment and who did not have an urgent or emergency condition were directed to a walk-in clinic, under the direct supervision of Julita Muzychka. This clinic provided a valuable service by shortening wait times and allowing Emergency staff to focus more on urgent problems. Attempts to have a walk-in clinic in the evenings and weekends operated by pediatricians on a fee-for-service basis were attempted in the mid-1980s, but did not last. The daytime walk-in clinic was phased out in 1987, when the new emergency department was opened.

As pediatric emergency medicine evolved in Canada, standardized protocols were introduced. In 1984, all pediatric patients at the Janeway had their vital signs (blood pressure, temperature, pulse, and respiratory rate) checked when a triage nursing position was initiated to determine the relative priority

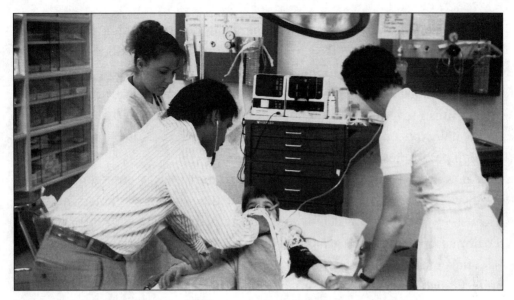

The emergency department, c. 1988.

for treatment. The Canadian Triage Acuity Scale was introduced in the late 1990s and quickly identified critically ill children.

In the early 1990s the Janeway introduced the Pediatric Advanced Life Support Program (PALS), which taught pediatric health care workers how to resuscitate and stabilize a critically ill child. PALS was created by the American Academy of Pediatrics and the American Heart Association. Physicians, including residents and interns, and nurses working in Emergency were expected to do this course. Before 1990 no dedicated pediatric cardiopulmonary course existed.

Pediatrician Rob Morris was appointed the first director of emergency services in 1985; prior to then, the emergency department came under ambulatory services. The emergency department was extensively renovated in the 1980s and was officially reopened in February 1987. This unit had six examining rooms, an isolation room, and a trauma unit with five or six beds, as well as a registration desk, sleeping quarters for the physicians, a quiet room, and an overnight observation room of six beds. The department was close to the laboratory and X-ray departments. These renovations added 5,000 square feet and cost $1 million.

At the new Janeway the pediatric emergency department is a modern facility with a spacious central desk, nine examining rooms, a six-bed observation facility with two isolation rooms, a fully equipped trauma room, a treatment room, a spacious waiting room with a registration desk, a triage area, offices for the administrative staff and the telephone call-in service, and a call room for the casualty officer. In 2011, a second casualty officer position was introduced for high peak times, decreasing the wait times.

An average of 90 to 100 patients come to the Janeway emergency department every day. Many of these are low acuity walk-in patients who come because most family physicians and private pediatricians do not provide after-hour services, and the availability of walk-in clinics in St. John's is limited.

The emergency department has been involved with national research projects including the Canadian Hospital Injury Reporting Prevention Program, which started in 1990, and the Immunization Monitoring Program-Active, which started in 1993.

In the late 1990s the Janeway Medical Advisory Committee and the chief of pediatrics felt that a full-time academic pediatric emergentologist would be needed to improve the department, initiate clinical research, and be a leader in academic education emergency medicine. The hospital and medical school made attempts to recruit a fully trained, board-certified pediatric emergentologist. Stephen Noseworthy, a graduate from Memorial's residency program, trained at the Children's Hospital of Eastern Ontario and was the first fully trained pediatrician at the Janeway with a subspecialty in emergency medicine. Noseworthy, who started in 2006, was succeeded by Robert Porter in 2008. Porter, a family doctor, was a full-time casualty officer at the Janeway and a certified emergency room physician. Porter has been active in research, teaching, and developing evidence-based recommendations.

Kevin Chan, a certified pediatric emergentologist, came to the Janeway as clinical chief in 2013 and as division head of the Janeway's emergency department. He brought new protocols from SickKids. In 2017, under Chan, manager Kim Pike, and patient-care coordinator Mary O'Brien, the department is extremely busy and provides up-to-date comprehensive care.

Dr. Julita Muzychka

General practitioner Julita Muzychka emigrated from Spain in 1960 with her husband, who had a faculty position at Memorial University. Muzychka, who did her internship at the General Hospital in 1961 and 1962, worked as a public health physician for a few months before moving to the Fever Hospital in November 1962 until the Janeway opened. Because of her experience with children at the Fever, she looked after patients on the infectious disease ward at the Janeway (1B). In 1968, under the direction of John Darte, she set up an outpatient walk-in clinic that served as an overflow clinic from the emergency room. She worked and taught there until she retired in 1989.

Julita Muzychka, 1966.

The walk-in clinic greatly improved the efficiency of the emergency department. As most of the patients were children with acute-care problems, it provided an excellent learning experience for medical students, interns, and residents. The clinic closed in 1989 when Muzychka retired. Although several attempts were made to open it, they all failed.

Joseph Squires's Story

I first met Joseph on the night of October 8, 2005, in the emergency department, when I was the casualty officer. He came in by ambulance near midnight and was unconscious and, because the nurses thought he smelled of alcohol, I initially thought he was intoxicated; however, a physical examination revealed blood in both ears and his mouth. I diagnosed a basilar skull fracture and knew he needed immediate ventilation,

Joseph Squires, 2016.

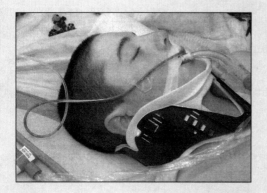

CT scans, and an assessment by neurosurgery. Dr. Debbie Reid, with an anesthetist from the Health Sciences Centre, performed a difficult intubation. A CT scan confirmed skill fractures but no fractures in his spine or other bones.

Neurosurgeon Falah Maroun determined that Joseph did not require surgery but he had to be sedated and ventilated for 14 days until the brain swelling subsided. Joseph's mother, Cynthia, was by his side the whole time, worried that he might die or be left with brain damage. Fortunately, his only lingering symptoms was some dizziness that lasted two years, but eventually subsided.

This story had a good outcome because the emergency room, anaesthesia, critical care, and surgery teams acted promptly. The lesson learned is that an unconscious teenager should never be presumed to be intoxicated or on drugs and an immediate thorough physical exam with appropriate investigations must be completed.

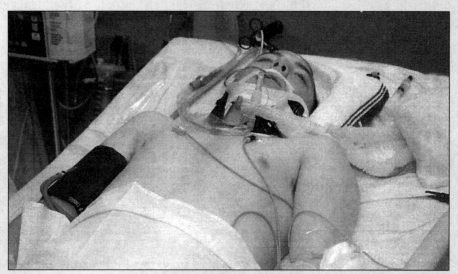

Joseph Squires in hospital in 2005.

LABORATORY MEDICINE

By Aiden Howell

In a diagnostic clinical laboratory, tests are done on specimens such as blood, urine, or tissue samples. The information obtained plays an integral role in the clinical diagnosis, treatment, and management of a patient by guiding clinicians in determining his or her health and, perhaps, illuminating any underlying illness or abnormalities. The Janeway laboratory opened in June 1966 with the appointment of Dr. A. William Janes as chief of pathology and director of laboratories, and Muir Gardiner as chief technologist. It was divided into clinical chemistry, special chemistry, microbiology, hematology, immunology, and genetics departments.

Aiden Howell.

The laboratory facilities and services were established on the ground floor. The laboratory office check-in, the patient waiting area, and blood and other specimen collection units were all centred in the same area. Initially six technical and six clerical staff were part of the department; the proposed staff complement was 30 technologists, six clinical personnel, and a second pathologist.

In September 1966 Janes and the Janeway's medical advisory committee expressed concern that staff shortages were having a significant impact on patient care. At night and during weekends, interns, residents, and some of the attending staff were obliged to provide basic laboratory procedures. More technologists were hired over the next few months, and services improved. By June 1967, however, Janes was still not satisfied that the Janeway could provide support for the full scale of laboratory services, and he resigned. He was replaced by Dr. Charles Hutton in July 1967.

Clinical Chemistry Laboratory

Many of the tests conducted by the clinical chemistry laboratory in 1966—tests for sodium and glucose and liver and kidney function tests—were done manually by technologists and required significant amounts of blood and

A. William Janes, first director of laboratories, 1966.

processing time. In the late 1960s and early 1970s, automatic analyzers, which required smaller samples of blood and could accurately conduct several tests on the same sample, were introduced. In 2017, these analyzers are programmed to test for a wide range of drugs and hormones.

The clinical chemistry laboratory participated in training programs of technical students of the College of Trades and Technology (renamed the College of the North Atlantic in 1997) before it integrated with the main Health Sciences clinical chemistry laboratory in 2001.

Special Biochemistry Laboratory

Under the direction of Dr. Madhavan Kutty, the special biochemistry division was developed. It offered specialized tests and provided more definitive diagnostic results than those in the routine biochemistry division. These services were offered on a provincial referral basis to pediatric and adult patients. Kutty introduced test procedures and directed the technical staff to analyze, standardize, and quality control these tests. The routine biochemistry section was expanded to include procedures transferred from special biochemistry as they became available and were offered on a routine basis. This freed up staff to

Madhavan Kutty, director of biochemistry.

develop procedures in special biochemistry, including testing amino acids by thin layer chromatography and organic acids by UV spectrophotometry, mass spectrophotometry, and gas chromatography, lipid profiling (triglycerides, HD2, and LDL cholesterols), lipoprotein electrophoresis, and hyperlipidemia typing. Tests for hemoglobin A1C, human growth hormone, insulin, T2, TSH, total and free testosterone, micropolysaccharides, VMA, and immunoglobulins were also available. Diagnosis of Tay Sachs and other inborn errors of metabolism, as well as other test procedures that could, in consultation with medical staff, make and/or confirm a diagnosis, were carried out.

During his tenure, Kutty applied for and received research grants, some for his own work and others in collaboration with other professional and medical staff. These grants provided funding for laboratory research assistants, supplies, and capital equipment needed to perform research projects. The equipment became the property of the Janeway laboratory at the completion of the project. The findings from these research projects were published in national and international journals.

Neonatal Screening Laboratory

To standardize results and to ensure their accuracy and quality, a neonatal screening program was established at the Janeway in September 1978. Before this program, a PKU stick (used to test for phenylketonuria, a rare inherited disorder which causes the amino acid phenylalanine to build up in the body) was dipped into a neonate's urine and tested. The neonatal screening program, which offered a more accurate PKU test, was developed and established in the laboratory by Kutty and June Hynes. Technical coordinator Albert J. Davis was also the medical coordinator.

Kutty and Hynes also developed a new technique for extracting blood from blotting paper, which simplified neonatal screening. Davis and Hynes visited provincial hospitals to demonstrate the technique of blood collection on the specially designed blotting paper attached to a neonatal screening request form. They impressed on the nursing staff the need for timeliness in blood collection and in the completion and submission of requisitions.

Microbiology Laboratory

A full microbiology service was established in 1966 and many of the procedures were established by Muir Gardiner.

The microbiology laboratory processed blood, cerebrospinal fluid, urine, stool, and the exudate from purulent wounds, and examined specimens for pathogenic bacteria under a microscope. Further samples could be cultured on culture media; the results could determine what bacteria contributed to a child's illness and, with further testing, the sensitivity of these bacteria to various antibiotics.

Respiratory syncytial virus and rotavirus were tested for in the Janeway. Most other tests for virus detection were referred to the Public Health Laboratories at the Miller Centre on Forest Road. A limited number of serology tests were done at the Janeway, such as infectious mononucleosis testing, but most of this testing was also referred to the Public Health Laboratories, as was most parasitology testing.

The microbiology laboratory participated in several proficiency testing programs. The American Association of Bioanalysts sent specimens quarterly for identification, culturing, and reporting, including serology and parasitology specimens. The Janeway's laboratory showed a high degree of accuracy. It also participated in the teaching and training of students in the Registered Technology Program. With the other laboratory divisions, the microbiology laboratory was included in computerization with the Meditech System. The Janeway laboratory closed in 1998 and its services are fully provided by the Health Sciences microbiology laboratory and Public Health Laboratories.

Hematology Laboratory

The hematology laboratory had three main purposes: examining blood cells, testing blood coagulation (blood clotting), and banking blood.

In 1966 blood cell examination was a manual procedure, but in the early 1970s automation was introduced. The first analyzer, the Heme W, measured hemoglobin, hematocrit, and white blood cells count. The installation of the Coulter S, followed by the Coulter S Plus, provided an expanded hematological profile consisting of hemoglobin (Hgb), hematocrit (Hct), red blood cells (RBC), white blood cells (WBC), mean cell volume (MCV), mean cell hemoglobin (MCH), mean corpuscular hemoglobin concentration (MCHC), and platelet counts. Whole blood specimens collected by venipuncture were tested on these analyzers, as were prediluted samples which required just 20 microlitres of blood. This provided the full range of testing abilities for all pediatric patients.

Automation was introduced later for coagulation testing: a Coag-u-mate Analyzer provided testing for pt (prothrombin time), ptt (partial thromboplastin time), and fibrinogen.

The Heme W, Coulter S, and Coag-u-mate analyzers were standardized and quality controlled daily by laboratory technical staff prior to testing patient specimens. Daily, weekly, and monthly preventative maintenance programs, as prescribed by the vendor, were carried out by laboratory staff.

Blood Banking

Blood bank services included ABO grouping, Rh typing, matching, and antibody identification. The Canadian Red Cross provided whole blood, packed cells, plasma, platelets, fresh frozen plasma, serum albumin, and cryoprecipitate to the blood bank for cross-matching and/or issuance for treatment of patients. Initially, the treatment of hemophilia factors VIII and IX deficiencies was by cryoprecipitate provided by the Red Cross. Factors VIII and IX were commercial products initially provided by the Janeway and later the Red Cross for treating hemophilia. Tragically, some of these products were contaminated with Hepatitis C and HIV in the early 1980s (see Infectious Diseases chapter).

The blood bank supervisor maintained a comprehensive procedure and policy manual. One policy advocated that patients less than two years old receive O-negative instead of group-specific blood. Newborns would receive cytomegalovirus (CMV) negative blood. The supervisor held regular in-service sessions with nursing staff on the proper handling of blood and blood products. Blood bank staff participated in the AAB (American Association of Bioanalysts) proficiency testing program; the results were always at 100 per cent agreement and controls assayed with each test or batch of tests. Detailed record books were maintained within the blood bank.

Immunology

The immunology division, originally housed in the main laboratory, was relocated in 1974 to the Janeway Apartments due to space constraints. It tested for a range of immunoglobulin antibodies with immunoelectrophoresis; for example, immunoglobulin E (IgE) is a marker that verifies an allergy.

The RAST (Radioallergosorbent Test), in conjunction with IgE testing, diagnosed allergic reactions in patients. A profile of common local allergens was established and skin testing performed in clinic by director of immunology Ranjit Chandra to determine allergies by reaction on the patient's skin. RAST allergen procedures were more expensive than most other allergen procedures—up to 10 times the in-house costs (e.g., $300 vs. $30 for a 10-test profile).

Other common tests included alpha-fetoprotein testing on serum and amniotic fluid. Ferritin was assayed on a gamma counter. The majority of immunology testing was by automation, which included known standards and quality control specimens.

Cytogenetic Laboratory

Cytogenetics is that branch of genetics concerned with the structure and function of the cell, especially the chromosomes. The cytogenetic laboratory began in 1967 under the direction of Janes, but the service was not in full operation until 1968. Susan Davis, the first technologist, developed the first karyogram (an ordered image of the chromosome characteristics of an individual), marking the beginning of the service.

Dr. Penny Allderdice took over as director of the diagnostic service in 1973. Allderdice, who had a genetic research laboratory at the medical school, loaned some of her equipment to the Janeway, the most significant being a fluorescent microscope with micro-camera attachments, to get its diagnostic services off the ground. Films of karyograms were developed, enlarged, and printed in a darkroom in Building 615.

The cytogenetics facility in the main laboratory soon became inadequate. A trailer, purchased in 1974, was attached to Building 615 to house the diagnostic service and four technologists. Another fluorescent microscope, a light microscope, several carbon dioxide incubators, and an ultraviolet sterile cabinet were purchased in 1974. Staff from both the medical school and Janeway laboratories used the equipment for diagnostic and research work. The diagnostic service included blood, amniotic fluid, and bone marrow specimens, along with products of conception. To introduce and establish more specialized testing with amniotic fluid and bone marrow, Allderdice and senior technologist Olga French visited cytogenetic laboratories in Montreal, Toronto, and Boston to learn and refine techniques at the Janeway laboratory.

A second trailer, purchased in 1978, had space for a sterile room equipped with a sterile cabinet, an inverted microscope, and two carbon dioxide incubators. Culturing in the sterile room was done on amniotic fluids, products of conception, and tissue specimens. Bone marrow karyotyping aided in diagnosing certain cancers, Philadelphia chromosome, the deletion of chromosome 22, and chronic myelogenous leukemia. Blood karyotyping aided the diagnosis of fragile X chromosome. Giemsa staining (g-banding) was developed to detect the deletion or addition of long chromosomes.

Allderdice discovered two chromosomes during her tenure: Allderdice Syndrome, or "Inversion 3 chromosome," was discovered in the Stephenville–St. George's area; "Inversion 9 chromosome," on Bell Island.

Anatomical Pathology Laboratory

Anatomical pathology is a medical specialty concerned with the diagnosis of disease based on the gross, microscopic, chemical, immunologic, and molecular examination of organs. Autopsies are also done in this laboratory, staffed by full-time physicians trained in pathology and certified by the Royal College of Physicians and Surgeons of Canada. Certified technologists prepare specimens for microscopic histological examination and do other procedures necessary for the diagnosis of disease. Most specimens come from the operating room or autopsies.

A full histology-pathology laboratory was developed in 1966 by Janes; Hutton took it over in 1967. Specimens from the operating room were received, logged, and assigned a surgical number. This number, a permanent identifier, was referred to at all stages of handling and processing. The pathologist prepared representative sections from the specimen and recorded a preliminary description. These sections were processed overnight in an auto-technician, embedded in paraffin blocks, cut at 7 microns, and then floated onto microscope slides and stained by hematoxylin and eosin stains. As requested and/or deemed necessary by the specimen type, special staining was done on additional slides, which were forwarded to the pathologist for microscopic examination. Pathology reports were forwarded to the surgical wards, a copy of which was retained in the laboratory for binding alphabetically at the year's end.

Autopsy services were also provided in this division, at the request of the attending physician, with the consent of parents and/or guardians. From 1967 through the 1970s, Hutton did about 50 autopsies a year. He resigned as chief of pathology and director of laboratories in 1986.

Chitra Pushpanathan, named clinical pathologist at the Janeway in 1987, retired in 2013; she was replaced by pediatric pathologist Kathryn Whelan.

All Janeway laboratories merged with the clinical laboratories of the Health Sciences Centre when it moved in 2001. The new Janeway has maintained a blood collection unit for children and women of the children's and women's health programs.

Chitra Pushpanathan, pathologist and director of laboratories, 1988–2010.

NURSING

Nurses play an essential role in the care of children at any pediatric health centre; if the Janeway were a ship, the nurses would be the engine driving it. They work tirelessly, covering the hospital 24 hours a day, often under stressful and demanding conditions. While their importance has never wavered, their training, roles, and responsibilities have evolved greatly.

The Department of Nursing and Patient Care started in April 1966 when Margaret Chesterfield, formerly of the Sheffield Children's Hospital in England, was appointed director of nursing. She had the difficult task of recruiting nurses to work throughout the hospital around the clock, usually in eight-hour shifts, and not just on the wards but also in the operating room, emergency department, ICU, and outpatient clinics. Although some nurses came from the pediatric units of other St. John's hospitals, it was difficult to recruit enough qualified nurses in the first few years. Very few available nurses had special pediatric training or experience. It was also difficult to recruit nurses because of the Janeway's physical isolation from the centre of the city and inadequate salaries. Graduate nurses often resigned after they had their own children, leaving a shortage in the system. It was difficult to find accommodations nearby until the Janeway Apartments opened in 1967. In 1967, a daycare nursery was opened in Building 615, near the Janeway, which also helped with the recruitment and retention of nurses.

In the 1960s, nurse training programs were offered at St. Clare's, Grace, and General hospitals in St. John's. Western Memorial Hospital, in Corner Brook, offered a program starting in 1971. These were three-year programs without university affiliation, and students were expected to participate in patient care and often covered night and evening shifts. Graduating nurses had limited training in pediatrics. Memorial University's School of Nursing opened in 1965 and celebrated its first graduates in 1970. These graduates held a Bachelor of Nursing degree and a Registered Nursing Diploma.

Elsie Hill, appointed director of nursing in 1967, held group conferences to discuss the National League of Nursing guidelines and involved Janeway nurses in planning their department. Changes resulted in more effective direction for head nurses, including daily ward conferences with physicians and allied health workers, improvements in nursing-care plans, and revision of patient records to make them more accessible. Staff were evaluated periodically.

In 1968, a division of continuing education for nurses was established under the direction of Una Kent. Monthly and weekly sessions were well attended, and the program continues to be very successful in 2017. Other continuing education programs, including extensive courses in neonatology, were completed by nurses. In 1970, a course in neonatal intensive care and recovery nursing was conducted at the Janeway.

In 1972, a 12-hour shift system was introduced to replace eight-hour shifts and was widely accepted. As staffing was still a challenge, in 1974 and 1976 nurses were recruited from Great Britain and the Philippines.

Several special programs were established in the early 1970s. The first parent-liaison nurse was Rita Walsh; her position evolved into Diabetic Nurse Coordinator. Liaison nurses were established in the emergency department, which greatly facilitated priorities and maintaining effective communication. This has evolved into an efficient triage system. Other programs developed with nurse specialists include perinatology, child development, oncology, cystic fibrosis, gastroenterology, rheumatology, neurology, pediatric surgery, diabetes, and rehabilitation. The nurses communicate with children and their families, discuss treatment with physicians, and liaise with other allied health specialists and the community. They are often the first line of contact when a problem arises. One of their major roles is educating children and their parents. This applies to all specialties, but particularly diabetes.

In the 1990s nurse practitioners were introduced. Nurse practitioners are registered nurses with additional education and training that allow them to order and interpret diagnostic tests, communicate diagnoses, prescribe pharmaceuticals, and perform specific procedures. The Janeway's nurse practitioners work in neonatology, adolescent medicine, and cystic fibrosis. This has improved the care of the children and adolescents in the program, both in acute and long-term chronic care.

In 1992, a single health care board for acute-care facilities was created in the city and the Janeway was no longer an independent health care facility. The introduction of program management did not change the practice of nursing or medicine, but it was a major change in the hospital's administrative structure and overall organizational culture. The Janeway no longer had its own CEO or director of nursing but became a "program" that incorporated children's and women's health. This program had a director and its divisions had managers, most of whom were nurses. A division manager was responsible for the nurses and other allied health workers in that division. A staff nurse, for example, on the surgical in-patient service would work in the division of surgery in the children's and women's health program.

In 2017, nurses generally have more advanced education and skills than they did in 1966. Their basic education includes a bachelor's degree; many obtain certification in specialty areas or continue to the master's or doctorate levels. Nurses now do many procedures that were once done by physicians, such as starting intravenous lines. They have more independence in their practice and are better informed and qualified to teach families and children. More nurses are involved in research, advocacy, and leadership; the Janeway's nursing staff have kept pace with the many innovations and advances in the standard of care and scope of practice.

My Nursing Story
By Mary O'Brien

My story starts when I was just 17 years old and I was accepted into the St. Clare's School of Nursing. When I graduated in 1974, jobs were scarce and, like a lot of my classmates, I left the province.

My first job was at Sunnybrook Hospital in Toronto. I worked on the adult hematology-oncology ward, and although I was happy to have a job, I often felt like something was missing. Longing to fulfill my dreams of being a pediatric nurse I was drawn back to the old Janeway Children's Hospital.

I returned to Newfoundland in 1975 and started nursing at the Janeway in PICU, NICU, the recovery room, and cardiac recovery. It felt like a beehive of activity on most days and I loved it! I worked alongside my classmates and many other nurses who taught me the lifelong lessons of patience, kindness, and critical thinking. I finally felt that I was working in a place where I belonged.

Our head nurse was Ramona Strong, an extraordinary teacher who willingly shared her knowledge. Taking us under her wing, she taught and cared for us young nurses as her own children. We worked with some of the most dedicated physicians: pediatric surgeons Richard Kennedy and Abdalla Hanna, pediatricians Austin Rick Cooper and Chaker Hobeika, pediatrician radiologists Spencer Bridger and Walter Heneghan, cardiac surgeon Gary Cornel, and neurosurgeon Falah Maroun. They were all excellent physicians and wonderful teachers.

This was a time when CT scans were not yet available, and doctors relied heavily on nursing assessments and careful monitoring of vital signs, which alerted us to changes in our patient's condition. Some of the most common injuries and illnesses I saw were head injuries, burns, and diseases that did not have protective vaccinations.

In the 1970s, wearing helmets was just starting to become more the norm. Many patients I saw suffered from severe head injuries due to the lack of safety equipment and public awareness around protective equipment. I treated many injuries resulting from bike, ATV, and car-pedestrian accidents. My colleagues and I had to keep a surgical drilling tool, also known as a burr drill, charged at the nurses' desk for emergency situations when the physicians had to drill into the skull (burr holes) in PICU.

Many homes were still without smoke detectors in the 1970s, and we provided care for many children healing from severe burns. I still remember the faces and names of the children I cared for and I have always kept them in my heart and prayers.

In the early days of the Janeway, routine immunizations were available but there were none for *Haemophilus influenzae* and *Neisseria meningitides meningitis* and septicemia (blood infection). I saw many patients in our unit ill from those terrible diseases, and they required intensive nursing care and monitoring. Thanks to life-saving vaccines, diseases

Care facilitator Mary (Roche) O'Brien, in 2016.

like meningitis and septicemia have almost become extinct. After seeing the damage and death that those dreadful diseases have caused, I feel very strongly about children receiving vaccinations to protect themselves and other children from these illnesses.

In 1979, I gave birth to my first child and decided to take a short break from PICU. I took a position with the Janeway float team. This was an extremely good fit for me and one of the most amazing experiences of my life as a nurse! I had the opportunity to work on every floor and in every department at the Janeway, giving me great insight and understanding of how other areas functioned. After a few months on the float, I went back to PICU; two years later, I had my second child. Following the birth of my third child in 1984, I transferred to the Janeway's emergency department, where I had the privilege of meeting and learning from Sheila Porter. I quickly fell in pace with the hustle and bustle. We never knew what was going to come through the doors. I quickly learned that teamwork and working at an extremely fast pace were key. After working together for a while, our team could anticipate each other's next move when working on a trauma or medical emergency.

May 24, 2001, was a day of great change for the Janeway. We closed our doors at the old Janeway hospital in Pleasantville and moved to our new home. We were all sad to leave, but we were hopeful that we would continue on as the Janeway family. The hospital is still a place of hope, healing, and happiness for many children, family, and staff all around the province.

As for me, I am still working in the emergency department as a care facilitator. To this day I continue to enjoy my job. I am able to appreciate the changes and advances that have taken place over the many years—from CT scans, MRIs, and a wide range of safety equipment and immunizations available to protect children against deadly diseases. I hope the awareness and importance of wearing safety equipment and immunizing children will be carried through future generations.

The Janeway's doors are always open to anyone who seeks care. The physicians, nurses, and staff do their best for each and every patient by providing safe, quality care during some of the scariest times of a young patient's life. At the Janeway, each child we care for has become like our own. As health care providers, we care for our patients, wishing nothing but the best outcome possible for them.

Nursing at the Janeway: My 22 Years
By Rita Dawe

I first worked as a nurse at the old Fever Hospital, where I worked with children who had infectious diseases. The Fever was a wooden building adjacent to the old General Hospital. Moving to the Janeway in August 1966 was quite a change—there was lots of space and families could stay with their children 24 hours a day. No visitors had ever been allowed at the Fever, not even the parents of sick children.

I became charge nurse on 2A at the Janeway and, to my surprise, it had a few beds, but little else—no crash cart for a child who became critically ill, no drug cupboard, and no books or toys. My first job was to change all that.

The ward was quite busy after it was set up, and many patients, mostly adolescents, had diabetes, asthma, or leukemia.

Many asthma patients were repeat patients. This situation didn't improve until we started an asthma clinic. In those days, children were placed in croup tents (a plastic "tent" placed over the upper body so that oxygen and cold air could be delivered to the child), and it was difficult to see them at night. One time a member of the cleaning staff accidentally unplugged an oxygen tube; however, it was discovered before the patient deteriorated.

One frequent patient who had always hated sports did much better after he learned to do the breathing exercises we taught him. The parents didn't realize the importance of their not smoking in the home—and inhaled steroids were not yet on the market.

Diabetic patients, too, had frequent admissions, and it wasn't until Dr. Albert J. Davis came in 1969 and set up a diabetic clinic that this situation improved. Doctors Chaker Hobeika and William Sprague also helped with the clinic.

I became a patient liaison nurse in 1971 and I was responsible for the health education of children and their parents. I taught children with asthma, diabetes, dermatology concerns, and hemophilia for a short time. I also orientated children (and their parents) who were having minor elective surgery by setting up a pretend operating room in the outpatient clinic on Saturdays; this proved to be effective.

Diabetes education was a large part of my work and, with the physicians, dieticians, especially Louise Dalton, and social workers, we started a diabetic camp.

I looked after one 12-year-old boy who had been a grade-A student until something changed. He became very angry and was often in the principal's office. He was sent to psychiatry but no one there could figure out what was going on. One day after he had kicked his locker, I had to talk with him, and I asked, "Why did you get angry and kick the locker?" He replied, "I can't see." We sent him to an ophthalmologist, who gave him glasses, and he did well after that.

I saw an 11-year-old girl with throat cancer, being cared for by Dr. Richard Kennedy, because the mother and child were upset and afraid. I told them to never give up hope. This girl did get better and eventually became a Janeway nurse.

Another child who had sore feet wouldn't talk to the doctor but would talk to me. It turned out that his sneakers were too small.

In the early 1970s we set up a province-wide teleconference with the help of Dr. Max House for health care workers about diabetes in children. The first of its kind in Canada, it was a resounding success.

I worked very hard when I was a nurse at the Janeway and I saw a lot of changes from the time I started working there until I retired in 1988.

ALLIED HEALTH

Pharmacy

The pharmacy department began operations on June 27, 1966, with chief pharmacist William Simmons and drug clerk John Ivany. It started as a small but functional service on the first floor of the Janeway, however, it was immediately obvious that the space was inadequate and the chief pharmacist's office was moved to another floor.

In 1967, with the assistance of the Pharmacy and Therapeutics Committee of the Medical Staff, a drug formulary was prepared and distributed and a program for reporting adverse drug reactions was implemented.

Donald Hillier.

Donald Hillier was appointed staff pharmacist in February 1970 and replaced Simmons as chief pharmacist in February 1972.

In addition to compounding and dispensing topical ointments, tablets, and solutions, the pharmacy was required to supply a wide range of specialty products, such as small volume parenteral solutions and specialized nutritional products. Since 1970 the department has been involved in intravenous hyper-alimentation (total nutritional intravenous maintenance of patients).

To assist in preparing these solutions and other sterile specialty products, a laminar air flow hood—a Class 100 Clean Air Centre—was installed. This equipment provides an ultra-clean work area by removing dust and other air-borne contamination through a microfiltration system.

In 1972 the pharmacy participated in the teaching program of the first class of the School of Pharmacy of the College of Trades and Technology. Prior to this, pharmacy students were trained under an apprentice program for five years and then assigned to a pharmacy. Most of these were retail pharmacies in larger centres such as St. John's.

Teaching students from the College of Trades and Technology, and after 1990, the Memorial University School of Pharmacy, was, and still is, an import-ant function for the Janeway's pharmacy department.

In 1976 pharmacy hours were extended to include three hours of sched-uled services on Saturdays, Sundays, and public holidays. On-call service was provided at all other times.

In 1977 a new physician's order form was introduced which provided the pharmacy with the original prescription. An electronic data processing pro-gram was initiated in 1980, which standardized inventory and cost control pro-grams and established a medication profile for each patient. This was the first online computerized pharmacy system in the province.

An additional pharmacist was appointed in 1980, improving the efficiency of the system.

In the 1980s, studies raised concerns over the safe handling of antineoplas-tic (anti-tumor) medications. In response, in 1985 a biological safety cabinet was installed to handle anti-neoplastic medications in a special room with external ventilation. At about the same time, the pharmacy introduced an admixture service to provide all parenteral cancer chemotherapy drugs in a premixed, measured, and ready-to-use format. The nurse and physicians were no longer required to prepare medications on the ward and the prescribed individual dose was delivered to the patient's bedside. The nurse, physician, and parent verified the correct dose. This reduced the potential risk of contact with che-motherapeutic agents and, more importantly, reduced the risk of a drug error.

In 1994 the hospitals in St. John's were consolidated and program man-agement was introduced. The clinical services of the Janeway came under the

Child Health program; however, laboratory, diagnostic imaging, and pharmacy became separate programs under the Health Care Corporation of St. John's and, later, Eastern Health. In 2017, the Janeway pharmacy operates under Eastern Health's pharmacy program, which oversees all hospital pharmacies in eastern Newfoundland, but it also operates independently.

In 2001, when the Janeway moved to the Health Sciences Centre, a small space was provided for the pharmacy. Originally, the Janeway pharmacy was going to be a satellite of the larger Health Sciences Centre pharmacy; it was later decided that it should operate independently—pediatric pharmacy deals with a different population with unique anatomy, physiology, and response to medications. Children's dosing is based on weight and the child's ability to metabolize a drug.

The pharmacists work closely with the Child Health program. They have a detailed knowledge of the patients and monitor their progress; they consult with physicians and nurses on a regular basis to discuss appropriate choice, dose, and duration of therapy.

The Janeway participates in "Medicine Reconciliation," an evidence-based initiative that further reduces the incidence of drug error. In most pediatric facilities in Canada, pharmacists are responsible for this program but, due to a shortage of pharmacy staff, the Janeway's nursing staff have taken on this role.

In 2017, four pharmacists and 1.5 pharmacy technicians work at the pharmacy.

The pharmacists provide care to pediatric patients in the form of intravenous medications, antibiotics, regular prescriptions, and total parenteral nutrition. They also access medications not routinely available in Canada under the Special Access Program. They are highly regarded by the Janeway medical and nursing staff, as well as patients and their parents for the excellent care they provide.

Respiratory Therapy

The respiratory therapy department at the Janeway started in 1966 with the appointment of John Hendriks. The focus of the department was the delivery of oxygen and aerosol therapy; later, ventilator management of neonates, chil-

Respiratory Therapy Directors

John Hendriks: 1966–1967

David Sheldon: 1967–1968

Allan Efford: 1968–1970

Brian Ryan: 1970–1978

Arthur Osborne: 1978–1999

Cheryl Bailey (clinical leader): 1999–present

(Source: Cheryl Bailey, Respiratory Therapist, Clinical Leader)

dren, and adolescents became important.

A respiratory therapist is a specialized health care practitioner who has completed a comprehensive program in a university or college and who has passed the provincial licensing exams. At the Janeway, respiratory therapists treat all aspects of cardiopulmonary care, from neonates to adolescents, and work closely with physicians and nurses in all areas of the hospital.

Respiratory therapists treat in-patients, day patients, and outpatients for a variety of conditions that may require treatments such as medical gas therapy, aerosol drug administration, bronchial hygiene procedures, and conventional and high-frequency ventilation and airway management, particularly for those who have a tracheostomy. They play an active role in high-risk deliveries, providing intubation meconium removal, suctioning, bag and mask ventilation, and administering surfactant.

Respiratory therapists play a vital role in neonate transport and are responsible for airway management, mechanical ventilation, respiratory assessment, and support and equipment maintenance. They travel with the team all over the province.

In NICU, they are responsible for ventilation, intubation, endotracheal tube care, and assessment of neonates with cardiopulmonary issues. They also participate in team rounds with the nursing and medical staff and help with the teaching of students and parents of sick neonates. In PICU, they are involved with ventilation, endotracheal tube care, and assessments of critically ill children.

On the medical and surgical wards, they are responsible for oxygen maintenance, respiratory assessment, discharge planning, and patient transport. In the emergency department, they assist with the resuscitation of critically ill children and assess those with respiratory conditions and facilitate transfers.

Janeway respiratory therapists follow outpatients with complex respiratory issues and provide teaching to caregivers. In fact, teaching is a major commitment for the therapists. As instructors in the hospital's simulation program they teach residents, nurses, and pediatricians in such programs as the Pediatric Advanced Life Support and the Neonatal Resuscitation Program (NRP). They also teach parents and give professional in-service lectures.

In the Janeway's early years, respiratory therapists played an important, but limited, role. In 2017 they intubate patients with endotracheal tubes to help them breathe and set up complicated conventional and high-speed respiratory ventilation. The first mechanical ventilator for infants and neonates, the Baby Bird, was acquired in 1974; in 2017 mechanical ventilators have digital components such as microprocessors, flow sensors, and Neutrally Adjusted Ventilator Assists that allow for precise, safe, and more sensitive ventilation that leads to better outcomes and fewer problems with chronic lung disease afterwards.

Physiotherapy

Pediatric physiotherapy is effective in the management of perinatal conditions, conditions diagnosed in early childhood, and injuries sustained throughout childhood and the transition to adult care. Pediatric physiotherapy improves physical function and quality of life. Its long-term benefits are significant and include reducing disability and the need for surgery or other costlier invasive interventions resulting in a decreased burden on future use of health care services.

"The Value of Physiotherapy," physiotherapy.ca

The Janeway's department of physiotherapy opened in 1967 with Barbara Ellis, MCPA, as its first director. In 1975, the department was reorganized with seven full-time physiotherapists, a physiotherapy aide, and a secretary. Three units were created: orthopedics, neurology; neurosurgery, burns, and infant stimulation; and cardio-respiratory. This separation allowed specialization

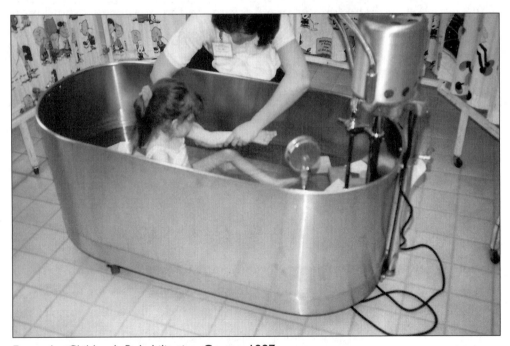

From the Children's Rehabilitation Centre, 1987.

and improved efficiency, morale, and staffing stability.

The department accepted physiotherapy students from Dalhousie University by the mid-1970s and continues to do so in 2017.

As the hospital expanded its outpatient services in the early 1970s, the need for physiotherapy increased.

In October 1996, the Children's Rehabilitation Centre moved to the Janeway, where newly renovated space was created to accommodate it while the new Janeway was being built. The rehabilitation and child development services were merged and designated space was provided for each team. Eight physiotherapy positions were designated to the rehabilitation/child development division and 5.5 to the acute-care division. The move to the new Janeway brought the two groups together in a shared physical space.

Since 2001, the rehabilitation team has provided a continuum of patient management from initial assessment through discharge planning for children/adolescents with physical disabilities. Children are often followed for many years, sometimes until they reach age 18. This team participates in travelling clinics to various parts of the province, as well as multidisciplinary clinics which are held regularly with other professionals including nurses, dieticians, occupational therapists, social workers, and physicians. Acute-care physiotherapist teams serve both in-patients and outpatients with a particularly busy outpatient orthopedic service.

The move to the new Janeway has allowed further innovation. The Motion Analysis Centre provides gait analysis for pediatric and adult clients and is used for clinical decision-making and research. A new physiotherapy position was developed and added to the Lifestyles Team—that team promotes physical activity and a healthy lifestyle for children.

The Janeway continues to provide clinical placements to physiotherapy students from across Canada. Staff physiotherapists are an integral part of the hospital and contribute to clinical rounds, in-services, and staff education.

The Children's Rehabilitation Centre 1994–1995
By Terry O'Brien

The Children's Rehabilitation Centre traces its history to the polio epidemics of the 1950s. Sunshine Camp on Thorburn Road near St. John's became the physical location for the provision of rehabilitation services.

Sunshine Camp, with the assistance of the Rotary Club, initially provided services for underprivileged children in 1937. Rotary's board of directors operated the Children's Rehabilitation Centre, and members of Rotary Club were also instrumental in starting the Newfoundland Society for the Care of Crippled Children and Adults in the 1950s (later renamed Newfoundland Society for the Physically Disabled and, in the 1990s, Easter Seals Newfoundland and Labrador). That organization still exists today but has not been involved in the operation of the Children's Rehabilitation Centre since the merger of hospitals in St. John's under Health Care Corporation of St. John's in 1994/1995.

During the 1950s and early 1960s rehabilitation services at the Sunshine Camp included nursing, occupational therapy, physiotherapy, social work, and medical services. These services were provided on both an in-patient and outpatient basis. Prosthetic and orthotic services were provided by the General Hospital at that time. In the early 1960s it was determined that a larger physical space was required to continue to provide appropriate rehabilitation services for children with physical disabilities.

Albert (Ted) Shapter, an orthopedic surgeon heavily involved in programs at the Sunshine Camp, lobbied the provincial government for use of the hospital in Pleasantville that was being vacated by the American military. Although that hospital became the Janeway, the government did agree to give the former American high school building, also in Pleasantville, to the Newfoundland Society for the Care of Crippled Children and Adults. Renovations to the building started in the early 1960s and its official opening came on April 1, 1968, although services were provided in the building prior to that date. In-patient services were increased to a 52-bed unit, and outpatient therapy services and interdisciplinary outpatient clinics offered. Cerebral palsy and spina bifida were the conditions most frequently seen, as well as polio patients from the 1950s.

The interdisciplinary team consisted of a clinical director (physical medicine specialist), medical specialists (orthopedic surgery, neurology, pediatrics, developmental pediatrics, psychiatry, urology, and rheumatology), nurses, occupational therapists, physiotherapists, and social workers. Prosthetic-orthotic services were provided by the General Hospital and a school established on site was staffed by teachers from the Department of Education. Psychologists, recreation therapists, and speech-language pathologists were later added to the team.

During the initial years in Pleasantville, Shapter and neurologist Norman Lush were key members of the medical team. A specialist in physical medicine became the clinical director for the rehabilitation programs. Dr. Gourdas Pal, recruited in 1972, was the longest-serving clinical director and remained with the program for 35 years. Also in 1972 it was determined that on-site prosthetic and orthotic services were needed. The Newfoundland Society for the Care of Crippled Children and Adults agreed to provide funding for this program, which continued until funding from the provincial government finally came through in the early 1980s.

Travelling assessment clinics, during which the rehabilitation team would spend two to five days at regional centres (Gander, Grand Falls-Windsor, Corner Brook, Stephenville, Goose Bay, and Labrador City) and provide assessment services, were developed in the late 1960s and early 1970s. On occasion, clinics were provided in St. Anthony and Burin.

The need for in-patient services diminished through the 1970s and the number of beds was reduced to 42 and eventually to 10. The Rotary-Janeway Hostel was built during this time and the Children's Rehabilitation Centre was able to access some beds at the hostel for patients and parents. Occupational therapy and physiotherapy treatment services were expanded in the late 1970s with the placement of a physiotherapist in Corner Brook and an occupational therapist in Grand Falls-Windsor.

An adaptive seating service was added to the prosthetic-orthotic program in the 1980s. This interdisciplinary service provided special seating to correct issues in children with disabilities. It also assisted in the integration of children with disabilities into the mainstream school system. During this decade, the need for in-patient services continued to decline and the in-patient unit was closed. An increased use of hostel services allowed parents to attend therapy sessions with their children and, if parents were unable to attend, arrangements were made to purchase in-patient services from the Janeway. Renovations were made to develop a day-patient area and to increase space in some therapy areas. The day-patient area addressed the needs of patients during periods between scheduled therapy sessions. Nurses who had been providing in-patient services were reassigned to the school system in St. John's so children with disabilities could better integrate into the regular school setting. This service was transferred to the Department of Health's community health nursing program in the late 1980s.

During the 1980s and early 1990s, the Children's Rehabilitation Centre took part in planning activities through the St. John's Hospital Council for the redevelopment of hospital services in the St. John's area. The provincial government decided in the early 1990s to redevelop services at the Health Sciences Centre site. This redevelopment would merge the Janeway and the Children's Rehabilitation Centre as the Janeway Children's Health and Rehabilitation Centre. All hospital-based services in St. John's would be incorporated under one board operating as Health Care Corporation of St. John's. All children's health and women's health services would be combined as the Child and Women's Health Program in new facilities at the Health Sciences Centre.

It was government's decision to immediately close the Children's Rehabilitation Centre Building in Pleasantville and move the services to the nearby Janeway, which happened in 1994/1995. The services moved with the new Janeway in 2001 and are currently part of Eastern Health.

Occupational Therapy

Occupational Therapy (OT) treatment focuses on helping people with a physical, sensory or cognitive disability be as independent as possible in all areas of their lives.

Kidshealth.org

Pediatric occupational therapists evaluate development skills through play and simple tasks such as colouring, printing, or cutting paper with scissors.

Although the Children's Rehabilitation Centre had occupational therapy services, it was not until 1994 that the Janeway appointed full-time occupational therapists, Sandy Delaney and Diane Bowman. The Centre was merged with the Janeway in 1996 and continued to have occupational therapy services.

In 2017 12.8 full-time equivalent occupational therapists work at the Janeway: 6.8 in child development, one in acute care, one in mental health, and five in rehabilitation.

Psychology

Kay Beatty and Elizabeth Daley were the first psychologists hired for the Janeway's child and adolescent psychiatry unit in 1966. Generally, child psychologists strive to help children cope with illness, disability, palliative care, conflicts with parents, and stressful events like divorce or the death of a loved one. They assist children who are suffering from anxiety, depression, hyperactivity, and school-related issues; they assess learning disabilities, attention deficit hyperactivity disorder, traumatic brain injuries, and the impact of neurodevelopmental conditions; and they help manage pain and eating disorders.

In the late 1980s and early 1990s psychologists were brought into the disciplines of child development and rehabilitation medicine. In 2017 three psychologists work within the Child Mental Health Program and eight within the Child Health Program. Within the latter program, two psychologists are dedicated to children's rehabilitation and neurology, two to child development, two to the lifestyles program, one to in-patient medicine, one to adolescent medicine, and one to women's health.

Six psychologists work at the Janeway Family Centre, an outpatient service in the Child Mental Health Program. Psychologists hired by Eastern Health in 2016 must have a PhD in psychology, one-year provisional registration working under supervision with staff psychologists at Eastern Health, and be licensed by the Newfoundland and Labrador Psychology Board.

Psychologists play an important role in many aspects of child health and are considered indispensable by physicians, nurses, and other allied health professions. As their services are in constant demand, patients wishing to see a psychologist may face a long wait list.

Social Work

Social work, an integral part of child health care, has been included in the professional services provided at the Janeway since 1966. Social workers, who usually have a master's degree in social work, help with the non-medical problems caused by illness and its effects on the whole family. They are involved in crisis intervention, providing help to families requiring financial and practical assistance, community liaisons, advocacy, child protection, and counselling on multiple issues. They teach parenting classes for parents and students in different programs and mentor social work students.

The Janeway's department of social work opened in 1966 and by 1986 it had a staff of 11 social workers. Before program management was organized in 1992, social work was a distinct department and social workers were assigned to different clinical services: child psychiatry, medicine and surgery, and outpatients. Their role expanded into child protection, child development, and individual clinics, such as cystic fibrosis and oncology. With the merging of the Children's Rehabilitation Centre and the Janeway in 1989, social workers were also involved with rehabilitation service.

The advent of program management eliminated a distinct department of social work; social workers were assigned to psychiatry, child protection, and children's rehabilitation. At the time, the Child Health Program oversaw all children at the Janeway, but in 1996 the Mental Health and Addiction Program took over child psychiatry. In 2017, both the Child Health and the Mental Health and Addiction programs employ social workers.

Dietary

Dietary services were contracted to private companies in the old Janeway. In 1966, Versa Foods was the first company to be hired, Arthur Sweet the food manager, and Mercedes Hennessey the chief dietician, with nutritional consultations by dietician Mary Pick.

In 1978, Albert J. Davis arranged with the province's Department of Health to create a provincial food bank for patients with inborn errors of metabolism, the most common of which was phenylketonuria, which would be associated with the National Food Distribution Centre for Inborn Errors of Metabolism in Montreal. It supplied special formulas and low-protein foods that were otherwise unavailable.

The principles and practice of dietetics has not changed much; however, the type of patient has. In the 1960s and 1970s, dieticians would have been consulted on infant formulas, children with diabetes, infants and children who failed to thrive, tube feedings for surgical patients with tracheoesophageal fistulas, and other conditions such as cerebral palsy. In the 21st century, dieticians increasingly deal with the obesity epidemic and anorexia nervosa. They work with children with inborn errors and decide what they *can* eat and work with autistic or anorexic children to determine what they *will* eat.

In 2017 six dieticians work at the Janeway; one is assigned to adolescent medicine, one to the lifestyles clinic. With program management, there is no "department" of dietetics; dieticians work with other health care professionals in the various departments.

SUPPORT SERVICES

Support services, including the communication centre, plant operations, material management, the Janeway Apartment complex, housekeeping and maintenance, and financial departments were amalgamated with the Health Sciences Centre and the Health Care Corporation of St. John's (later, Eastern Health) when the Janeway and the Child Health Program moved to the new site in 2001.

Clinical Support Staff

Clerical workers are an integral part of any health care facility and are often overlooked and underappreciated. Donald Kelland in his book *The Dr. Charles A. Janeway Child Health Centre* does not mention this group.

The duties and responsibilities of clerical workers have changed dramatically over the years due to the Information Technology revolution, paperless charts, private MCP billings, and automated telephone systems.

Three main groups of clerical workers are stenographers, who type dictated clinical notes (who are being replaced by voice recognition devices); clerks, who admit patients to various services, for example, day surgery, outpatient clinics, and in-patient services and perform various other duties such as filing, and data entry; and secretaries assigned to various physicians and professional groups. Often the first point of contact, clerical workers must have special skills in communicating with the public. They are often responsible for arranging schedules and prioritizing patient calls. Physicians, in particular, often have a close professional bond with their secretaries and depend on them to organize their day and keep track of patient files.

Despite their changing roles, clerical support staff offer a valuable service without which the hospital could not function.

Personnel Department

This department was organized several months prior to the opening of the Janeway. Robert H. Pike, appointed on May 3, 1966, served for many years as its director. His department came under the Health Care Corporation of St. John's with the Janeway's move in 2001.

Communication Centre

The switchboard, often referred to as the "heart of the hospital," plays an important role in routine and emergency situations. When the Janeway opened, a single, manually operated switchboard with pull-cord plugs operated 24 hours a day, seven days a week. In 1972 two internal emergency lines and a public emergency line (911) were added. A hospital pocket pager system was added in 1973.

Although a switchboard is often taken for granted, a hospital could not function without it. In 2017 a central switchboard service serves Eastern Health in St. John's, including the Health Sciences Centre (including the Janeway), St. Clare's, the Waterford Hospital, and the Miller Centre.

Housekeeping and Maintenance

Housekeeping services were contracted out to commercial organizations when the Janeway opened in 1966, but the hospital took them over in 1975. Linen services, originally a separate department, was amalgamated with housekeeping in 1984.

The maintenance department is responsible for maintaining hospital equipment and buildings and enhancing their physical appearance, which is essential to the care and well-being of patients, visitors, and staff. Fire and safety is also a major responsibility of the maintenance department.

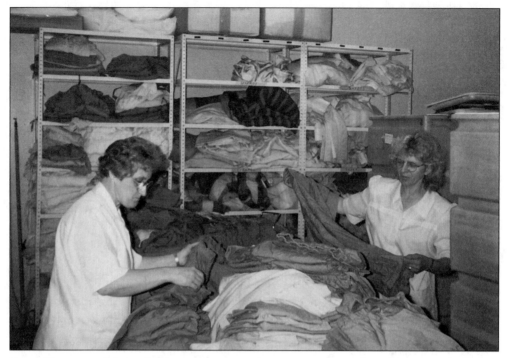

Vivian Thorne and Anita Dyer, support services.

Plant Operations

This department is responsible for the operation and maintenance of all pressure vessels, as well as for steam heating, ventilation, refrigeration, medical gases, sterilizer systems, air conditioning in the total hospital plant and ancillary buildings, and hospital security and traffic control. From 1973 until 2001, plant operations co-operated with Cabot Institute by providing on-the-job training for students in its Power Engineers Certification Program.

The Janeway Apartment Complex

The Janeway Apartments, a complex of three buildings built across the street from the Janeway Hospital, opened in 1967. The complex, with 82 units, was operated by the Children's Hospital Corporation to provide housing for hospital employees. Its role changed over time, and by 1977 10 bedsitting rooms were allocated as a hostel for parents and children admitted to hospital or scheduled for outpatient appointments.

In 1983 the Northwest Rotary Janeway Hostel opened; these rooms were used for hospital divisions requiring additional space, and several services—child development, genetics, finance, and social work—were relocated there. By the time the new Janeway opened, most of the apartments were occupied by various divisions of the hospital and the buildings were seldom used as actual apartments.

Material Management

At first, the Janeway purchased supplies from the provincial departments of Health and Supply. The role of the hospital's material management department expanded dramatically over the years as ICUs, operating rooms, emergency departments, laboratories, and radiology units expanded. In 1971 material management participated in the group purchasing program organized by the Newfoundland Hospital Association.

Financial Services

The Janeway's financial services department was developed according to the requirements of the hospital insurance regulations of the Department of Health.

The 1967 budget included a total revenue of $2,197,701. Of that, $1,291,367 was allocated to salaries, $416,167 for drugs and supplies, and $474,117 for service departments. In 1978 a new IBM computer was installed to provide services.

By 1976 operating revenues had risen to over $12.5 million to cover salaries of $8,632,000. Medical and surgical supplies and drugs cost $724,000.

By 1986 the revenue was $25,652,000.

Pastoral Care

Pastoral care has been an essential component of the Janeway's services since 1966. Chaplains provide emotional and spiritual support to patients and families coping with the illness or injury of a child, the stress of terminal illness, and unexpected bereavement. Pastoral care has always been open to all faiths and cultures. In 2017, all faiths, including non-Christian religions, are represented, and officials from these faiths regularly visit the hospital and have made tremendous contributions over the years.

In November 1974, Gordon White became the full-time director of the Janeway's Pastoral Care and Counselling Service. White worked with the chaplains to coordinate counselling and spiritual care to children and their families in their own faiths. This was recognized as an essential service, available 24 hours a day.

Since 1977, the Canadian Council on Hospital Accreditation has formally required pastoral services in every hospital. In 1983, a quality assurance program and a pastoral care advisory committee were established to evaluate and ensure quality of care. The old Janeway did not have a chapel, but a quiet room was established in 1984.

The Janeway's pastoral care team merged with that of the Health Sciences Centre in 1995 and in 2017 one department of pastoral care services both hospitals. There is a central chapel in the Health Sciences Centre.

The Miracle of Life
By Sister Mary Molloy

Some time ago I was called to the Janeway's NICU. The nurse informed me that a new baby required surgery and that the parents had requested that the baby be baptized. The mother and grandmother were from St. Pierre and were unable to speak English.

I usually ask the medical condition of the patient when I receive an urgent call, but for some reason I neglected to ask on this occasion. I immediately rushed to the hospital—I wonder sometimes how I escaped getting a speeding ticket.

At the NICU I was greeted by several of the medical staff, including a pediatrician and nurses, as well as an interpreter. All were anxious for me to get on with the baptism.

I began to administer the Sacrament in the presence of all, including the mother and grandmother. In all my 15 years of service as a chaplain at the Janeway, dealing with families and extremely sick children, this was the most touching. The interpreter added so much; he was gracious and compassionate. As I administered the Sacrament, the interpreter very serenely translated for me.

After the baptism was completed, I stepped aside to allow the medical team to care for the baby. It was at this point that I saw the serious condition of the baby. I could feel my body cringing at what I saw before me.

The baby had gastroschisis, which occurs while he or she is growing in the uterus. The abdominal wall fails to close completely (usually to the right of the umbilical cord) and the abdominal contents (mostly bowel) come out through the hole. There is no protective sac around the contents. Usually the condition is diagnosed before the birth of the baby, as was the case with this little treasure from St. Pierre.

The defect must be closed surgically. This is often not possible in one step, as the abdomen is small and the bowel that is outside is often quite swollen. A pouch is placed over the exposed bowel and is sutured to the skin. The bowel gradually goes back in by gravity (which is why it is kept upright); every other day the pouch is rolled down, like squeezing a tube of toothpaste to get everything to the top. When all the bowel is inside the abdomen, the abdomen is surgically closed. The baby is kept on a ventilator during this process because the pressure on the abdomen as the bowel is being replaced exerts pressure on the diaphragm, making it difficult for the baby to breathe.

This particular baby went home and did very well.

I have always used the rose as my symbol of pastoral care. A rose is sometimes very delicate and fragile—and isn't all of life like that, especially human life? From the time the rose begins its life, it opens a little more each day. The warmth of the sun, the soft summer rain, and the gentle breeze are all life-givers to the rose. Aren't we, in our care and gentleness, our prayers and presence, the same kind of life-givers to our patients and their families? Their emotional, spiritual, and even physical life is fed by the care of those who minister to them.

The patients we contact each day (especially the darling fragile infants) call us to love and serve without rush and haste. I think of those red stickers on packages which say "Fragile: handle with care." All of life is like that. Adults, adolescents, and children are all fragile, especially the sick infants and the elderly in our hospitals. We must handle them with care and prayer.

As a result of my experience with this seriously ill child, I feel I am marked in some way, just like the little marks on the petals of the rose. The presence, dignity, and professionalism of the medical team was an inspiration. It was truly a sacred moment.

Child Life Services

A program of therapeutic play and recreation was launched at the Janeway on September 1, 1966, under the direction of play therapist Eve Weiser, and the help of nursing assistants, student nurses, and volunteers. The program, which evolved into Child Life Services, filled an important role in restoring hospitalized children to complete health.

Child Life Services emerged in Canada in the early 1960s through the pioneering work of Emma Plank, who used the principles of child development to promote psychosocial development and effective coping strategies for children admitted to hospital and their families. But until the Janeway opened, few such services were available for Newfoundland children, and parents' visiting hours were limited.

In 2017, the Janeway's Child Life Services team provide recreation for children and their families. It acknowledges the specific emotional issues related to hospitalization faced by patients, as well as their families. Children often harbour fears of coming to a strange place, of being separated from their family, and of the medical procedures they may have to undergo. This stress can interfere with a child's recovery and well-being. Child Life Services attempts to reduce stress and promote normal growth and development through play. Children also learn to master new skills, express themselves, and create. Having a "safe zone" away from treatments, therapies, and needles is important for children during their hospital stay; it provides security in a sometimes-frightening environment.

The in-patient playroom is a brightly lit room resembling a small toy store; cabinets and shelves are filled with craft supplies, games, and books to entertain and occupy children during their stay. The staff focus on each child's needs and interests during their playroom visit and if a child requires a help or encouragement, the staff is quick to provide it. If a child is not well enough to go to the playroom, staff provide in-room activities. The Child Life Services team also plan group activities and special events; they may also have some involvement with outpatients.

Two types of play are organized: recreational, which is spontaneous and unstructured; and therapeutic, which involves activities with a specific goal or skill development in mind.

Playroom and bedside activities include crafts, video and computer games, movies, board games, puzzles, books, colouring sheets, toys, Internet use, card games, and painting. Group activities include movie day, concerts, guest visitors, and special or holiday events. Outpatient activities include toys, books, colouring sheets, and video games. A popular pet therapy program sponsored by St. John Ambulance was introduced in 2009.

In 2015, UPOPOLIS—an online network for children and teens in hospitals—was introduced. An exciting innovation embraced by Child Life Services, UPOPOLIS is a safe online community that allows patients to stay connected to family and friends, share experiences, and create their own unique content. Sponsored by Kids' Health Links Foundation and architected by Telus, UPOPOLIS is for children and youth between the ages of 10 and 19 who are receiving medical care. It is currently offered in 10 hospitals and health care centres across Canada.

Child Life Services is fulfilling its primary objectives of helping children cope with the stress and anxiety of the hospital experience and promoting the child's normal growth and development.

Administration

Prior to the creation of the Children's Hospital Corporation in 1966, Lord Brain's Royal Commission on Health recommended A. Victor Neale, professor of child health and dean of the medical faculty of Bristol University, for the position of chief of staff of the new children's hospital. Neale started in the fall of 1965. He appointed a scheduling committee to organize its development. The committee successfully worked out many of the details involved in forming a children's hospital and met numerous times until it opened in 1966.

On March 25, 1966, the Children's Hospital (Management) Act was passed in the House of Assembly and created the Children's Hospital Corporation. Health minister James McGrath appointed members of the corporation, including its chair, Campbell MacPherson. This was the first time in the province that a public hospital had become a corporation run by a board of directors.

The first executive director of the Children's Hospital Corporation, Donald Kelland, appointed on March 7, 1966, had the difficult task of administrating the hospital when it opened; he remained in that position for 20 years. Kelland was succeeded by Richard Nurse in 1986 and George Tilley in 1992. Tilley stayed in the position until the hospitals in St. John's were amalgamated under the Health Care Corporation of St. John's (HCCSJ) in 1994 and Eastern Health in 2006.

The hospital did not have a medical director or medical chief of staff until 1991; prior to this the chair of the medical advisory committee assumed those responsibilities. On February 25, 1975, Dr. John Darte, outgoing committee chair, wrote a report to the Joint Conference Committee (a hospital organization composed of the board of governors, administration, and medical staff representatives). He stated that the chair of the medical advisory committee could not make the same decisions as a chief of staff. He felt that the hospital

Executive Directors
Donald E.J. Kelland: 1966–1986
Richard C. Nurse: 1986–1992
George Tilley: 1992–1995

Directors of Nursing and Patient Care
Margaret G. Chesterfield: 1966–1967
Christine Callanan (acting): 1967
Elsie Hill: 1967–1978
Eleanor Ellis: 1978–1984
Bertha Paulse: 1984–1985
Velma King (acting): 1985–1989
Marilyn Pardy: 1989–1994

Directors of Child Health Program
Marilyn Pardy: 1996–2003
Lynn Crosbie: 2003–2006
Patricia Pilgrim: 2003
Carol Chafe: 2006–2011
Joy Stuckless: 2011
Jeanne Robertson: 2011–2015
Arlene Scott: 2015–present

Medical Directors
Kevin Hogan: 1991–1995

Chairs of the Board of Directors
Campbell MacPherson: 1966–1972
James Greene, QC: 1972–1974
E. John Short: 1974–1978
Robert Wells, QC: 1978–1987
John Baker: 1987–1994

Clinical Chiefs
Albert J. Davis: 1995
Wayne Andrews: 2000–2004
Austin Rick Cooper: 2004–2006
Victoria Crosbie: 2006
David Price and Austin Rick Cooper: 2007–April 2008
Ken Henderson: April 2008–2013
Kevin Chan: January 2013–present
Victoria Crosbie (acting): 2016 (January–May)

George Tilley, executive director, 1992–1995.

Richard Nurse, executive director, 1986–1992.

was poorly represented in certain areas, especially those that were multidisciplinary. The medical advisory committee was overextending itself in making minor decisions, he added, and pressured the executive director to make decisions that may not have been his prerogative, resulting in disagreements among the medical staff. Darte strongly recommended establishing the position of medical director or chief of staff immediately. This did not happen, and the administration, medical advisory committee, and department heads continued to sort out problems as best they could. The lack of a medical director before 1991 was a significant problem for the hospital. However, that year, Dr. Kevin Hogan was appointed its first medical director.

The long delay in establishing this position was due to a poor provincial economy, difficulty in finding a suitable candidate, and acceptance of the status quo by the medical staff. During the 1970s and 1980s, the other four major hospitals in St. John's had medical directors.

The duties of the medical director, appointed by the board of directors and responsible to the executive director, were outlined in the Janeway's bylaw rules and regulations, July 1991 (see sidebar).

In the beginning the hospital was organized into "departments," including clinical, administrative, and allied health services. In 1994, the administration of the Janeway changed with the formation of the HCCSJ, whose Child and Women's Health Program was created in 1996. Although officially amalgamated, these two programs continued to operate as separate entities.

In 2017 the Child and Women's Health Program has a director, who works with the vice-president of clinical services, and two clinical chiefs, one for child health and one for women's health. Six divisional managers and a program consultant work under child health. The clinical chiefs, who are physicians, report to the vice-president of medical services.

Janeway Auxiliary Presidents

Name	Date	Name	Date
Evelyn Crosbie	1968	Barbara Kelland	1993
Evelyn Crosbie	1969	Barbara Kelland	1994
Margaret Darte	1970	Jean Lewis	1995
Margaret Darte	1971	Jean Lewis	1996
Elizabeth Munn	1972	Jean Lewis	1997
Elizabeth Munn	1973	Jean Lewis	1998
Irene Duffett	1974	Judy Curtis	1999
Irene Duffett	1975	Jean Lewis	2000
Jean Davis	1976	Jean Lewis	2001
Jean Davis	1977	Jean Lewis	2002
Rosemary Carter	1978	Mabel Best	2003
Rosemary Carter	1979	Mabel Best	2004
Jean Bruneau	1980	Mabel Best	2005
Jean Davis	1981	Marilyn Pardy	2006
Jean Davis	1982	Marilyn Pardy	2007
Mary Green	1983	Marilyn Pardy	2008
Mary Green	1984	Judy Murphy	2009
Mary Green	1985	Judy Murphy	2010
Mary Green	1986	Judy Murphy	2011
Marina Beanlands	1987	Judy Murphy	2012
Marina Beanlands	1988	Pat Corrigan	2013
Jean Lewis	1989	Pat Corrigan	2014
Jean Lewis	1990	Mary Baker	2015
Doreen Dinn	1991		
Jean Lewis	1992		

Donald E.J. Kelland

Donald Kelland was appointed administrator of the Janeway on March 7, 1966. As a young man, he joined the civil service and worked his way up through the ranks.

As administrator and executive director he had many challenges and difficulties to overcome, but he oversaw the transformation of an empty building into a first-class, fully accredited pediatric health care centre. He retired in 1986.

During his tenure, Kelland was noted for his superb management skills, a calm and non-biased approach to physician and staff complaints, and his continual support and empathy for the children and their families.

Donald Kelland.

In his retirement he undertook two herculean tasks: publishing a comprehensive book on the Janeway and establishing the Janeway archives.

Kelland, born in Heart's Content, moved to St. John's at the age of eight and lived on Leslie Street and attended Bishop Feild College. He was totally dedicated to his wife, Barbara, and their three children, David, Donna, and Andrea.

I owe a great deal of gratitude to him because without the archives he created and his book it would have been difficult for me to publish a book in 2017 about the Janeway.

The Janeway Auxiliary
By Marilyn Pardy

Two years after the Janeway opened, Margot Reid led an organizing committee to form the Janeway Auxiliary. Evelyn Crosbie accepted the office of founding president, and the auxiliary's first meeting was held in January 1968. Between 1991 and 1998 there were 83 active and eight associate members.

Initially the auxiliary provided services on two wards from 10 a.m. to 11:30 a.m. and 2 p.m. to 3:30 p.m. daily. Several members came in for the lunch and dinner periods and assisted staff in admitting and discharging patients, helped to relieve patient anxiety, escorted children to the wards, assisted with diagnostic services, and supplied reading materials, toys, and games. In March 1968, services were started in the admitting and outpatient departments.

Additional services were added for play therapy in the psychiatric unit, wards, and patient areas. Members helped children compose letters to parents, assisted at the children's library and medical library, organized handicrafts, purchased supplies, assisted with child feeding, and lent a hand in radiology, volunteer services, ICU, recovery, and public relations. The goal of volunteers was not to replace hospital staff or parents but to supplement and provide the many extras children need during hospitalization.

The auxiliary raised money to provide essential equipment to diagnose and treat children. In 1970, it organized the first Janeway Day at the Races, which became a major fundraiser until the Goulds racetrack closed. When the track re-opened in 1991, the Janeway Foundation revived the event and organized it annually, until it again closed in 1999.

Daphne Maunder, an auxiliary member since 1968, was appointed full-time director of volunteer resources and public relations in September 1975. Of great assistance to the auxiliary, she was responsible for recruiting and orientating volunteers and volunteens (junior volunteers).

Another major fundraiser for the auxiliary, the Janeway Gift Shop, originally opened as a small shop in the outpatient area of the old hospital; it continues in the new Janeway in a larger walk-in gift shop. The busy shop, which provides services to children, parents, and staff, is run by auxiliary and student volunteers.

As health care has evolved, the role of the auxiliary has changed. In-patient beds have decreased dramatically and many of the health care needs of children are now being met on an ambulatory basis. Day surgery allows children to have procedures done in the operating room and return home the same day. Technology has

Evelyn Crosbie, Auxilary president, 1968–1969.

advanced rapidly and made tremendous improvements to children's health. The need for auxiliary members on in-patient units decreased as fewer children were hospitalized and the acuity level of those who were admitted increased.

The Evelyn Crosbie Scholarship was started in 1988 in memory of the auxiliary's first president. This $500 scholarship was awarded annually to a registered nurse on staff at the Janeway pursuing professional development in a post-secondary institution. In 2006 the amount was increased to $750 and the criteria changed to make it available to all pediatric staff.

Since 2002 the auxiliary also has also awarded two $500 scholarships to student volunteers working in the Janeway. In 2011 it was renamed the Jean Lewis Scholarship in memory of a dedicated auxiliary member.

When the Children's Rehabilitation Centre merged with the Janeway in 2002, the name of the auxiliary changed to the Janeway Children's Health and Rehabilitation Auxiliary.

The Pillar Project was a special project of the auxiliary to celebrate its 35th anniversary in 2003. The grey support structures (pillars) in the new hospital did not blend in with the beautiful colour schemes elsewhere. Local artists were commissioned to paint 36 concrete pillars, transforming them into tropical forests, puffins flying past a lighthouse, sea life, butterflies, and more. In addition, 100 mini quilts were received from three local quilting guilds with the theme "playtime" and displayed throughout the hospital. The auxiliary was honoured to receive the 2006 Canadian Auxiliaries Recognition of Excellence (CARE) Award from the Canadian Association of Healthcare Auxiliaries.

In 2012 the auxiliary was again honoured to receive the CARE Award from the Canadian Association of Healthcare Auxiliaries for Music Therapy. A six-month pilot music therapy program, funded by an outside agency in 2008, received positive feedback from staff and families. The auxiliary ensured that this beneficial program could continue and, beginning in October 2009, it funded one day per week of music therapy at a cost of $12,000 per year. The second year, funding increased to $24,000 and, since 2013, it been increased to $30,000. Other funding sources have become available, including through the Janeway Foundation. The auxiliary is very proud to have been responsible for initiating this invaluable service.

In 2008, to celebrate the auxiliary's 40th anniversary, $40,000 was allocated for "comfort and care" items: commercial-grade wooden glider rocking chairs, desks and chairs, a digital camera, portable DVD players, MP3 players, televisions, and other furniture. A family room in the Child Development and Learning Division was refurbished, including a new sofa and loveseat, and dedicated to the memory of auxiliary member Jean Lewis. To close the 40th anniversary celebrations, an afternoon tea was held in October and staff and past presidents were invited. An exhibit depicting the history of the auxiliary was created and displayed.

The auxiliary continues to be an active group in 2017. Fundraising is a major activity and, as of 2015, $1.9 million has been raised. The gift shop continues to be a major fundraiser supplemented by bake sales, a used-book sale, and other activities. Evening coffee and tea service is provided to parents. The auxiliary provides a morning coffee with homemade goodies each year at the Christmas sale with proceeds going back to the hospital. Knitted goods are received from around the province and include baby bonnets, finger puppets, baby sweater sets, and Linus blankets. This knitting is distributed throughout the hospital and at times items are sold in the gift shop.

Audiovisual Services

In the years before 1980, Jim Thistle, who worked at Memorial University, came to the Janeway when a photographer was needed. In 1980, Janeway Audiovisual Services was created and Philip Escott appointed the visual technician. He was succeeded by Barry Bradbury, who is still active in the role in 2017. Bradbury provided an excellent service over the years and many of his photographs are still available in archived material.

Medical Library

A medical library opened at the Janeway in 1966 and served the staff and students well. In the years before the Internet, it was a valuable and important component of the hospital, servicing research education and clinical care. Librarian Joan Wheeler started in 1967 and was there for many years. In 2017, the Health Sciences Library serves the medical school, pharmacy, nursing schools, and Eastern Health, including the Janeway.

Janeway School

Before the Janeway opened, teachers visited the sanatoriums in St. John's and Corner Brook to teach adult and child patients. School lessons were also provided to the children at the orthopedic division and pediatric wards of the General Hospital in St. John's.

The Janeway school was initially part of the regular school system under the Special Services Division of the Department of Education; later it fell under the Avalon East School Board and, in 2017, comes under the English School District.

The Janeway school was started in November 1966 under the guidance of Mercedes Marshall, who had been the principal of the Children's Teaching Program of the General Hospital. Several other teachers worked with Marshall. Running a hospital school has always come with logistical challenges in that the children often require frequent medical procedures.

The Children's Rehabilitation Hospital had teachers on staff until it closed its children's ward in 1970, and the sanatorium on Topsail Road had a teaching program until it closed in 1975 and one of the teachers, Mary Keough Callanan, joined the Janeway.

In the 1960s and 1970s the number of children admitted to hospital was larger, and their stays much longer than they are in 2017. Teaching was crucial to allow children to keep up with the school curriculum and, in many cases, they were offered individualized tutoring in areas in which they had weaknesses.

The Janeway school originally had two classrooms: one for medical patients, one for psychiatry patients. In 1969 the psychiatric classroom was deemed too small, and two additional classrooms were provided in Building 615 across the street. In 1973, the hospital employed seven teachers and by 1990 that had increased to 13. About 180 pupils participated in the year 1982/1983. In 2017, five teachers are on staff, but the in-patient census has decreased.

The school follows the set curriculum of the Department of Education and liaises with the patient's home school to ensure that each patient has the appropriate lessons. Bedside teaching is offered in addition to classroom teaching. Many children are fully caught up with their curriculum by the time they are discharged.

Bonnie Pennell, a teacher from 1975 to 2013, says: "All teachers would agree it was a privilege to work with the children of the Janeway. We did not only engage with the child but with the whole family during what was usually a difficult time."

Pinkie Duff outlined her career as a teacher at the Janeway:

> I began my career at the Janeway in 1974 on the Psychiatric Unit. I taught there seven years and then moved to the medical/surgical units for the primary grades—half-time bedside and half-time classroom. During that time I became vice-principal. I moved back to Psychiatry in the 1990s, still carrying the vice-principal's duties, and teaching elementary grades. I retired in 1998.
>
> The best feature for me was the levity and lack of formality that children brought to teaching, despite their illness. We were teachers, mentors, and friends to both child and parent, often bridging between medical and academic fields.

PART III
RESEARCH AT THE JANEWAY

Research, 1966–2001

The main objective of those planning the Janeway in the 1960s was to create a first-class pediatric health centre to meet the needs of the province. Education, but not specifically research, was a mandate of the hospital. After the hospital opened, the emphasis remained on establishing good clinical services, and no active plans for a research program were in place.

A university-hospital affiliation agreement between Memorial University and the Janeway was signed on July 2, 1968; its goals included "the conduct of medical research with the aims of adding to human knowledge and improving methods for the prevention and treatment of disease." Its main emphasis, however, was the establishment of sound teaching programs and administrative structures. Subsequent correspondence among the medical school's pediatric faculty refer to educational and administrative issues. The education of medical students, interns, residents, and nursing and allied health students was a priority; actual research programs with designated space did not come until much later.

Madhavan Kutty, appointed director of biochemistry at the Janeway in 1968, conducted several research projects on lipid metabolism, specifically pseudocholinesterase. Penny Allderdice, who set up a medical genetics laboratory at the Janeway in 1973, conducted some of her research there. Ranjit K. Chandra, who in 1974 came to the Janeway, and the medical school as a visiting research chair of pediatrics, actively researched the relation of diet and nutrition to immunity and resistance to disease and the prevention of allergic diseases in young children. In 1977 he was made a research chair in pediatrics at Memorial's medical school. In 1989 Chandra helped establish the World Health Organization Collaborating Centre for Research and Training in Nutritional Immunology, based at the Janeway and operated jointly by Memorial and the Janeway; it closed after five years of operation without official notice.

The Janeway Children's Hospital Foundation, established in May 1985, designated some of its funding for pediatric research. Since 1985, it has supported 50 child health research projects, and, since 2001, a number of women's health projects.

In 1988, a director of pediatric research position was created by Memorial and the Janeway's Department of Pediatrics. Chandra's responsibilities, as its first director, included organizing the annual Janeway research forum, determining how research funds should be disbursed, and facilitating appropriate projects for research with department members and residents.

See Appendix A: Research by selected physicians and scientists at the Janeway.

The Janeway Pediatric Research Unit

By Roger Chafe

The move to the new Janeway in 2001 coincided with attempts to increase research capacity and to establish an active pediatric research hospital. In 2008, funding for a research unit was raised through donations from the Janeway Foundation and the Colonel Harland Sanders Foundation and support from Eastern Health. Located in the Janeway hostel, the research unit as of 2017 includes office space for pediatric clinical faculty, a research coordinator, research nurses, and other research staff. A clinic room to examine patients involved in research projects is available, as is a biomedical room to analyze and store patient samples. The unit officially opened on February 23, 2011.

The research capacity of the Janeway also expanded around this time with the appointment of the first full-time PhD faculty member in the division of pediatrics, responsible for training pediatric residents and supporting research across the Janeway. With the appointment of Roger Chafe, pediatrics residents increased the already active role that they played in research there. Since 2010, these residents have published articles on a broad range of topics: the rates of autism spectrum disorders (ASD) on the Avalon Peninsula, electrocardiogram interpretation, recommendations of early childhood nutrition, community-associated methicillin-resistant *Staphylococcus aureus*, resident performance evaluation, and a new screening tool for identifying possible eating disorders in type 1 diabetes patients.

After the establishment of the research unit, the clinical faculty interested in research moved to formally create the Janeway Pediatric Research Unit (JPRU) within Memorial University's Faculty of Medicine. Established in July 2014, it serves as a nexus for pediatric research conducted at the Janeway and the Faculty of Medicine. The unit started with 12 members; by 2015, it had 17.

Recognizing the importance of serving the youngest members of our society, JPRU's vision is to improve children's health in Newfoundland and Labrador and beyond through high-quality health research. Faculty and staff associated with the unit conduct clinical and applied health research. Over 50 research projects were either under way or completed in its first two years on a range of childhood-related topics: rheumatology, childhood obesity, oncology, emergency medicine, gastroenterology, neonatology, genetics, autism, neurology, breast feeding, arthritis, pediatric Crohn's disease, medical education, eating disorders, and vitamin D insufficiency. These projects include those focused on the local Newfoundland population and those which are part of national and international studies. Chafe became the first JPRU director and Dr. Leigh Ann Newhook associate chair of clinical pediatric research.

Janeway Pediatric Research Unit (JPRU): Janeway Hostel

Pediatric research in Newfoundland and Labrador continues to grow. In 2015, research manager Rana Aslanov was hired to supervise research staff and students and to support researchers and medical residents in implementing their projects. Pediatric residents undertake research projects during their residency training and present their work annually on Pediatric Resident Research Day. JPRU director and Memorial associate professor Roger Chafe is involved in the newly developed (2016) research project "Improving outcomes for youth with type I diabetes in transition to adult care through strengthening integration with primary care: An exploratory, cross-provincial study," in collaboration with Ontario program lead Astrid Guttmann. In both Newfoundland and Ontario, improving the transition from pediatric to adult care has been identified as a priority research topic.

Chafe, who has been involved in projects related to the transition to adult care since 2013, has worked with pediatric populations with cancer and chronic diseases and conditions. He serves as an academic supervisor for graduate students' and pediatric residents' research projects.

Research on pediatric type I diabetes remains active. Newhook is involved with TrialNet, a global network of researchers in 18 diabetes research centres, in the US, Canada, the UK, Finland, Italy, Germany, Australia, and New Zealand.

TrialNet has already initiated several studies and the Newfoundland team, led by Newhook, has participated in its "Natural history study of development of type I diabetes" since 2005 and its "Oral insulin for prevention of diabetes in relatives at risk for type I diabetes mellitus" since 2008. TrialNet's goal is to perform intervention studies to preserve insulin-producing cells in individuals at risk for the condition and those with new onset type I diabetes. Another of Newhook's projects is "Exploring the reasons why birth by C-section is a risk factor for type I diabetes mellitus in Newfoundland and Labrador," a provincial project with research centres in St. John's, St. Anthony, Stephenville, Corner Brook, Labrador City, and Grand Falls-Windsor; another examines the "Association of type I diabetes mellitus and drinking water contamination in Newfoundland and Labrador." Newhook is also one of the leading investigators of breast-feeding rates and challenges in the province. Breast-feeding rates in Newfoundland and Labrador are the lowest in Canada; increasing them is complex, as they are shaped by cultural context, social structures and support, and life circumstances.

Pediatric rheumatologist Paul Dancey is a member of the Canadian Alliance of Pediatric Rheumatology Investigators. Starting in 2016 all Canadian children with newly diagnosed chronic arthritis are enrolled in a long-term outcome study. A second study on childhood arthritis considers how interactions between a child's genes, environment, and lifestyle may help predict childhood arthritis outcomes. The Janeway is an active participant in the Canadian Pediatric Surveillance Program and Dancey a principal investigator in four simultaneously running studies of the program.

A Canadian Children Inflammatory Bowel Disease Network Biobank Registry was initiated in 2014 with its main office at SickKids in Toronto. The Janeway is a participant of this national registry. Pediatric gastroenterologist Jeff Critch is a principal investigator at the Newfoundland and Labrador site. Critch and Jerry McGrath also continue a GEM (genetics, environment, and microbial interactions in the cause of inflammatory bowel disease) research project which started in 2008.

Pediatric infectious diseases specialist Natalie Bridger is participating in two large national projects, "National program of hospital surveillances system for vaccine-related events—Canadian Immunization Monitoring Program Active (IMPACT)" and the "Canadian Perinatal HIV Surveillance Program," as a part of the Canadian Pediatric Surveillance Program.

Pediatric endocrinologist Tracey Bridger is part of three clinical trial projects, including "Determining the gut microbiome profile of NL children in the Janeway lifestyle program," funded through the Janeway Foundation in 2015, and "Trial to reduce insulin-dependent diabetes mellitus in the genetically at risk."

Pediatric gastroenterologist Pushpa Sathya's new research project "Milk protein intolerance in infants" received a full ethics approval in September 2015. Its goal is to evaluate the role of formula change or maternal dietary changes (in exclusively breast-fed infants) in the prognosis of children with cow's milk protein intolerance. This will be achieved by documenting, comparing, and contrasting different management styles of the individual practitioners participating in this study. Her second project, a pilot study "Role of omega-3 fatty acids (n-3PUFA) in controlling inflammation in pediatric NAFLD," is still in the process of developing appropriate documentation and is awaiting approval from Health Canada.

Emergency department physician Robert Porter is the principal investigator of two studies: "Translating emergency knowledge for kids" and "Adverse events in the emergency department." He also conducted a trial in 2016 on the use of intranasal fentanyl; in October 2015, he completed the qualitative study "Strengthening transitions in pediatric emergency care."

Dr. Anne Drover is working on two research studies in 2017: the observational study "Breast feeding initiative" and the qualitative study "Ten steps of the baby-friendly hospital initiative."

Other Research, 2001–2017

Endocrinology Group

Endocrinologist Joseph Curtis is involved in several studies that focus on the pediatric population. "Bone mineral density in Newfoundland children aged 8–18 years," a study of healthy Newfoundland children, which aims to average norms for bone density in healthy children before, during, and after puberty, will be completed in 2018. Little research has been done on the vitamin D status of Newfoundlanders. Lifestyle changes—sunscreen use, spending less time outdoors, and insufficient intake of vitamin D-rich foods, as well as living at a northern latitude—may affect the vitamin D status of Newfoundlanders.

With doctors S. Tsai, Ara Healey, and Bridget Fernandez, Curtis is also conducting a study of Addison's disease. This is a descriptive analysis on the presentation of children with this condition and their progress over years of treatment. The research team is also attempting to identify any genetic markers of this rare disorder.

In addition to being involved in a large study on the epidemiology of type 1 diabetes in Newfoundland, conducted by Newhook, Curtis is co-investigator with doctors Benvon Cramer and Suryakant Shah on a study of large vessel complications that can arise in children with diabetes. Its goal is to ascertain whether a significant lowering of blood glucose is associated with a reduction in the risk of early atherosclerosis.

Pediatricians in Endocrinology as of 2017: Joseph Curtis, Albert J. Davis, Donald Hillman, Leigh Ann Newhook, Ara Healey, and Heather Power.

Neonatal Research

Neonatology has had an active research program since the mid-1970s, involving active collaboration with scientists in other disciplines and national neonatal organizations.

Research topics and publications include the prevention of nosocomial infection, iron supplementation in breast- and bottle-fed infants, acute care of at-risk newborn (ACORN), blood glucose levels in newborns, peripherally inserted central catheters, neonatal resuscitation, Newfoundland's genetic burden, postnatal steroids for chronic lung disease in neonates, evidence-based use of surfactant in preterm infants, evaluation of neonatal resuscitation skills, visual acuity in term infants, determinants of breast-feeding success, morbidity and mortality of very low birth weight infants, hearing loss with use of high-frequency jet ventilation, early childhood neurologic disability, extracorporeal membrane oxygenation: a systematic review, molybdenum requirements in low-birth-weight infants, vitamin requirements in premature infants, and improved outcomes of premature infants delivered in tertiary-care centres.

Researchers in Neonatology as of 2017: Khalid Aziz, Wayne Andrews, Brian Simmons, James Friel, Geoffrey Downton, Poh Gin Kwa, Derek Matthew, Shoo Lee, David Long, and Donald Reid.

Acute Rheumatic Fever Study

A study of acute rheumatic fever in the pediatric population was published in March 2007. Pediatric cardiologist Christina Templeton undertook the study with co-investigators Austin Rick Cooper, Paul Dancey, and Proton Rahman as part the Canadian Pediatric Surveillance Program. Cooper was influential in bringing this study to the Janeway and in raising the funds needed for the project.

Although acute rheumatic fever is extremely rare in the Canadian pediatric population, medical treatment is required in all confirmed cases, often with multiple medications. Memorial University researchers found that the most common major manifestation was carditis, or inflammation of the heart, occurring in 59 per cent of cases. Of those, 35 had mitral valve disease, 23 had aortic disease, and 18 had both. Arthritis occurred in 54 per cent of patients.

Thirty-eight per cent of the 68 children studied experienced chorea, or jerky spasmodic movements of the limbs, trunk, and facial muscles.

Templeton's three-year surveillance study, the first published study of rheumatic fever in the Canadian pediatric population, showed that this is a rare disease, with only 2.9 cases per million population per year.

Autism Research

A multidisciplinary team of clinicians and molecular geneticists have been working since 2001 to understand the genetic aberrations that underlie ASD. The Autism Genome Project team is led by doctors Steven Scherer (SickKids) and Peter Szatmari (McMaster University). Geneticist Bridget Fernandez leads the Newfoundland and Labrador team, which consists of Janeway child development pediatricians Cathy Vardy, Sandra Luscombe, and Victoria Crosbie.

Cohorts of autistic patients have been assembled by investigators in Toronto, Hamilton, Edmonton, and Newfoundland and Labrador. In the latter, about 180 affected individuals are included, of interest because they come from the founder population of the province.

Fernandez is interested in the subset of autistic individuals who have facial dysmorphism and/or other birth defects, those with "complex ASD" and who do not have an identifiable genetic syndrome. The hypothesis is that these ASD patients are genetically distinct from those that lack these features. She has developed a dysmorphology protocol, which has been adopted by the broader research team. Fernandez has performed detailed dysmorphology assessments on all Newfoundland and Labrador participants and their parents; one-third of this cohort has been classified as having a complex form of ASD, and half of these do not fit into any known syndrome. This clinical information will be incorporated into Scherer's molecular strategies. The team has also identified and phenotyped several Newfoundland and Labrador families containing three to six autistic individuals.

Fetal Alcohol Syndrome
Theodore Rosales (1982–2014)

Pediatrician Theodore Rosales is an expert in fetal alcohol syndrome disorder (FASD), an umbrella term which describes a range of effects that can occur in an infant whose mother consumed alcohol during pregnancy. It is the leading cause of preventable mental disabilities in first world countries. Rosales's publications include joint authorship of "Canadian Guidelines for Diagnosis of FASD," published in the March 2, 2005, issue of the *Canadian Medical Association Journal*. He has worked on FASD in co-operation with the Innu and Inuit of Labrador and the island of Newfoundland with health, social services, education, and justice agencies in the communities.

Rosales has also researched neural tube defects, chromosome disorders, Wilson disease, hereditary convulsive disorders, bone marrow transplantation for metachromatic leukodystrophy, molecular analysis of cystic fibrosis, gonadal dysgenesis, hereditary hemorrhagic telangiectasia, microcephaly, and child protection.

Vitamin D Research

Vitamin D deficiency is associated with poor bone health, as well as an increasing list of other diseases, including colorectal cancer, type 1 diabetes, and multiple sclerosis. A resurgence of vitamin D deficiency rickets has been noted in certain high-risk Canadian children. Two national health-related societies in Canada have made recommendations for vitamin D supplementation, yet little research has been done on the vitamin D status of Canadians.

The vitamin D status of specific groups of Newfoundlanders and Labradorians, including pregnant women, newborns, and children with and without type 1 diabetes, is being studied locally by doctors Leigh Ann Newhook, Laurie Twells, Scott Sloka, Ed Randell, and Christopher Kovacs. The results indicate that vitamin D concentrations in most subjects are either in the deficiency or insufficiency ranges. Further research is important as vitamin D insufficiency may be a significant modifiable health issue for these groups.

Incidence and Genetics of Epilepsy

In researching the incidence and genetics of childhood epilepsy, Dr. Sue Moore and doctoral student Krista Mahoney have discovered that the incidence of idiopathic, or genetic, epilepsy in Newfoundland and Labrador is three times that in other parts of the developed world.

As of 2017, 121 families have been identified, 86 of which are actively participating in the study. In most families, epilepsy is caused by a complex interaction of genes; in a minority, it is inherited in an autosomal dominant manner: any child of an affected parent has a 50 per cent chance of inheriting the gene. Several families with autosomal dominant epilepsy are in the study. A novel mutation of an epilepsy gene has been identified in one family, and the remaining families are being screened to identify the responsible gene or genes. Further understanding of the molecular genetic basis of epilepsy will enable neurologists to optimize the management and therapy of affected individuals.

The molecular work on the epilepsy research is being done in the Faculty of Medicine by Terry-Lynn Young and Mahoney.

Pediatric Neurology

Several active research projects in pediatric neurology involve pediatricians David Buckley and Muhammad Alam and nurse coordinators Sharon Penney and Dianne McGrath.

An ongoing study, started in 2007, follows children who present with demyelination syndrome (changes in the white matter of the brain) to determine what percentage experience recurrence and subsequently are diagnosed with MS. The study will also look at biological and clinical predictors of outcome. This major multi-centre Canadian study is the first to study MS in children in a large population. Prior to this, MS was always considered to be a young adult disease. This study, "Clinical and genetic epidemiology of pediatric epilepsy in Newfoundland and Labrador," is being done in collaboration with other researchers from Memorial University.

A multi-centre Canadian study of the health-related quality of life, as seen through the parents' eyes, in children with epilepsy during the first two years after diagnosis is ongoing. According to Buckley, this study will lead to a better understanding of the experiences of children with epilepsy and those of their families and, ultimately, to a determination of how both can be better supported. Information is being gathered through parent questionnaires over a two-year period.

A cerebral palsy (CP) database is being developed to identity all children in Newfoundland and Labrador with CP and to assess the extent of their disabilities. In collaboration with Dr. Sherell in Montreal, this has become an ongoing country-wide project.

An international pediatric stroke registry begun several years ago as a Canadian project has recently become international; Memorial's pediatric researchers have been part of this registry since its inception. The purpose of the registry is to learn more about childhood stroke and to answer research questions about various kinds of strokes, causes, treatments, and degree of recovery. It shares knowledge internationally. In 2017, 150 co-investigators at 91 centres spanning 22 countries are involved.

A retrospective study of Newfoundland children who failed first treatment for epilepsy, which is being carried out by Memorial's pediatric neurologists, examines the influence of a child's age, epilepsy cause, seizure type, and specific medications.

A nursing study, "Evaluation of the role of the epilepsy nurse specialist from a parent/patient perspective," done in collaboration with epilepsy nurses from Calgary and Edmonton, used parent/patient questionnaires to evaluate the role/benefit of specialized nurses in the epilepsy clinic. It concluded that specialized nurses have a definitive role in the care of children and adults with epilepsy.

Neurologist J.C. Jacob's study "A clinical genetic and pathological study of neuronal ceroid lipofuscinosis (NCL) in Newfoundland and Labrador as a prototype for pediatric neurodegenerative disease" is ongoing. Newfoundland and Labrador has the highest incidence of Batten disease, one of the most prevalent forms of NCLs in North America

The first case of infantile botulism in an infant was diagnosed in Newfoundland and Labrador by doctors Muhammad Alam and Melissa Langevin in 2010. Infantile botulism results from a powerful toxin excreted by *Clostridium botulinum*, a bacterium ingested by the infant, which can result in muscle paralysis.

Perinatal Program

Considerable research is ongoing within the perinatal program. Research interests and projects include Provincial Perinatal Surveillance Program (PPSP), Canadian Perinatal Program Coalition (CPPC) and Database Committee (CPDC), Newfoundland and Labrador Congenital Anomalies Surveillance System, smoking and pregnancy, maternal obesity and breast feeding, pre-gestational diabetes in pregnancy, maternal and neonatal outcomes of women using methadone in pregnancy, neonatal outcomes of infants born to glucose-tolerant obese mothers compared to infants born to diabetic mothers in Newfoundland and Labrador, maternal and fetal outcomes in preterm with pre-labour rupture of membranes, lifestyle survey of new moms, the effect of gestational weight gain by body mass index on maternal and perinatal outcomes in twin pregnancies, impact of maternal short stature on maternal and perinatal outcomes, outcomes of term neonates after threatened preterm birth, and false preterm labour and adverse perinatal outcomes.

Researchers with the perinatal program in 2017: Lorraine Burrage, Joan Crane, Geoffrey Downton, Chris Holden, Marty Keough, Phil Murphy, Leigh Ann Newhook, James Quinlan, and Barb Young.

Perinatal Clinic Physicians (1966–2015)

Maroough Aldabaugh	Maeve Kelly
Yasmeen Akhtar	Poh Gin Kwa
Kim Blake	Sandra Luscombe
Anna Cornel	Clare Neville-Smith
Vickie Crosbie	Mary Noseworthy
Margaret Cox	Jennifer O'Dea
Padmavathy Guntamukkala	Ebru Ozkerkan
Ann Johnson	Marsha Smith
Pali Kamra	Cathy Vardy

Perinatal Program Nurse Managers (1966–2016)

Edna McKim
Cathie Royle
Lorraine Burrage

HIGH-RISK FOLLOW-UP CLINIC ADMISSION CRITERIA

The occurrance or recognition of one of the following in the first 28 days of life:

1. Birth weight < 1500 grams or gestation < 32 weeks

2. Mechanical ventilation for 48 hours or more

3. Central nervous system
3.1 Seizure confirmed by abnormal EEG, or as a result of metabolic etiology (such as hypoglycemia)
3.2 HIE
3.3 Stroke
3.4 Meningitis/Encephalitis
3.5 Hydrocephalus
3.6 Intraventricular hemorrhage, grade 3 or greater
3.7 Periventricular leukomalacia

4. Complex surgery
4.1 Thoracic
4.2 GI
4.3 GU

5. Cardiac
5.1 Cyanotic congenital heart disease
5.2 Cardiac surgery requiring bypass < 30 days of age

6. Prolonged hypoglycemia >3 episodes of blood glucose, 2.6 mmol/L in a 24-hour period

7. History of prenatal exposure to alcohol as a result of maternal alcohol intake characterized by substantial, regular intake or periodic binge drinking during pregnancy (Motherisk Program, 2006)

8. History of prenatal exposure as a result of maternal dependence during pregnancy to illicit substances such as amphetamines (e.g., Adderall), cannabis, club drugs (e.g., ecstasy), stimulants (e.g., cocaine, Ritalin), opioids (e.g., heroin, Oxycodone, Percocet), and solvents

9. Prenatal exposure to Methadone as a result of maternal participation in a Methadone Maintenance Treatment (MMT) program during pregnancy

10. Specific physician request

11. In the event of a multiple birth, all babies are followed if one meets a criterion for clinic admission

PART IV
PERINATAL PROGRAM

Perinatal Program Newfoundland and Labrador (PPNL) evolved from the need to improve the quality of perinatal (maternal/newborn) care in the province. PPNL's mandate, as directed and supported by the Provincial Perinatal Advisory Committee, is to improve pregnancy outcomes and provide a follow-up clinic to infants at high risk for developmental delay.

Dr. Derek Matthew started a clinic in April 1977 to follow up high-risk infants. A perinatal committee was also established at the Janeway.

Pediatrician Ann Johnson prepared a detailed review of perinatal services in the province in 1978. This report examined perinatal statistics for 1975–1977, reviewed retrospectively all births occurring in one month, and designed a birth certificate that would provide useful data. Johnson recommended uniform documentation of vital statistics in the neonatal period, a more aggressive approach to the pathological definition of the causes of neonatal deaths, and a continued co-operation and coordination of perinatal services throughout the province. Her report, submitted to the Janeway medical advisory committee in late 1978, was approved. It was then forwarded to the medical advisory committees of the St. John's Hospital Council, St. Clare's Hospital, and the Grace Hospital. Her recommendations were fully supported by all, including the nurses and physicians caring for neonates. The Department of Health funded the program starting in 1979.

Physicians and staff involved with the initiation of the perinatal program included doctors Poh Gin Kwa, Johnson, Anna Cornel, Clare Neville-Smith, and Peg Cox, as well as Flo Downey.

The clinics and offices of the program were initially housed in Building 615 across the street from the old Janeway, and later in the nearby Janeway Apartments. In the new Janeway, the program operates out of a suite of rooms on the main floor across from the cafeteria.

The initial objectives of the program were to organize the follow-up of infants in designated high-risk categories, to aid in the collection and analysis of perinatal statistics for the province, to work with centres providing obstetrical and neonatal care to achieve the best possible results, and to provide resources for perinatal education to health care professionals and the community.

In April 2005 the reporting structure of PPNL changed from reporting to the Department of Health and Community Services to reporting to Eastern Health. The provincial Perinatal Advisory Committee is still in place and supports the program in its mandate.

The current mandate of PPNL was adopted following a program evaluation in 1996 and reaffirmed by the Perinatal Advisory Committee in 2012/2013. The mandate encompasses the following terms of reference: organization and implementation of the perinatal follow-up clinic for high-risk infants; developing and implementing a provincial perinatal database system; facilitating and supporting research and quality assurance initiatives in perinatology and developmental outcomes; developing guidelines for perinatal care, including obstetrical and neonatal care; reviewing and implementing appropriate nationally developed programs related to perinatal health; offering educational services and resources to centres providing perinatal care; and prevention and health promotion and advocacy in improving perinatal outcomes.

The program is actively involved with the Baby-Friendly Initiative and supports the Baby Friendly Council of Newfoundland and Labrador, which is strongly committed to increasing the initiation and duration of breast feeding in the province.

The program continues to provide clinics, including the perinatal high-risk follow-up clinic and, more recently, in 2001 a breast-feeding clinic. Admission criteria for the perinatal high-risk follow-up clinic (2015) is listed in sidebar "High Risk Follow-Up Clinic Admission Criteria." One hundred and twenty-three babies met the criteria for the perinatal high-risk follow-up clinic in 2013/2014. Information about follow-up cases can be found in Table 1.

This clinic is the only developmental follow-up program for high-risk infants in the province. Its primary objective is to identify areas of concern early in the growth and development of these children and provide early intervention.

Children are usually seen at 4, 8, 12, 18, and 36 months at the Janeway by a pediatrician, nurse, and psychologist. Travelling clinics are held twice a year in western and central Newfoundland by pediatricians only. Children in the follow-up clinic who live in the Labrador-Grenfell region are followed by a pediatrician who resides in St. Anthony.

The PPSP captures maternal and neonatal data from the four provincial health authorities and publishes its findings in an annual report. PPNL continues to be a part of the Canadian Perinatal Program Committee and the Canadian Perinatal Surveillance System-External Advisory Committee. Other initiatives involving PPNL are capturing breast-feeding data for the province, implementing universal hearing screening, and operating the province's congenital anomalies surveillance system.

PPNL is involved with research projects which are listed in the Annual Report for 2014/2015. It has created guidelines for the development and advocacy of the advancement of perinatal care services in Newfoundland and Labrador. These initiatives include breast feeding, maternal newborn policies, and the provincial child and maternal death review.

PPNL has been actively involved with several provincial/national programs and education initiatives: ACORN, Neonatal Resuscitation Program (NRP), Advanced Life Support in Obstetrics Program (ALSO), Advances in Labour and Risk Management (ALARM), simulation of emergency clinical skills, substance abuse, Advanced Pediatric Life Support (APLS), fatal health surveillance, hypoxic ischemic encephalopathy, breast-feeding education, baby-friendly initiative, and managing obstetrical risk efficiently.

PART V

MEDICAL EDUCATION

Memorial University's medical school was established in 1967. Before it became officially affiliated with Memorial in July 1968, the Janeway was involved in post-graduate medical education, and doctors from McGill and Dalhousie medical schools completed a portion of their post-graduate training in pediatrics at the Janeway. For several years the Janeway also enjoyed an association with the Mayo Clinic in Rochester, Minnesota. Its orthopedic residents could elect to do a six-month elective rotation in pediatric orthopedics at the Janeway.

On July 2, 1968, Memorial University and the Children's Hospital Corporation signed an agreement making the Janeway an affiliated teaching hospital with Memorial. Its goals were to provide high-quality patient care and community service, to develop and maintain high standards in medical education, and to conduct medical research with the aim of adding to human knowledge and improving methods for the prevention and treatment of disease. Clinical teaching was deemed to be in the interest of both the university and the hospital. After the signing of this agreement, a joint liaison committee was established under John Darte, the medical school's first permanent chair of pediatrics and the Janeway's chief of pediatrics. At the initial meeting, July 2, 1968, the first order of business was to appoint several senior Janeway physicians to the medical school. The first appointments included Clifton Joy, clinical associate professor of pediatrics; Richard Kennedy, chief of surgery, clinical associate professor of surgery; Charles Henderson, chief of anesthesia, clinical associate professor of anesthesia; and Walter Heneghan, chief of radiology, clinical associate professor of radiology.

Bernard Boothroyd-Brooks was appointed assistant professor of psychiatry and director of the Division of Psychiatry with the Janeway's Department of Medicine on January 11, 1971; Martin Lewis, chair and professor of pathology

Pediatric Residency Program Directors

Clifton Way

Albert J. Davis

Kaiser Ali

Robert Morris

Wayne Andrews

Surya Shah

Tracey Bridger

John Martin

Chairs of Pediatrics

John M.M. Darte: 1969–1975

Donald A. Hillman: 1976–1982

Rudolph Ozere: 1982–1987

Albert J. Davis: 1987–1996

Austin Rick Cooper: 1996–2008

Cathy Vardy: 2008–2015

Kevin Chan: 2015–present

at the medical school and chief of pathology at the Janeway, March 1, 1971; and laboratory director Charles J. Hutton, clinical associate professor in pathology, September 1, 1971. Clifton Way, appointed assistant professor in 1969, was also acting chief of pediatrics after Joy's resignation and before Darte's arrival in 1968.

See Appendix B for a list of Janeway pediatric residents and their year of appointment.

Memorial University Full-time Pediatric Faculty and Year Appointed

Clifton Way	1968	Khalid Aziz	1996
John Darte	1969	Mohsin Rashid	1996
Albert J. Davis	1969	David Buckley	1997
Chaker Hobeika	1970	Suryakant Shah	1998
Gordon Gosse	1972	Anna Dominic	2000
Damodar Vaze	1973	Leigh Ann Newhook	2000
Austin Richard Cooper	1974	Tracey Bridger	2001
Ranjit K. Chandra	1974	Victoria Crosbie	2002
Derek Matthew	1976	Jeff Critch	2002
Donald Hillman	1976	Anne Drover	2004
Elizabeth Hillman	1976	Mary Noseworthy	2004
Shyamo Virmani	1977	Susan Moore	2005
Wayne Andrews	1978	Stephen Noseworthy	2006
Kaiser Ali	1979	Jeff Burzynski	2007
Geoffrey P. Sharratt	1981	Paul Dancey	2007
Rudolph Ozere	1982	Robert Porter	2008
Theodore Rosales	1983	Akhil Kumar Deshpandey	2008
Robert Morris	1984	Colleen Crowther	2009
Gabriel Ronen	1984	Denise Hickey	2010
Donald Reid	1984	John Martin	2010
Joseph Curtis	1987	Jennifer O'Dea	2010
Keith Goulden	1988	Tyna Doyle	2010
Elizabeth Ives	1988	Pushpa Sathya	2010
David Long	1988	Roger Chafe	2010
Cathy Vardy	1988	Shahzad Waheed	2011
Vincent M. Osundwa	1992	Natalie Bridger	2011
William Sprague	1992	Julie Emberley	2013
Kim Blake	1994	Mary Jane Smith	2013
Brian Simmons	1994	Kristina Krmpotic	2014
Jill Barter	1995	Kevin Chan	2015

John Darte

Pediatrician John Darte was the first chair of pediatrics in the Memorial University medical school. During his tenure, from 1968 to 1974, he was also the Janeway's chief of pediatrics. Darte's experience was extensive: he subspecialized in pediatric oncology and medical radiotherapy and had completed extensive research in leukemia and other hematology-related concerns at SickKids in Toronto.

John Darte, first chair of pediatrics at Memorial University's medical school.

Darte had worked with renowned hematologist John Dacie at Hammersmith Hospital in London, England, in 1952/1953 and with Dr. Edith Pattison at the Christie Hold Radium Institute in Manchester, England, in 1956/1957. Between 1957 and 1968 he treated children with cancer and researched full body radiation and bone marrow transplantation at SickKids and at Princess Margaret Hospital. Darte had a keen interest in research, extensive experience in the diagnosis and treatment of children with cancer, expertise in teaching, and a profound compassion for his patients, most of whom had a life-threatening disease.

Physically, Darte was a giant of a man—6 feet 6 inches tall and 250 pounds—with a great sense of humour and a loud laugh. He was kind and generous and loved by his patients and colleagues.

Darte arrived at the Janeway and the medical school in September 1968 before the curriculum had fully been developed, and before the first students had graduated. The Janeway was making steady progress but many obstacles needed to be overcome and programs developed.

A good leader, Darte was quick to identify problems and fully supported colleagues who had solutions. Dr. Albert J. Davis met with Darte in 1972 to outline his concerns about the hospital's ability to help sick neonates and about issues related to their transport to the Janeway. Davis suggested that the province needed a newborn transport system. Darte listened intently and then, in a loud friendly voice, said, "Bert, that's a great idea—just do it; you go to government and anyone else who will support it, and I will support you, but you do it." With that encouragement, Davis did, and the transport system became a unique, well-run service.

During Darte's tenure, the pediatrics department at the Janeway and the discipline of pediatrics at Memorial University, which were almost inseparable, developed academically and clinically to meet national standards. This was done with the full support of the pediatricians, several of whom were full-time faculty members at the university.

Darte was respected and fully accepted by the local Janeway chiefs, physicians, and staff. This spirit of cooperation throughout pediatrics was the envy of many other disciplines at the medical school. Through his leadership, Darte directed the practice and study of pediatrics in Newfoundland in the right direction and allowed it to develop into the success it is today.

Memories of First-Year Residency
at the Janeway, 1967

By Poh Gin Kwa

After completing her residency training at the Janeway and the IWK Hospital, Poh Gin Kwa returned to the Janeway and Grace General Hospital in 1971 as a pediatrician. She worked in neonatology at the Grace and in Child Development and the Perinatal Clinic at the Janeway. She also founded the Down Syndrome Society of Newfoundland. As of 2017 Kwa has been a full-time pediatrician for 44 years.

My family was from southern China but I grew up in Indonesia, one of 10 children of a poor immigrant worker father. I really wanted to be a physician but this was impossible for financial reasons until, in 1958, I received a scholarship to attend the National Taiwan University in Taipei. This medical school was very modern and most of the faculty were American-trained in prestigious university teaching hospitals.

I did my rotating internship at the General Hospital in St. John's, from July 1966 until June 1967. My first rotation was pediatrics on the old Alexander Ward and the Victoria Ward and it

Poh Gin Kwa.

was there I meet Clifton Joy, chief of all the pediatricians in the city. He was very kind to me and was my mentor. He asked me to become a resident at the new hospital which was about to open up. I could only do one year because the Royal College of Physicians and Surgeons would only approve the program for one year. I completed the rest of my training in Halifax, Nova Scotia.

At the Janeway I worked very hard and was on call every second day and every second weekend, covering the wards as well as the emergency ward. We would admit on average 10 to 12 patients a day to the ward with a variety of conditions.

There was not a lot of supervision by the attending pediatricians; however, Dr. Norah Elphinstone Browne was a wonderful teacher and an expert on acid-base balance and other chemical problems in sick children. She was very kind and compassionate and generous with her time. Dr. Joy was a very busy man, but kind and appreciative of all our hard work. In the year I spent at the Janeway there were three other residents and several rotating interns from Dalhousie University and foreign medical school graduates from the General Hospital.

The nurses on the wards and in the emergency room were usually very experienced. We learned a lot from the patients. In those days there was no academic half days, just grand rounds in medicine and surgery and some teaching in radiology. There was no time off after being on call.

There are a few stories I would like to mention.

At that time, there were no butterfly needles (small needles with plastic "wings" to hold during insertion) to access a vein; the only small needle was a size 25 straight needle. At that time there were many children with infectious diseases being admitted to 1B (isolated unit). They were very sick and so "shut down" that it was impossible to find a vein when they came into the Janeway. I had to do a cutdown around their ankle area to find the vein to set up their IV. There were no surgeons to teach me how to do a cutdown and I had to read the surgical procedure textbook and get the information to do a cutdown and set up an IV solution of fluid for all these sick children to save their lives.

Children with spinal abnormalities or very severe TB meningitis cases sometimes came in. It was very difficult to do a spinal tap to obtain their spinal fluid to make the right diagnosis of meningitis. I needed to do a cisternal puncture (if the child's anterior fontanel was closed) or do a subdural tap (if the child's anterior fontanel was opened). I did all of these procedures without any supervision or without being taught by a staff physician. I had to read the

245

procedure textbook and figure out how to do it by myself. I was lucky that I didn't run into any complications with these procedures.

The administrators and nursing supervisors had a lot of power in the hospital because there was no residency director and the pediatricians were often in their offices uptown. The time changed in the spring to one hour earlier and I did not know about it; I was late coming to the hospital to work in the morning. The administrator and nursing supervisor gave me a very hard time. They told me if I was late again they would report to the Royal College of Physicians and Surgeons of Canada and my residency training would not be counted.

Dr. Joy and his family loved Chinese food and one evening he asked me to come to his house to cook for him and his family. I did it, and we had a good meal and a good time. That night I was so full and so tired that I overslept the next day and I was late going into the hospital to work. I was scared to death that the administrator would report me to the Royal College of Physicians and Surgeons of Canada and my first-year residency training would not be recognized. I told Dr. Joy about this and he went to see the administrator and spoke to him on my behalf and explained why I was late coming to work. I was off the hook and I was so happy. I have never forgotten Dr. Joy's kindness.

Overall, I had a good year as a first-year resident. I learned a lot and made some good friends. Dr. Elphinstone Browne and Dr. Joy were exceptionally nice and they gave me plenty of advice, teaching, and confidence.

My Internship at the Janeway, 1967
By William Sprague

I did my internship in July and August 1967 at the Janeway. I had planned to do internal medicine, but those two months at the Janeway and the influence of Dr. Joy changed my mind.

As interns, we were pretty much on our own. We looked after children on the wards and ICU. The only neonates at the hospital had congenital anomalies; they were not premature. We worked every second night and every second weekend and got paid about $187 per month.

I remember looking after very sick patients in ICU. One was Dr. Rufus Dominic's patient who had Hemolytic-Uremic Syndrome, whom we ventilated but subsequently died.

Dr. Collins also had a patient who was ventilated. In those days, a staff member's involvement was minimal and as an intern you carried a lot of responsibility. Residents were not involved that much, at least during the summer of 1967. Once a child had status epilepticus and I gave IV valium to stop the seizures.

Overdoses had to go to the General Hospital emergency room first and then be admitted to the Janeway. One pediatrician, Dr. Clifton Way, was very good at discharging patients but the others sometimes kept patients weeks or months, particularly diabetic patients.

The top third floor of the Janeway was empty and we slept in patient rooms up there. The hospital was newly renovated and was much better than the old Halifax Children's Hospital or SickKids in Toronto.

There were very few pediatricians around that summer. Dr. Norah Elphinstone Browne, who started Child Development, was chief of the infectious disease ward. She gave wonderful talks on fluid and electrolyte balance and the sort of things which carried me through my career. She was a great clinician and teacher.

There was a shortage of nurses that summer and we had to help feed the babies. I got into trouble, as I am prone to, when a rat ran across the floor and I had informed the administration and other people that rats are in the hospital and John Butt, associate executive director, was upset with me because he didn't want the news to get out.

It was the Tom Sawyer era and one of our diabetic patients went missing every afternoon but he always came back for supper. We later found out that he went swimming in the creek up on back where they later built the Janeway Apartments.

As I mentioned before, some of the children were admitted for a long time and one evening I took some of the children to the circus because they had been in the hospital all summer long and I thought they needed time out. I took them to the circus at the stadium and I brought them back. We didn't have permission from the parents or administration. The next day John Butt, very kindly, very diplomatically, said, "It was very kind of you to take the children to the circus but that isn't the way we do things here."

Another time I got in trouble when I set up a Thomas splint on a boy with a fractured femur. A Thomas splint is a splinting device to reduce pain that uses straps attached over the pelvis and hip at one end and weights or a traction device at the distal end. In those days we used weights as traction; however, I couldn't find any weights and went down to the kitchen and got several large unopened cans and used those. I thought I did a great job but the next morning Dr. Richard Kennedy, a pediatric surgeon, came by and in a loud voice told me that was not the way we set up a Thomas splint and that I knew nothing. I guess you can't please everyone.

Overall it was a difficult but productive summer. I learned lots of things and took an interest in pediatrics and eventually trained in pediatrics and became a pediatrician.

Dr. Sprague returned to the Janeway in 1973 as a general pediatrician and stayed until 1997.

PART VI
THE JANEWAY FOUNDATION

From its beginning, the Janeway has been the recipient of the overwhelming generosity of Newfoundlanders and Labradorians. Funding provided by the provincial government through the Hospital Insurance Program was adequate for maintaining a tertiary-care hospital for children (and, after 2001, for women's and children's health), but it was not enough to initiate research projects, purchase state-of-the-art specialized equipment, or pay for certain renovations and capital projects.

In 1967, the Janeway's board established a public relations committee and authorized it to emphasize fundraising. The committee consisted of board members J. Douglas Eaton (chair), William Tiller, and Archibald R. Frost, whose duties were to develop ways and means of raising funds and establishing a foundation for the hospital.

The Janeway received several generous unsolicited donations in the early years; however, the need for capital items went beyond the available money. The Department of Health was sympathetic and health minister James McGrath arranged a government grant of $10,000 to be used for special projects. This became the nucleus of a board fund, which was later augmented by substantial fundraising efforts.

Daphne Maunder.

The first Christmas appeal in 1969 netted $10,000 and was a valuable experience. Obviously, the people of the province were interested in assisting the Janeway purchase essential equipment to carry on its role as the provincial child health care centre.

In 1984, director of volunteer services Daphne Maunder—who had expressed an interest in fundraising—developed and implemented a new approach by directly mailing a pamphlet to 25,000 people in the province. That effort raised $103,000 and was considered a great success. This initiative, which was part of the annual Christmas Appeal, as well as generous donations from the Janeway Auxiliary, were significant sources of capital funding.

In 1970, the Auxiliary held the first Janeway Day at the Races. This became a yearly event wherein the St. John's Racing and Entertainment Centre and the Newfoundland Harness Horse Owners Association donated the proceeds from the horse races that day to the Janeway. This continued until 2000.

The Janeway Children's Hospital Foundation was incorporated on May 30, 1985, with the mandate to assume responsibility for all fundraising activities. Daphne Maunder was appointed manager and a board of directors appointed under chair Elmer Harris.

Donald Kelland, Daphne Maunder, and Premier Brian Peckford announce the Janeway Foundation in 1984.

In the same year, the Janeway joined other children's hospitals in Canada and the United States in the Children's Miracle Network Telethon. This initiative raised $350,000.

The Foundation has continued to thrive and, although the Janeway Telethon is a major fundraiser, the foundation also raises much-needed funds from planned-giving programs, the Christmas appeal, an annual golf tournament, bequests, and in memoriam and corporate donations.

The funds raised are spent on equipment, research, and education. This equipment includes fetal heart monitors, an MRI-compatible ventilator, cardiac monitors, a rhinolaryngoscope, and simulation equipment which provide medical and nursing students, physicians, and nurses with up-to-date knowledge and treatment techniques. At the old Janeway, Foundation funds provided for much-needed upgrading in the physical building as well as new equipment.

The Foundation provides funds annually to support educational opportunities throughout the hospital in pediatric oncology, cardiology, neurology, and surgery.

The Foundation has funded more than 50 active research projects, allowing the practice of better evidence-based medicine. This research will have long-term impacts on children who suffer from eating disorders, childhood obesity, and adverse drug events, for example. Several initiatives supply support to specific child health programs such as lifestyles, eating disorders, and diabetes. The Foundation also supports the Women's Health Program, which relates to obstetrics and is a part of the Janeway site.

The Foundation has had a profound impact on the care the Janeway has provided to the children of Newfoundland and Labrador from conception to their 18th birthday. These generous contributions have made a difference to the next generation by giving the staff what they need to provide the best care.

Appendix A

Research by selected physicians and scientists at the Janeway

Kaiser Ali, pediatric hematologist-oncologist, 1979–1991
Ali completed a longitudinal cohort study to determine the effectiveness of Anti Rh(o) (D) in chronic ITP. His other research included the absence of carcinoembryonic antigen (CEA) expression by neuroblastoma with monoclonal and polyclonal antibodies, CT scans following VP shunting in children with brain tumors, and familial intracranial gliomas.

Penny Allderdice, geneticist, 1973–1977
Allderdice was the director of the cytogenetics laboratory at the Janeway and a professor in cytogenetics at Memorial. A well-established scientist in her field, she came to the Janeway and Memorial in 1973 and retired in 1997.

Allderdice is widely known for original investigations into cytogenetic syndromes in Newfoundland and Labrador. Her thorough follow-up to identify carriers at risk and to correlate theoretical outcomes with the provision of services to members of extended families has been matched by few others. In 1975 she identified and published a new chromosomal syndrome duplication, 9q34, a developmental disorder of children. This syndrome was subsequently named after her and her research on it was published in the *American Journal of Human Genetics* (volume 27) in 1975.

Allderdice collaborated with geneticists across North America, many of whom also received research support from the Medical Research Council of Canada. Together they contributed to the human gene map using samples and segregation data from Allderdice's own research.

By providing genetic counselling to many Newfoundland families, Allderdice became aware of social and environmental factors which contributed to the effect of inheriting a chromosome rearrangement or Mendelian gene.

Allderdice published many papers and received funding from the National Research Council of Canada. She was appointed a member of the Genetics Grant Review Committee of the Medical Research Council from 1976 to 1980, a member of the Medical Research Council Scholarship Committee in 1988, and a member of the National Research Council of Canada from 1976 to 1980.

Kim Blake, general pediatrician, 1992–1997

Blake developed undergraduate teaching methods that used simulated pediatric scenarios, constructed a Down Syndrome database for Newfoundland and Labrador, and studied children with hypersensitivity to sound frequencies.

Kevin Chan, pediatrician, emergency medicine

Chan's research included strategies for patient-oriented research (with Chris Aubrey-Bessler Kevin Chan, Bruce Cooper, and Marshal Goodwin), emergency room guidelines, evaluation of rapid group A streptococcus in the emergency room (with Peter Daley), and X-ray requirements for scaphoid fractures (with Jonathan Porter and Bob Porter).

Ranjit Kumar Chandra, pediatric immunologist, 1974–2002

Chandra came to the Janeway and Memorial in 1974 as professor of pediatric research. He quickly established himself as an expert in the relationship of diet and nutrition to immunity and resistance to disease. He published new approaches to the prevention of allergic disease in young children as well as on nutrition and immunology. He received many awards and honorary degrees and was made an officer of the Order of Canada.

In the late 1980s Chandra undertook a study for Ross Pharmaceuticals, a maker of infant formula, to see if their products could prevent babies from developing allergies; it was subsequently published in the *British Medical Journal* in 1989. He also did a study for Nestle and Mead Johnson, two pharmaceutical companies that also manufactured infant formula.

In 1994 Chandra's research nurse, Marilyn Harvey, reported concerns with the research to Albert J. Davis, chair of pediatrics at Memorial: fewer subjects had been recruited for the study than were reported. The university appointed an independent panel who spent three months interviewing witnesses and examining Chandra's publications. Their reprt was held confidential until the CBC obtained a copy in 2005 and broadcast the panel's conclusions— including that Chandra was guilty of scientific misconduct—on *The National* on January 30 and February 1, 2006.

Despite the Committee's conclusion, the university did not take any action against Chandra.

In 2001 in a paper published in *Nutrition*, Chandra concluded that a specific multivitamin and mineral formulation greatly enhanced the memories of seniors. In 2003 a *Nutrition* editorial questioned the validity of Chandra's findings. Chandra was critical of their comments.

Chandra retired from Memorial University in 2002. He launched a lawsuit against CBC and Memorial University—CBC for libel and invasion of privacy, Memorial for losing some of his data—in 2015. After 60 days of testimony, he lost his case and the judge exonerated the CBC. Chandra was ordered to pay the court costs of $1.6 million.

A retired editor of the *British Medical Journal*, Richard Smith, was a witness for the CBC at the trial in July 2015. In an article in the journal he criticized Memorial, the scientific journals that published Chandra's work, and Chandra. On October 29, 2015, the *British Medical Journal* announced that it was retracting a 1989 paper by Chandra on the influence of maternal diet during lactation and the use of formula feeds on the development of atopic eczema in high-risk infants.

Austin Rick Cooper, pediatric infectious disease and general pediatrics, 1974–present
Cooper's research includes CMV disease in newborns, "I" cell disease, systemic candidiasis, rheumatic fever, bacterial meningitis, and the history of medicine.

Gary Cornel, cardiac surgeon, 1974–1990
Cornel studied the familial co-arctation of the aortic arch.

Benvon Cramer, pediatric radiologist, 1984–2014
Cramer researched urinary tract imaging in children, nephrocalcinosis in rabbits, segmental multicystic renal impairment, cisterna magna clots, and the clinical and genetic epidemiology of Bardet Biedl Syndrome.

Albert J. Davis, pediatrician, 1969–2010
Davis's research included diabetes, lipid metabolism, growth hormone, precocious puberty, neonatal screening, pediatric gastroenterology, and medical education.

Poh Gin Kwa, pediatrician
Gin Kwa completed a cross-sectional study on postpartum women from Newfoundland and Labrador and their levels of omega-6 polyunsaturated fatty acids in breast milk and cord blood compared to other Canadian women. She also studied molybdenum requirements in low birth weight infants.

Keith Goulden, pediatric child development specialist and neurologist, 1988–1992
Gouldan studied posterior fossa asthrocytomas, the effect of radiotherapy on cognitive function, and clobazam monotherapy.

Elizabeth Ives, geneticist, 1988–1999
Ives, a distinguished researcher in clinical genetics, who received MRC grants, published research on Battens disease, Huntington disease, the genetics of deafness, myotonic dystrophy, and atelosteogenesis type III.

Lawrence F. Jardine, pediatric hematologist-oncologist, 1992–1999
Jardine conducted randomized clinical trials with the Children's Cancer Group, as well as an extensive review of children with leukemia and lymphoma over 27 years. His other research interests included venous thromboembolic complications in children, monitoring factor concentrates with the Canadian Hemophilia Registry, Intrathecal Leucovorin following an overdose of Intrathecal Methotrexate, and evaluating protein C for Immuno Canada.

Kdapasambil Madhavankutty (Madhavan Kutty), biochemist, 1968–1995
Kutty conducted research at the Janeway and published on serum cholinesterase activity in hyperlipidemia; ultramicro technique for the assay of serum cholinesterase; globoid cell leucodystrophy; late infantile amaurotic idiocy; alpha fetoprotein levels in patients with cystic fibrosis; and lymphocytic resetting and the effect of serine and phospholipase D and its possible implications on membrane structure.

Falah Maroun, neurosurgeon, 1966–present
Maroun's research includes cerebrovascular lesions in children, the incidence of intracal neoplasms in Newfoundland, diastematomyelia, familial intracranial gliomas, recurrent meningitis in children, modified hemispherectomy for epilepsy, intracranial ventricular shunts, leptomeningeal spread of primary brain tumors, and neural tube defects in Newfoundland.

Rob Morris, pediatrician, 1984–present
Morris was the local director for the Canadian Hospital Injury Reporting and Prevention Program (a multi-centre study sponsored by Health and Welfare Canada), from 1990 to 2004; a principal investigator (with Kutty and Damoder Vaze) for a study on the efficiency of oral enzymes in improving malabsorption status in patients with cystic fibrosis (1989–1992); local investigator with the Pediatric Investigators Collaborative Network on Infections in Canada (1990–1993); and a local investigator for IMPACT, the Immunization Monitoring Program–ACTive (1993–2011).

Bhanu Muram, pediatrician and casualty officer, 1989–present
Muram participated in several asthma studies, including a study of the efficacy and safety of repeated nebulized therapy combining Ipratropium Bromide 0.25 mgs plus Salbutamol Sulphate 3.0 mg versus Salbutamol Sulphate 3.0 mgs alone in children with acute asthma (a multi-centre study across Canada in 1993); and a multi-centre, randomized, double-blind, double dummy, parallel-group clinical trial to determine the clinical equivalence between Fluticasone Propionate 400 mcg/daily versus Diskus and Budesonide 800 mcg/daily via Turbuhaler administered for six months in pre-pubescent patients aged four to 12 years with asthma. Muram was also an investigator in a multi-centre study across Canada in 1994–1995 on the efficacy of Ceftin in treating Group A Streptococcal infections in children.

On the topic of gastroenterology, he has studied safety and symptom improvement with Esomeprazole in adolescents with GE reflux disease, and the effects of Esomeprazole treatment for GERD on quality of life in 12- to 17-year-old adolescents.

His studies on infectious disease and immunology include immunogenicity and safety of two dose levels of Thimerosol-free Trivalent seasonal influenza vaccine in children aged six to 35 months, and immunogenicity and safety study of GSK Biologicals Quadrivalent influenza vaccine when administered in children.

Rudolph L. Ozere, pediatrician, 1982–1990
Ozere's research included Reyes syndrome, chlamydia trachomatis pneumonia, and hemolytic uremic syndrome.

Asuri N. Presad, pediatric neurologist, 1996–1999
Presad extensively studied the dietary therapy of epilepsy.

Chitra Presad, geneticist, 1997–1999
Presad's research included the role of diet therapy in the management of hereditary metabolic diseases, prolonged QT interval (a measure of the heart's electrical cycle) as a clue to impending cardiac arrhythmia in metabolic myopathies, and Niemann-Pick disease type C.

Chitra Pushpanathan, pediatric pathologist, 1986–2014
Pushpanathan's research included complications of perinatal care; an experimental study on the therapeutic effect and drug toxicity of anti-cancer drugs with the cancer research group at Memorial; experimental induction of nephrocalcinosis (with radiologist Benvon Cramer); and pancreatic echogenicity in premature and newborn infants.

Gabriel Ronen, pediatric neurologist, 1984–1991
Ronen published a Canadian retrospective study of the treatment of refractory epilepsy with Clobazam. His other research interests included cerebrospinal fluid levels of acetylcholinesterase and pseudocholinesterase in neonates with hypoxic ischaemic brain injury; molecular, genetic, and biochemical analysis of benign familial neonatal convulsions; the epidemiology of epilepsy with Rolandic spikes in childhood (a population study in Newfoundland and Labrador), and brainstem auditory evoked potentials in Chiara II malformation.

Pushpa Sathya
Sathya completed a multidisciplinary human study on the genetic, environmental, and microbial interactions that cause inflammatory bowel disease. He also studied the role of omega-3 fatty acids (N3 PUFA) in controlling inflammation in pediatric in non-alcoholic fatty liver disease; cow's milk protein intolerance in infants; celiac disease in children, Canadian progressive familial intrahepatic cholestasis, and the epidemiology of pediatric hepatitis C infection in Manitoba. He was also involved in the Canadian biliary atresia register, the Canadian Pediatric Survey of Access to Gastroenterology, and the guideline for the diagnosis and treatment of non-alcoholic fatty liver disease in children.

Raj D. Seth, pediatric neurologist, 1991–1993
Seth's research focused on intractable pediatric epilepsy.

Geoffrey P. Sharratt, pediatric cardiologist, 1982–1993
Sharratt researched left axis deviation in otherwise healthy children; Gaucher's disease with mitral valve calcifications; arrhythmias in normal infants; the predictive value of early response to Indomethacin in assessing the final outcome of PDA closure in premature infants; and co-arctation of the aorta.

Geoffrey Smith, pedodontist, 1978–2012
Smith studied sugar-free medications, sugar-free antibiotics, dental trauma, and reprocessing (sterilization of single-use items used in dentistry).

Appendix B

Janeway pediatric residents and their year of appointment

Imelda Abear	1979	Scott Bryant	1986
Martin Abenheimer	1978	David Buckley	1993
Andrew Adade	1981	Megan Burke	2014
Danielle Adam	2014	Polineni Butchamamba	1974
Ajit Ahluwalia	1981	Camila Carneiro de Lima	2016
Yasmeen Akhtar	2002	Rebecca Cases	1979
Muhammed Alam	2000	Allison Carroll	2006
Norma Alba	1977	Pamela Case	1981
Muroog Al-Dabbagh	1999	Carolyn Cashin (Connors)	2012
Todd Alexander	1999	Paula Chalmers	1974
Samina Ali	1996	Marisa Chard	2011
Syed Kaiser Ali	1972	Bharat B. Chawla	1990
Leigh Anne Allwood	1993	Malcolm Cheng	1993
Ibrahim Al-Nassir	1975	Mammen Cheriyan	1994
Francisca Alonzo	1981	Kwok Wai Chiu	
Zenaida Antonio	1977	Jarmila Chrappa	1980
Manutchehr Assemi	1985	Peter Church	2006
Nadia Aumeerally	2007	Jo-Anna Clark	2014
Karen Backway	1999	Joy Clements	2015
Gurumukh Das Batra	1975	Julie Clowater	1994
Rajendra Berharry	1981	James Coffey	2003
Kathleen Berry	1981	Mark Cohen	1978
Emily Biden	2011	Anna-Claire Coleman	2006
Ashley Blagdon	2014	Carrie Comerford	1992
David Bond	1978	John Compton	1978
Enrique Borja	1990	Colin Cooper	1973
Lynette Bowes	1995	Jeffrey Critch	1995
Heather Bremner	2006	Catherine Cronin	1989
Tracey Bridger	1994	Colleen Crowther	2009
Natalie Bridger	2004	Victoria Crosbie	1990
Mark Brodsky	1981	Joseph Curtis	1987
Jason Brophy	1999	Sarah Curtis	2000

Paul Dancey	1998	John (Jack) Hand	1997
Jennifer Davis	2013	Omer Hamud	2012
Heather Davis	2004	Marguerite Hanoman	1979
Heather Dawson	1974	Lisa Harris	1997
Beth DeBruyne	2010	Elizabeth Harvey	1982
Joanne Delaney	2016	Trinda Hayden	2015
Haresh I. Desai	1979	Alison Haynes	2008
Delores Doherty	1973	Ara Healey	2002
Anna Dominic	1993	Katharine Herrington	2012
Adhad Dowlut	1982	Denise Hickey	1997
Geoffrey Downton	1977	Jennifer Hilliard	2007
Tyna Doyle	2002	Linda Hillier	1983
Anne Drover	1997	Amanda Hogg	2010
Thanh H. Duong	1981	Peter Howland	1979
Tracey Dyer	2016	Pein-Pein Huang	1980
Minnie Earle	1978	Jo-Anna Hudson	2014
Makram Ed-Bardessy	1974	Linda Huh	1999
Carlos Enriquez	1990	Jonathan Hummell	1985
Heather Escott	2004	Richard Huntsman	1998
Carolyn Escudero	2007	Robyn Hutchings	2006
Liam Fardy	2013	Thresiamma James	1985
Luana Farren-Dai	2016	Lawrence Jardine	1987
Kate Fathi	2010	Furrakh Javed	2003
Loretta Fiorillo	1982	Michael Jeavons	1975
Sheila Fitzgerald	1978	Sivaami Jeevanandam	2006
John Fitzsimons	1983	Jusli Pin-Mu Jeh	1974
Anthony Ford-Jones	1976	Shashtkant Joglekar	1976
Michael Forrester	2015	Isaac John	1981
N. Jane Forsey	1975	Barbara Kaczmarsha	1992
Christopher Foster	1975	Anjali Kamra	2008
Alisha Gabriel	2014	Palinder Kamra	1984
Jennifer Garland	1996	Anand Giottam Kantak	1978
Balbinder Gill	1990	Kescha Kazmi	2014
Clive Glazebrook	1975	Heather Kee (Barter)	1979
Lisa Goodyear	2001	Catherine Maeve Kelly	1982
P. Goonawardena	1973	Francis Kelly	1977
Vojtech Gregus	1987	Peter Kent	1977
Josias Grobler	2001	Vinod Kesavan	1988
Masoud Grouchi	1992	Samir Khoury	1996
Gregory Guilcher	2001	Carmelita Kintanar	1982
Padmavathy Guntamukkala	1997	Sheila Kiruluta	1975
Louise Guolla	2015	Shirley Korula	1978
Azad Singh Guron	1987	Hayim Krespin	1979
Michael Hall	1988	Kristina Krmpotic	2013
Azza Hamed	1994	Anna Kubow	2009

Narinder Kumar	1986	Shasta Moser	2011
Poh Gin Kwa	1966	Christa Mossman	2000
Haladhra Laishram	1991	David Mowat	1975
Melissa Langevin	2007	James Muller	1978
Kam-Yung Lau	1976	Munawar Mumtaz	1988
David Le	2009	James Munro	1985
Hoaan Le	2009	Bhanu Prasad Muram	1985
Robyn LeDrew	2012	Anne Murphy	1998
Donald Heaton Lee	1979	David Murphy	1977
Shoo Kim Lee	1987	Tricia Murphy	1995
Chumei Li	2001	Kimberley Myers	2002
Marina Liscano	1977	Anandhan Naidoo	1977
Ted Logan	1982	Michael Nash	2002
Alison Lopez	2013	Abid Nawaz	1978
Hanna Lotocka-Reysner	1998	M. Dokiso Nchama	1973
Tianyan (Tanya) Lui	1992	Leigh Anne Newhook	1997
Sandra Luscombe	1995	Alana Newman	2012
Timothy Lynch	1994	Susanna Sau-Ngau Ng	1974
Robert MacCari	1982	Pius Ngassa	1978
Jillian MacCuspie	2011	Que Ngyen	1981
Andrew MacIntosh	1977	March Nicholson	2002
Joan Kathryn MacIssac	1981	Faith Nixdorff	1982
Louisa MacKenzie	2001	Colleen Nugent	2009
April MacPhee	2009	Wendy Nusche	1988
Peter MacPherson	2012	Gabriel Nwaesei	1988
Brenda MacQuarrie	1985	Vincent Nwosa	1980
Thomas George McGarry	1977	Colleen O'Brien	2003
Marianne McKenna	2005	Cecil Ojah	1982
Catherine Mah	1998	Andrew O'Keefe	2008
Hilje (Hilda) Makken	1998	Heather Onyett	1974
Santina Malaguti	1987	Vincent Oswundwa	1978
Paul Maloney	2007	Hayley Oulton	2012
Cherry Mammen	2003	Ebru Ozerkan	2006
Janice Manthorne	2000	Indira Pachai	1982
Noelle Marsh	2016	Philsamma Padamadan	1982
Sarah Amanda Marsh	2013	Harpreet Pall	1999
John Martin	2004	Kamlesh Kumar Patel	1989
Patricia Massicotte	1990	Kirit Patel	1978
Erin Maszczakiewicz	2014	Parul Patel	1990
Mary Mattar	1979	Rikin Patel	2009
Linda Matthews	1974	Serina Patel	2005
Paul Moorehead	2004	Pedraza	1973
Robert Morris	1976	Lorine Pelly	2008
Jennie Morrison	2011	Pauline Penner	1987
Mfed (Ed) Mosely	2000	Sande Perlis	1984

Vijayalakshmi Perumal	2003	Barbara Stanford	1981
Theyanisha Pillay	2005	Joel Stemmer	1989
Norman Pinder	1975	Sandra Stevenson	1996
Martin Pollard	1973	Smeeksha Sur	2001
Kenneth Porter	1980	Chin Chai Tan	1973
Heather Power	2010	Tracy Tan	2013
Patrick Power	1977	Shamim Tejpar	1979
Asuri Prasad	1991	Christina Templeton	1995
Chitra Prasad	1991	Steven Thicke	1981
Andrzei Radzikowski	1979	Maria Thomas	1976
Salimur Rahman	1974	Van Nham Tran	1981
P. Rajasekaran	2001	Sarah Tsai	2005
Mahesh Raju	1986	Heng-Hsiung Tschen	1976
Sowmith Rangu	2016	Tara Tucker	1993
Gudimetla S. Reddy	1975	Padmini N. Turlapati	1984
R.V. Reddy	1975	Gordon Turner	1979
Ramakrishnan Redheendran	1975	Lesley Turner	1997
Debbie Reid	1990	Michele Ulrich	2005
Sergei Reznikov	2014	Raj Uttamchandani	1979
David Rice	1980	Jiri Vajsar	1987
George Robbins	2006	Jacob Rijk Van Gelder	1987
Hannah Roberts	2013	Cathy Lynn Vardy	1983
Theodore Rosales	1970	Damodar Vaze	1973
Spencer Rose	2003	Laura Vivian	2004
Susan Russell	2003	Andrew Warren	1993
Mohamed Sabet	1975	Emery Weber	2011
Michael Saginur	2007	Caroline Weisser	2013
Shakuntla Sahni	1980	Eileen White	1979
Abdul K. Samman	1986	Hubert White	1977
Donna Scott	1986	Robin Williams	2005
Bazir Serushago	1994	Ellen Wood	1980
Ali Shaabat	1984	Samantha Woodrow-Mullett	2015
Aruna Uday Shah	1979	Michael Wright	1975
Suryakant Shah	1990	Qasim Yar	1987
Lalit K. Sharma	1974	Ali-Akbar Yazdi	1974
Natalie Shiff	2002	Janina Zaremba	1986
Cheryl Simmonds	1974	Mark Zarestsky	2012
Avash Singh	1990	David Zielinski	2003
Ram Nivas Singh	1986	Caroline Zuijdwijk	2005
Mary Jane Smith	2006	Claudia Zuin	2004
Mila Smrz	1986		
Mark Sorial	1993		
Katie Soper	2010		
Lana Soper	2008		
William Sprague	1972		

References for Part I

"Announce Children's Hospital at Fort Pepperrell." *Evening Telegram*, March 5, 1964.

A Plan to Rationalize Hospital Services in St. John's: Benefits and Cost Implications. Memorial University Medical School, Health Sciences Library, Faculty of Medicine Founders' Archives, Coll-001 20.01.048.

Adamson, J.B. "Medical Survey of Nutrition in Newfoundland." *Canadian Medical Association Journal* 52, no. 3 (March 1945).

Appleton, V.B. "Observations of Deficiency Diseases in Labrador." *American Journal of Public Health* 11 (1921): 617.

Aykroyd, W.R. "Beri-beri and Other Food Deficiency Diseases in Newfoundland and Labrador." *Journal of Hygiene* 30 (1930): 357.

Aykroyd, W.R. "Vitamin A Deficiency in Newfoundland." *Irish Journal of Medical Science* 6 (1928): 161.

Baker, Melvin and Janet Miller Pitt. "A History of Health Services in Newfoundland and Labrador Child Welfare." In *Encyclopedia of Newfoundland and Labrador*, Vol. 2. St. John's: Harry Cuff Publications, 1984.

Brain, Russell. *Royal Commission on Health*, January 1966. Memorial University Medical School, Health Sciences Library, Faculty of Medicine Founders' Archives, WA 546 DE 2.1 N4 R6R, 1966.

Butler, D.L. "Observation on a Proposal to Extend Newfoundland Health Facilities so as to Improve Free Medical, Dental and Eye Care for All Children up to 16 Years." Letter, October 31, 1956. Memorial University of Newfoundland, QEII Library, Archives and Special Collections Division, Smallwood Papers, Coll. 075.

Cadigan, Sean T. *Newfoundland and Labrador: A History*. Toronto: University of Toronto Press, 2009.

Canadian Pediatric Society. "A program for Child Health in Newfoundland." Memorial University of Newfoundland, QEII Library, Archives and Special Collections Division, Coll. 285, 1303.005.

Collins, J.F. "Sick Children and the Public." Letter, *Evening Telegram*, February 2, 1962.

Coward, N. Barrie. "Scurvy, Recent Experiences." *Canadian Medical Association Journal* 63, no. 6 (December 1950): 549–52.

Crandon, John H., Charles C. Lund, and David D. Bill. "Experimental Human Scurvy." *New England Journal of Medicine* 223, no. 10 (September 1940): 353–69.

Cuthbertson, D.P. *Report on Nutrition in Newfoundland*. London: H.M. Stationery Office, 1947.

Davies, V.W. "Lessons from the Newfoundland Gastroenteritis Epidemics of 1963." Editorial. *Canadian Medical Association Journal* 96 (February 25, 1967): 484–85.

Dobbin, Lucy. *Report on the Reduction of Hospital Boards*. February 1993. Memorial University Medical School, Health Sciences Library, Faculty of Medicine Founders' Archives, W84 DC2.2 N4 D632, 1993.

Easter Seal Meeting Minutes. March 15, 1961, July 1962. Private collection.

Elphinstone, Norah. Brief of The Royal Commission on Health Services for Newfoundland from the Chair of the Special Services Committee of the NMA for the Children's Health Services, April 1965. Newfoundland and Labrador Medical Association Archives.

"Fly in the Ointment." Editorial, *Evening Telegram*, February 21, 1966.

Gibbons, Margaret. "The Child Welfare Association 1919–1939." Hons. thesis, Department of History, Memorial University, May 1996.

Haggerty, Robert J. and Frederick H. Lovejoy. *Charles A. Janeway, Pediatrician to the World's Children*. Cambridge: Harvard University Press, 2007.

Health Research Unit, Memorial University of Newfoundland Division of Community Medicine. "The Health Status of the Children of Newfoundland and Labrador," July 1996. Memorial University Medical School, Health Sciences Library, Faculty of Medicine Founders' Archives, W19 N4 M4 MR 1965.

Heslop, Lisa and Karen Frances. "Case Study of Program Management in Canada." *Nursing Leadership* 18, no. 2 (June 2005), http://hospitalquarterly.com/content/19029.

Hickman, Alex. Letter to M.O. Morgan, September 25, 1968. Memorial University Medical School, Health Sciences Library, Faculty of Medicine Founders' Archives, Coll-001, 2.12.001.

House of Assembly Proceedings, February 25, 1964. House of Assembly Library, Confederation Building, St. John's.

Janeway Medical Advisory Committee. Minutes, March 1991; March, October, July 1992; January, April, September, November 1993; January, February 1994. Private collection.

Janeway Medical Advisory Committee. Quarterly report, September 1992, September 1994; annual report, 1993. Private collection.

"Joseph R. Smallwood Claims Ten Experts Approved Location of Children's Health Centre." *Western Star*, February 26, 1966.

Joy, Clifton to J.R. Smallwood, 15 February 1964. Memorial University of Newfoundland, QEII Library, Archives and Special Collections Division, Smallwood Papers Coll-075, 3.15.016.

Joy, Clifton. Letter to author.

"Joy Makes Maiden Speech—Concerned over the Shortage of Children's Hospital Beds." *Daily News*, April 22, 1963.

Kelland, Donald. *The Dr. Charles A. Janeway Child Health Centre: The First Twenty-Five Years, 1966–1991*. St. John's: Children's Hospital Corporation, 1991.

Legislature of the Province of Newfoundland and Labrador. Budget Speech, March 26, 1992, House of Assembly Library.

Little, J.N. "Beri-beri Caused by Fine White Flour." *Journal of the American Medical Association* 58 (1912): 2029.

MacFarlane Commission. "Report of a Survey of the Feasibility of Establishing a Medical School at Memorial University of Newfoundland," 1965. Memorial University Medical School, Health Sciences Library, Faculty of Medicine Founders' Archives, W19 N4 M4 MR 1965.

McDevitt, E. "The Vitamin Status of the Population of the West Coast of Newfoundland with Emphasis on Vitamin C." *Annals of Internal Medicine* 20, no. 1 (1944).

Metcoff, J., Grace Goldsmith, A.J. McQueeney, R.F. Dove, Ellen McDevitt, and F.J. Stare. "Nutritional Survey in Norris Point, Newfoundland." *Journal Laboratory Clinical Medicine* 30, no. 475 (1945): 475–87.

Mitchell, H.S. "Nutrition Survey in Labrador and Northern Newfoundland." *Journal of American Dietetic Association* 6 (1931): 29.

Mitchell, H.S. and M. Vaughan. "A Continuation of the Nutrition Project in Northern Newfoundland." *Journal of American Dietetic Association* 8 (1933): 526.

Mosdell, H.M., Department of Health & Welfare. "Encouragement of Dairy Production: Supply of Whole Milk to Relief Recipients in St. John's." The Rooms Provincial Archives of Newfoundland and Labrador, GN 33, Box 56-1-2.

Nickerson, G. "Chief Pediatrician, Royal Victoria Hospital, Montreal Says Medical Facilities Are Badly Needed." *Daily News*, October 19, 1963.

NMA Newsletter 7, no. 3 (Convention 1965). NLMA Archives.

O'Neill, Paul. *A Door of Hope: The Story of the General Hospital* (unpublished manuscript, 1978). Memorial University Medical School, Health Sciences Library, Faculty of Medicine Founders Archives, 466.

Pepperrell Hospital Committee. "Children and Convalescent Hospital, 1960–61." Report to the Executive of the Newfoundland Medical Association. NLMA Archives.

"Provide New Rehabilitation Centre." *Evening Telegram*, April 30, 1964.

Report on Provincial Hospital Facilities, 1958. NMA-NLMA Archives.

Roberts, J.B. "The Children's Health Service in Newfoundland." Paper presented at Canadian Medical Association annual meeting, June 16, 1960. *NMA Newsletter* 2, no. 6 (July 1960): 6.

Royal Commission on Hospital and Nursing Home Costs. February 15, 1984. Memorial University of Newfoundland, Health Sciences Library, WX157 N547r, 1984.

Severs, David. "Immunization in Newfoundland." *Newfoundland Medical Association Journal* 21, no. 1 (February 1979): 19–21.

Severs, David, P. Fardy, S. Acres, and J.W. Davies. "Epidemic Gastroenteritis in Newfoundland during 1963 Associated with E. coli 0111.4." *Canadian Medical Association Journal* 94 (1966): 373–78.

Severs, David, T. Williams, and J.W. Davies. "Infantile Scurvy—A Public Health Problem." *Canadian Journal of Public Health* 52 (May 1961): 214–20.

Slang, A.S. and A. Joshi. "The Evolution of Free Standing Children's Hospitals in Canada." *Pediatrics and Child Health* 11, no. 8 (October 2006): 501–506.

"The Speech from the Throne." *Daily News*, March 8, 1964.

St. John's Hospital Council. *Provision of Clinical Services and Programs: A Study to Determine Future Requirements*. January 1979. Memorial University Medical School, Health Sciences Library, Faculty of Medicine Founders' Archives, Coll-001, 2.12.034.

Statistics Canada. Annual Year Books, 1867–2016. http://www.statcan.gc.ca/pub/11-402-x/index-eng.htm.

Wallace, W. Steward, ed. "Economic History of Newfoundland." *The Encyclopedia of Canada*. Toronto: Marianopolis College, 1949. 23–36.

Williams, Robert. Letter to author.

Young, Victor, chair. Government of Newfoundland and Labrador, *Royal Commission on Renewing and Strengthening Our Place in Canada*. St. John's: Office of the Queen's Printer, March 2002.

Acknowledgements

I would like to thank my secretary, Sharon Hookey, who has spent many hours transcribing and preparing this book, for her hard work and dedication; Stephanie Porter, my editor, who has made many suggestions and helped me with the elements and style of the written word; Joseph Curtis, John Crellin, Derek Matthew, and Albert J. Davis, who edited several sections for accuracy and medical content; and those who wrote sections of the book: Aiden Howell, Joanne Simms, Terry O'Brien, and Patricia Rose.

I would particularly like to thank those who took the time to write and share their own stories or the stories of their children.

Many individuals on staff or retired with Eastern Health, the old Janeway, and Memorial University have made valuable contributions, which are greatly appreciated. My thanks to Cheryl Bailey, Mary Baker, Germaine Barnes, Jill Barter, Lorraine Burrage, Janice Bursey, Bill Callahan, Bev Carter, Kevin Chan, John Collins, Jim Connors, Gary Cornel, Peg Cox, Charlene Daley, Paula Dalley, Paul Dancey, Albert J. Davis, Heidi Davis, Joanne Dawe, Larry Dohey, Cheryl Fosdec, Renu Gill and staff, Melissa Glover, Shania Goudie, Pamela Griffiths, Chaker Hobeika, Stephanie Horlick, Cindy Howell, Janine Hubbard, Flo Joy, John Joy, Donna Kelland, Richard Kennedy, Kristina Krmpotic, Falah Maroun, Rhonda Marshall, John Martin, Edna McKim, ßRobert Morris, Phil Murphy, Katheryn Nichol, Mary O'Brien, Arthur Osborne, Marilyn Party, Ean Parsons, Bonnie Pennell, David Price, Pinkie Renouf, Lisa Rose, Diane Ryan, Arlene Scott, Marjorie Scott, Kim Scruton, Mary Frances Sculley, Joanne Simms, Rick Singleton, Geoff Smith, Faith Stratton, Terry Upshall, Damodar Vaze, Pearl Vokey, Rita Walsh, Clifton Way, Linda White, Bob Williams, and Marion Yetman.